AT HOME
AT HIGHCLERE

The Countess of Carnarvon

Entertaining at
THE REAL DOWNTON ABBEY

CONTENTS

Handwritten visitors' book with signatures, dates, and an ink sketch of a castle.

Left page:

Hawkins

August 15. 1867

October 22nd 1867

22 Oct. 67

23. Oct 1867

23 Oct 1867

Right page:

...ton Wellesley 24 Oct 67

Ashley October 25 - 67

Harriet Ashley October 25th 1867

Edward ..... October 27 - 1867

J G Shaw Stewart 28 October 1867

Hardinge Nov. 2nd 1867

WELCOME

This is a book that offers a glimpse into real life at Highclere Castle with stories from the past and the present. It contains anecdotes and recipes that reflect years of tradition, passed down through the centuries. The art of entertaining remains as important at Highclere today as it ever was, even if on a smaller scale and with less frequency than was common before the Second World War.

The anecdotes and stories focus on four different historical weekends at Highclere Castle supplemented by observations of life today, with the menus and recipes.

The scenes and seasons of the year here will be so familiar to millions of people as the home of the fictional Crawley family of the TV series *Downton Abbey*. Each season has its own character and there is much pleasure to be had enjoying the natural fruits offered as each month presents its seasonal best.

The kitchens at Highclere stand on a site that has probably served a similar purpose for close to a thousand years. More recently, food and dining have played an important social role in the lives of Earls of Carnarvon, bringing people together formally and informally, fostering conversation, relationships and sharing laughter.

Until the advent of supermarkets in the last few decades, Highclere was self-sufficient, depending on its kitchen garden and an abundance of game and meat from the estate and farm, as well as fish from its lakes.

Today, the supply of home-grown vegetables is modest, but we still source local produce on the basis that all cooking begins with good ingredients; our chef's key demand is for the highest possible quality.

Over the years, Highclere has welcomed royalty, statesmen, Egyptologists and pioneers of technology and the Visitors' Books also record weekends with guests from the worlds of music, art and letters. The etiquette of the invitation, the format of the weekend house party, the *placement* at dinners and the general entertainment of guests has preoccupied each generation at Highclere. Today we still welcome friends, family, politicians, artists from the worlds of literature and music, as well as guests from the modern worlds of TV and film.

Highclere's future depends on its ability to adapt in a changing world. The Castle has built on its reputation for exceptional hospitality and it is a pleasure to create convivial weekends for gatherings of the influential people of the day. I hope this book gives a glimpse inside a great house, with recipes, tales from upstairs and downstairs, as well as remarkable photographs from the archives to compare with those of today. The Castle was built to be a much-loved, spectacular home, to entertain and host weekend house parties.

'So perhaps the best thing to do is to stop writing introductions and get on with the book.'

A.A. MILNE — *Winnie-the-Pooh*

FIONA – 8TH COUNTESS OF CARNARVON

View from the Saloon

FROM ARCHITECTURE TO POLITICS

Disraeli, the Right to Vote and the Canadian Federation

October 1866

Benjamin Disraeli was a Victorian Conservative politician who achieved position, fame and *gravitas* wholly on his own merits. Highly intelligent, ambitious and politically adroit, he had been appointed Chancellor of the Exchequer by the Prime Minister, Lord Derby, in 1866. This was, in fact, for the third time and, like all his tenures as Chancellor, it was short-lived. His previous two budgets had brought the government down, first in 1852 and then again in 1858, though Disraeli was not solely responsible for the country's loss of confidence in his party.

With hindsight, putting him in charge of the country's finances was ironic, given the problems he had in regulating his own. Early ill-conceived business ventures led to debts, which were only to some extent alleviated by his marriage to a wealthy widow. Financial insecurity plagued him for much of his political career and indeed life.

ABOVE
Excerpt from Highclere Castle Visitors' Book, October 1866

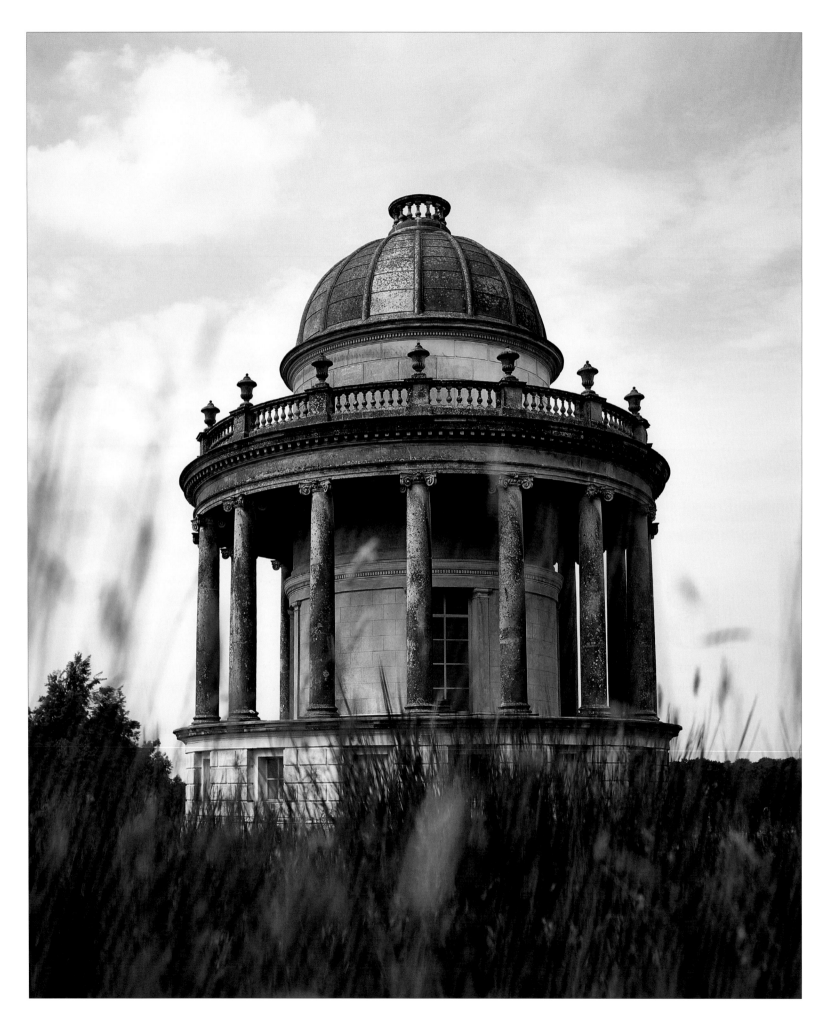

The Temple of Diana today, as seen by guests on their arrival

Benjamin Disraeli (1804–1881)

Benjamin Disraeli and his wife Mary Anne had spent much of the summer at Hughenden, their house in Buckinghamshire. They had been making many improvements there; Mary Anne particularly enjoyed working in the garden and they had comfortably established themselves in the roles of country squire and his wife.

Anticipating the invitation to Highclere from Henry Howard Molyneux Herbert, 4th Earl of Carnarvon, who was a fellow Privy Council member and Secretary of State for the Colonies, Disraeli had directed his private secretary Montagu Corry to forward all ministerial correspondence to Highclere for the weekend, after which the Disraelis would return by train to London as Parliament began its autumn session.

On the afternoon of Friday, 26 October Lord Carnarvon's carriage had collected them at Highclere railway station and now Mr Disraeli was very much enjoying the drive from the London Lodge entrance of Highclere Park towards the Castle. The carriage had just passed through a dense plantation of rhododendrons before the horses went trotting smartly up the incline to the Temple of Diana, a circular, classically inspired building prominently situated above Dunsmere Lake. The stands of oaks and beeches were ablaze with the golden hues of autumn. 'But is this Home Park not most delightful, madam?' exclaimed the Chancellor of the Exchequer to his wife.

The horses picked up speed as the carriage proceeded up the drive towards the bridge. As they slowed to cross it, Mrs Disraeli delighted in the sight of the two swans making their way across the water, which was dotted with tiny islands. She had herself named their own two swans, on the trout stream in the garden at Hughenden, Hero and Leander.

It would be another half a mile before the horses' hooves began to crunch across gravel as the carriage slowed in front of the Castle. Disraeli leaned out, better to admire the intricate and pleasing façade as the light was fading. It was his first visit to Highclere Castle and it looked to be a truly magnificent building.

UNG· IE ·SERVI ·RAI

A · D · MDCCCXLII

ELEVATION OF DOORWAY

PLAN

ELEVATION OF RETVRN OF

DOORWAY

Charles Barry   6th May 1842

ON THE DOORWAY

Westminster Feb.ᵗ 12ᵗʰ 1842

Sir Charles Barry's drawing for the front portico of the Castle,
February 1842

The 3rd Earl of Carnarvon had decided

to commission the eminent architect Sir Charles Barry to
remodel the existing Georgian house at Highclere. The great
project began in 1842. Following the 1834 fire at the Palace of
Westminster, Barry had won the prestigious commission to
rebuild the Houses of Parliament on which work had begun in
1840. He was indeed the pre-eminent exponent of Italianate
architecture and engineer of his time and greatly in demand;
whilst Highclere was more or less completed by 1860, the
Houses of Parliament took a further decade. Following his
father's death, the 4th Earl of Carnarvon completed the
interiors of the Castle and thus began the era of his celebrated
'weekend house parties'.

Standing at the front door of the Castle, waiting to
conduct Mr and Mrs Disraeli inside, was Allan the house
steward. Ever-conscious of his own importance, as well as
that of the guests, Allan had instructed Thomas the butler to
stand slightly behind him. The footmen stood lined up to one
side before hurrying forward to lower the carriage steps and
help the guests down.

Allan conducted them into the Saloon where

the family gathered before tea. Lady Carnarvon smiled sweetly
as she came forward to enquire after their journey. She related
that Lord and Lady Cranborne (who later bore the title Lord
and Lady Salisbury) had just arrived. Cranborne was tall and
bearded, a man who loved to laugh in the company of close
friends and had a strong streak of self-mockery. He had fallen
in love with his wife Georgina in 1856, to his parents' fury.

Sir Charles Barry's scheme for the Saloon

The 4th Earl and Countess of Carnarvon

The Cranbornes, however, remained devoted to one another and she became his emotional mainstay and confidante. They were both clever, renowned for their intellect and love of culture rather than any devotion to society or sport. Immensely proud of his family, whether in terms of its heritage or his own children, Cranborne was not a traditional Conservative, preferring to test conventional wisdom before he espoused it.

Disraeli had very much hoped that Lady Carnarvon's mother Lady Chesterfield would be at Highclere for this particular weekend. He knew her husband had, alas, just died but was ready to offer his condolences and support. Mary Anne Disraeli, on the other hand, was rather relieved that Lady Chesterfield was at Bretby House in Derbyshire that weekend. Mr Disraeli bowed and conveyed his condolences to Lady Carnarvon on the death of her father. Some years later, by then himself a widower, Disraeli laid his heart at the Dowager Lady Chesterfield's feet several times and tried to persuade her to marry him. He was completely enamoured. However, Lady Carnarvon remained strongly opposed to the match and in the end neither Disraeli nor Lady Chesterfield remarried.

After the usual pleasantries, the Disraelis were led up the wide oak staircase to the Gallery and guest bedrooms. Mary Anne was delighted with the little corner sitting room in the tower at the far end of her room. It was a charming place to rest. Fires had been lit in the rooms and a maid stood by to help her change for tea. Mary Anne had not been feeling well of late but did not wish to trouble her husband by raising the subject. He waited to accompany her downstairs when she was ready.

Some of the house party had already gathered for afternoon tea in front of a welcoming fire in the Saloon. Outside the October evening drew in, the low light gently fading. Voices from the Front Hall signalled the return of Lord Carnarvon and some more of his guests after a brisk walk around the Park. After shedding their coats, George Verdon and Frederic Rogers happily followed their host in search of warmth and tea. Verdon had emigrated to Australia when he was just seventeen years old, later returning to England to represent the interests of the state of Victoria. He was a frequent guest at Highclere. Sir Frederic Rogers was Permanent Under-Secretary of State for the Colonies, the Colonial Office of the time being conducted along the lines of a gentlemen's club. Thanks to the erudition of all who worked there, it was a famously efficient department despite the short hours and long holidays it enjoyed. Lord Carnarvon had served as Under-Secretary of State for the Colonies under Lord Derby from 1858–9, and in July 1866 had been given overall responsibility for the department.

The large figure of Lord Cranborne joined them. Ever polite, he remained some thirty minutes with the ladies before retiring to the Library, a footman following him carrying a tray of tea – Lord Cranborne was well known for drinking a prodigious amount of it. A somewhat enigmatic and aloof man, he was passionately interested in books and his great friend and host Lord Carnarvon had assembled

Guests outside the Castle Library, about 1866.
From left: Lord Derby; an unidentified lady;
Montagu Corry (Benjamin Disraeli's personal
secretary); George Verdon; Lady Carnarvon;
another unidentified lady.

In the Library, Cranborne had ensconced himself comfortably in a deep-red wing-backed armchair by the elaborately decorated fireplace. Frederic Rogers stood nearby. He worked in the Colonial Office under six successive Secretaries of State and possessed a formidable mind. Educated at Eton, he then won a scholarship to Oxford where he attained a double first in mathematics and classics. Good-looking and presentable, with a most attractive smile, he was a firm favourite with all the society hostesses.

Rogers and Carnarvon were discussing the not inconsiderable task that faced them in the next year: creating an independent Canadian Federation.

It had originally been expected that John A. Macdonald would arrive in England as part of the Canadian delegation. There were suspicions that the delay in his arrival was due to his 'notorious vice'. Carnarvon judged him 'the ablest politician in Upper Canada', yet was quite incensed that Macdonald could be 'so drunk as to be incapable of official business for days altogether'.

Carnarvon had received a telegram explaining, however, that for various reasons some of the Canadian delegates had been delayed, which he noted made their colleagues already here 'very impatient'.

If the Canadians were missing, Australia was well represented: George Verdon had become a regular guest at Highclere over the summer and this weekend he hoped to take the opportunity to approach Disraeli on a matter of paramount importance to the future of his home state.

a fascinating collection in his new Library at Highclere. There were by then over 5,000 volumes, some of them rare, from an early book, *Orlando Furioso* by Ariosto (1538) to *Silva*, Evelyn's famous discourse on trees, published the previous century, a fourth edition (1685) of Shakespeare's plays and Thomas Hobbes's tracts published in 1682. These were painstakingly catalogued and arranged on the Library's veneered mahogany shelves that were embellished with carvings of the leaves and fruits of field and orchard. The beautifully proportioned and decorated room had been completed by the architect Thomas Allom following Barry's death in 1860.

Georgina Cranborne remained chatting with her hostess, glancing fondly after her husband as he left the room. Lady Carnarvon poured the tea whilst the footmen stood ready to pass the tiny slices of plum cake, the crumpets and sandwiches.

Books shelved in Highclere's magnificent Library, enjoyed by the visiting Lord Cranborne

A rare seventeenth-century edition of Shakespeare

The Chancellor of the Exchequer was aware that Verdon had his own agenda, wishing to raise the question of the naval defence of Victoria – specifically, he hoped to raise funds for a warship. He intended to initiate any and every opportunity this weekend to promote his cause. He had already engaged the attention of Lord Carnarvon, as Colonial Secretary, when staying at Highclere the previous month. Verdon was now embarking on a charm offensive to win over the man who could finance the ship that would help to safeguard Australia's shores.

Verdon was an enthusiastic companion and attentive guest. He had already used his winning smile over tea to persuade Mrs Disraeli to further his cause with her husband. Compared to the other challenges Disraeli was facing after the defeat of Russell's electoral reform bill in the summer and the subsequent riots in London, the Australian request was a comparatively simple matter.

Georgina and her hostess, Evelyn Carnarvon, remained in the Saloon and drew Mary Anne Disraeli into conversation. The latter was now seventy-four years old, twice their age, with a tendency to lose her train of thought. She was more than happy to talk about her new Italian Garden, though, and Evelyn complimented her on her husband's new appointment. Mary Anne was unreservedly devoted to the husband she always called 'Dizzy' and regarded as an utter genius. On this happy note she retired to change for dinner, whilst Evelyn and Georgina slipped up to visit the nurseries on the top floor of the Castle, where they could say goodnight to their children.

The Carnarvon family name is 'Herbert' whilst the Cranbournes' is 'Cecil' – the friendship between the two families was such that Evelyn's daughter was given 'Cecil' as her middle name and the Cranbournes' next son 'Herbert' as his. Each man stood as godfather to one of his friend's children. Evelyn's two-year-old daughter Winifred and baby son George were under the care of Nurse and her nursery-maids.

The Nursery was, by virtue of its location at the top of the house, conducted almost as a separate establishment, with both day and night nurseries. Nurse ranked only after Lady Carnarvon's lady's maid in terms of precedence below stairs. Always dressed in a white washing gown, as she bustled happily around her domain she was ordered and sensible but also affectionate.

Little Lady Winifred toddled merrily across the rugs to fall into her mother's arms. Baby George at three months old lay swaddled warmly in his cradle, a nursery-maid sitting attentively nearby. The tiny figure of the old Carnarvon

Nanny, Mrs Morton, was installed in a rocking chair in the corner. She was much loved by Lord Carnarvon and, although ninety-three years old, remained bright as a button if very frail. The nursery footman had just carried up more coals for the fires and been sent back down for warm milk from the kitchens. Lady Carnarvon loved to see her children for tea but otherwise had little time to spend with them during such a weekend. Her husband was even more remote and busy.

The chime of the long clock outside the Library reminded the gentlemen of the need to retire. Weekend house parties at this time would usually number no more than nine or ten people, unlike the larger gatherings popularised later in the century. Nevertheless, formal dress was expected after 6 p.m. The great Castle was lit by both sconces of candles and the new paraffin oil lamps – there were so many that it was one man's sole daily employment to light and extinguish all

LEFT
Toys from the past gathering dust in old nursery rooms

RIGHT
Mary Anne Disraeli (1792–1872)

the lamps as well as cleaning and maintaining them. He would progress around the galleries, landings and passages, both upstairs and downstairs, taking up to two hours to complete his duties each morning and evening.

Footmen carried up jugs of hot water and ladies' maids discreetly appeared to assist the process of dressing. Each of Lady Carnarvon's guests travelled with a maid, who was always neatly turned out; she would need to be able to dress hair, look after her mistress's clothes, make repairs and choose clothes and accessories suitable for every eventuality. The role was prized as it was not merely well paid – ladies' maids also benefited in kind by receiving their mistress's outdated or cast-off clothing, which they could reuse or sell. The maids' importance in the household was such that they would invariably change into a modified style of evening dress themselves before eating dinner in the staff dining room.

They were not the only members of staff who would need to find time to change. The footmen would hasten towards their rooms at the rear of the Castle to change into their evening attire – silk stockings, knee breeches, livery coats, white gloves – and finally to carefully position their wigs. Immaculate and upright in stature, they would lend additional formality and dignity to the events of the evening.

Just like the world above stairs, downstairs was run according to a strict timetable of duties, with suitable attire to be worn at all times. As they were upstairs, roles and titles were often passed down through families, and the butler and housekeeper followed a strict code of duty in their own right. Managing such a large and busy household, with up to

sixty members of staff living in and around the Castle, was a logistical challenge. Chief Steward Mr Allan and housekeeper Mrs Laverick held positions of considerable responsibility.

Having rested, Lady Carnarvon and her female guests began the business of changing for dinner, with their maids deftly arranging hair and jewels. After checking their appearance and selecting shawls to guard them against any draughts, the ladies set off down the Gallery, escorted by their husbands, before descending the great oak staircase. The high-necked decorous day dresses of earlier had been replaced by beautiful, low-cut evening gowns, in sumptuous satin and intricate lace, worn, of course, with evening gloves.

Mary Anne Disraeli, now feeling better, trod happily down the staircase on her beloved husband's arm. Adorned with a few too many diamonds and feathers, and with her face painted, she was less restrained in her dress than the other wives were. Like her husband, she enjoyed the extravagant costumes of the preceding era, with their layers of lace, ribbons and decorative *fol-de-rols*.

As dinner was announced, Lord Carnarvon offered his arm to the good-natured Mrs Disraeli and placed her to his right at the table. Meanwhile, Mr Disraeli took his hostess, Evelyn Carnarvon, to her place opposite her husband. The rest of the party, including a cousin of Lord Carnarvon's

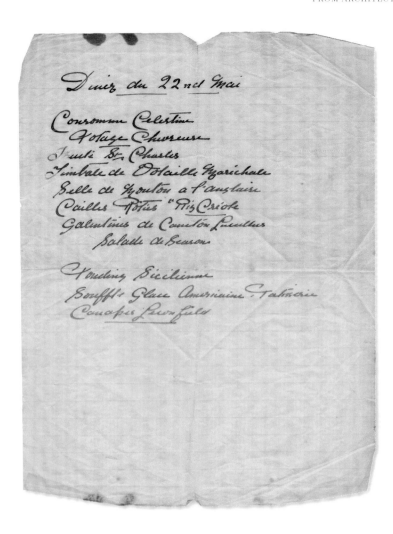

Chef's notes for a typical late-Victorian dinner menu *à la Française*, as enjoyed by Disraeli and the other guests at Highclere, including two soups, trout, a chicken *timbale*, lamb, roast quails, a duck *galantine*, a pudding and an iced soufflé …

years later Disraeli acknowledged to Quaker politician John Bright during the 1866 reform debates that he had always intended to 'create a sensation, occupy the limelight … to act a part on the greatest stage in the world'.

Lady Carnarvon had carefully agreed the

menus for the weekend well in advance with her French cook, Monsieur Baptiste, and the House Steward. The dinners served were grand although not as extensive as in other great houses. Dinner at Highclere was still served *à la française*, which meant that the first course was already set out on the table before Lady Carnarvon led her guests into the Dining Room. This would generally consist of one soup or more, to be followed by *relevés* of roasted or stewed meats, poultry or fish. Each course was 'removed' as further dishes were brought in. Dishes of meat, poultry or seafood were then accompanied by *entremet*s with small sweet or savoury preparations. And so the dinner would progress, with a larger main course, again served with sweet or savoury *entremets*, and puddings of cheese, pastries and fruit. Ices and petits fours would bring the dinner to a close.

Disraeli wrote that he usually found the sheer quantity of food served on such occasions overwhelming although fortunately, at Highclere, he should be able to take some exercise the following day.

who was in the diplomatic service and his youngest sister, followed in pairs, according to rank and social status.

Dorothy Nevill, herself a renowned hostess as well as a regular guest at Highclere, commented that the house parties there had an intellectual and social charm that was largely due to the personality of the hostess. Evelyn Carnarvon had gained a reputation for her ability to gather people of conspicuous talent at Highclere whilst her husband was notable for his outstanding courtesy.

Lady Nevill had just been staying with them and was sad to miss 'Dizzy'. She had known him since he first arrived in London in 1832 with his black velvet dress coats and tasselled canes. He was by now a more sober-suited statesman, often grave and pensive. Dorothy had lived opposite him in Upper Grosvenor Street and well recalled the struggles of his younger years. His first attempts to enter the House of Commons failed. During his early days in London, he was often distracted and disappointed in love, his father writing to him in distress to complain about such erratic behaviour. But

The vaulted ceiling of the Front Hall of the Castle designed in 1870 by George Gilbert Scott

Lord Carnarvon gently quizzed Mrs Disraeli, striking a sensible balance in his conversational style. He neither wished conversation to lapse in case she dozed off nor to encourage her to talk so unselfconsciously that it drew attention. Even Queen Victoria was witness to unguarded chatter and was apparently amused when Mary Anne commented *à propos* a remark about some lady's pale complexion, 'I wish you could see my Dizzy in his bath!'

Benjamin Disraeli's devotion to his wife was, however, a matter of public record and it was considered a remarkable alliance. Despite the years, age had not dimmed her blue eyes nor yet much altered her narrow waist. Like her husband's Byronic locks, her dark hair remained untouched by grey, though she gaily admitted to all their friends that she dyed her husband's. A little miniature of Disraeli was pinned as ever high on her velvet bodice.

Benjamin Disraeli was seated opposite his wife; he was a well-built, powerful man with a high broad forehead and sunken eyes. In fact, with his black curly hair and beard, Lady Carnarvon thought he seemed both mysterious and impressive. He conversed in a low, almost monotonous voice, but his skilful, well-informed hostess quietly encouraged easy, comfortable exchanges. Disraeli greatly depended on the sympathy of his friends, especially the women, although his letters reveal that he set no store by their intelligence. His own story, however, was unique: a man of vision, daring and adroitness who, wholly on his own merits, was now Chancellor of the Exchequer and one of the closest confidants of Queen Victoria.

Disraeli was also a romantic novelist and an early edition of his 1845 work *Sibyl* could be found in the Library at Highclere. He was not the only writer present that weekend.

SYBIL

OR

THE TWO NATIONS.

BY THE

RIGHT HONORABLE B. DISRAELI.

'The Commonalty murmured, and said, " There never were so many
Gentlemen, and so little Gentleness." '   BISHOP LATIMER.

NEW EDITION.

LONDON:
LONGMANS, GREEN, AND CO.
1871.

All rights reserved.

The title page of Disraeli's novel *Sybil*, a copy of which sat on Highclere's Library shelves at the time of the author's visit, as it does today. The inscription on the title page makes clear the politician's touching devotion to his wife Mary Anne:

> I would inscribe this work to one whose noble spirit and gentle nature ever prompt her to sympathise with the suffering; to one whose sweet voice has often encouraged, and whose taste and judgment have ever guided, its pages; the most severe of critics, but—a perfect Wife!

Lord Cranborne had also earnt his living from writing until his prospects improved on the sad death of his blind elder brother.

Lady Carnarvon finally brought the conversation around to the matter of honours for a very dear mutual friend, the MP Sir William Heathcote, who had been Lord Carnarvon's guardian after his father's death. She would later remark to her husband that she felt encouraged by Mr Disraeli's reception of her comments.

After fruit was placed on the table, Lady Carnarvon rose from her chair, which was the signal for the ladies to leave the gentlemen and retire to the Drawing Room. Mr Disraeli immediately stood up, followed by the remaining men, whilst Lord Cranborne, who was seated nearest the door, held it open; all remained courteously standing as the ladies withdrew.

The men could then return to their discourse,
inevitably to discuss matters of state and current concerns –

it must have seemed a troubled time. There had been vast pro-reform riots in Hyde Park in London during the summer. Iron railings had been pulled down and the Home Secretary, Spencer Walpole, apparently burst into tears. The question of who should be allowed to vote was dividing all the parties. Across the Atlantic, the American elections had just taken place, the first after the Civil War. In addition, there had been a war between Austria and Prussia with Italy forming an alliance with Prussia, ensuring Bismarck's victory and strengthening his political position.

George Verdon awaited his opportunity to discuss with Mr Disraeli and Lord Carnarvon the financial support needed for the naval defence of Melbourne. He was promised HMS *Nelson* as a training ship and £100,000 towards the cost of the armour-plated monitor ship *Cerberus*, which became one of the first vessels in the Royal Australian Navy. This was a real coup as Disraeli had been trying to curb naval expenditure in order to help his balancing of the nation's books.

The butler, Thomas, remained discreetly by the green baize-lined door to the Saloon waiting for a signal that the party would retire to join the ladies, who had been happily chatting in the Drawing Room. Lord Carnarvon did not keep his guests up late but, nevertheless, it would require hours of work to clear and reset the tables before Thomas and the footmen could go to their rooms at the back of the Castle and turn in for the night. As each couple carefully ascended to the Gallery bedrooms, holding a candle to aid their progress, their ladies' maids and valets would be dutifully standing by to help them undress.

Saturday dawned with fine clear October weather. The air smelt fresh and Lord Carnarvon proposed to Disraeli that they set off together for a walk in the Park after breakfast. Carnarvon had written, in his letter of invitation, that 'it would give us very great pleasure to show you the place ... I should rejoice in getting a quiet half hour's talk with you on several matters of importance'.

Naturally their conversation revolved around the 'reform' question. Who should be able to vote in Britain: just men of property or any man with an income? Carnarvon and Cranborne wished to establish secure principles. Disraeli commented that, for his part, he wished the Tories would 'hold our hand till later' and 'see what public opinion is'. He also mentioned the idea of a Commission but Lord Carnarvon felt Disraeli was 'obviously undecided ... sometimes inclining to one side, sometimes to another'.

Carnarvon himself preferred a cautious approach to any extension of the franchise, although he also thought that there was no justification for excluding women. Disraeli then proposed they should bring in a surprise amendment in the autumn, which Lord Carnarvon considered 'a dodge'. Disraeli seemed to nod in agreement to this and the subject was abandoned for the remainder of the weekend. They returned across the lawns and through the 'American Garden' back to the Castle. Disraeli, however, was first and foremost a politician and had gained fresh insight into his colleague from even that short exchange.

Later that day, Carnarvon and Cranborne again discussed reform, specifically the resolutions they believed would be brought before Cabinet during the next six months. Lord Carnarvon, however, would be concentrating on foreign affairs: he would be wholly engaged with both the North American delegates and the drafting of the Bill for the 'Confederation of the Dominion of Canada'. Lord Cranborne had already demonstrated attention to detail in his speeches about India. His priority was to help as many as possible in the case of famine and, like Lord Carnarvon, was intent upon allocating any budget possible to support education in India.

Lady Carnarvon always took breakfast in bed but had arranged to meet whoever wished at eleven o'clock to set off towards the Monks' Garden, to see the recently restored peach house. The new mushroom house behind it was by now nearly completed as well.

It was a busy time of year on the estate with new cottages being built for servants and estate workers, and the stables and cowsheds being overhauled before winter. As they walked, Evelyn told Lord Cranborne that they were still dealing with some defects in the construction of the Saloon, and most importantly the main staircase. The problem stemmed partly from the fact that the previous Earl's paperwork was incomplete, and partly from the reluctance of the original builders to return due to arguments over money. Since Barry's death, both Thomas Allom and Gilbert Scott had been involved in trying to complete the detailing but there had subsequently been variations, necessitating new contracts.

The party then continued towards the ruined temple in the garden. George Verdon followed behind, escorting Lady Cranborne and Mrs Disraeli. Mary Anne exclaimed in delight at all she saw; she had herself created a much-praised Italian Garden at Hughenden. She explained that her husband adored her work there and nothing made him happier than planting trees. They had planted a 'German Forest' on a small hill, so they could walk amongst dark evergreens, recalling their visits to forests in Bohemia. Between gardening and reading, the past summer had seemed to fly by. Her companions listened attentively and walked slowly.

LEFT
Front door of Highclere Castle photographed c.1890.
The words inscribed in stone above the door and around
the Castle read 'UNC JE SERVIRAY' – old Norman
French for 'Only One Will I Serve'

RIGHT
A view across Dunsmere Lake, c.1905

Aware of Mr Disraeli's preferences, Lady Carnarvon sought to provide a choice of dishes, whilst her husband proposed walking parties.

Lord Carnarvon meanwhile had quietly avoided the usual country sporting pursuits such as shooting or hunting. He had been brought up to do neither, and was a terrible horseman. He had hunted once or twice and on the field could easily be distinguished in his bright green velveteen, unable to get off because, as he himself commented, he would never be able to get back on. Lord Carnarvon infinitely preferred the project of remodelling his house and gardens and thought them restored to the way they had been in the time of the Cavaliers, full of colour and cheer. He greatly enjoyed researching the history of the house, its architectural development as well as the associated family history. The numerous portraits of his ancestors were to him a constant reminder of those previous generations: their histories and personal stories set against the times in which they had lived. Disraeli, by contrast, had commissioned portraits of men he knew or admired.

After lunch, Disraeli, Cranborne and

Carnarvon withdrew to undertake their correspondence. Lord Carnarvon suggested that Disraeli should borrow his Study past the Breakfast Room, whilst Cranborne and he used a top-floor retreat. Lord Carnarvon's Study was lined with books by Greek and Latin authors, which Mrs Disraeli knew would make her husband very happy. Disraeli began on the work forwarded by Montagu Corry. Monty also knew Lord Carnarvon and had stayed at Highclere. He was a dapper young man with a repertoire of amusing songs, which led to much success with women. During his short employment to date by Disraeli, he had already won the heart of Mary Anne and become part of the couple's life together.

The day moved on towards afternoon tea followed by another dinner, with perhaps turtle soup succeeded in turn by *suprème* of chicken and *boeuf à la provençale*. Mrs Disraeli worried that 'Dizzy' would not only get bored, 'but take to eating as resource' and then become 'dreadfully bilious'.

On Sunday morning, Lord Carnarvon had

arranged for a short service to be held in the Saloon at the Castle as the new church at Highclere was not yet completed. Afterwards, he suggested to Mr Disraeli that they should walk to Dunsmere Lake together.

'How scenical, how scenical!' exclaimed Disraeli as he stood outside the high, iron-studded walnut door in the front elevation of Highclere Castle. From here he could look north across the parkland towards the hills, knowing that

Oxford lay just beyond; to the north-west his own beloved Hughenden. Leaving the other guests behind in the Castle, the two men set off on foot towards the lake. Disraeli had always appreciated the romance of the countryside. He paused several times to admire the sylvan scenes and afterwards Lord Carnarvon recorded:

> ... walked to the lake with Disraeli ... he admired everything, the sun was shining brightly and the trees flaming with autumn colours and talked agreeably on all subjects *inter alia* Copernicus and Pythagoras and ancient astronomy ...

The alternative walk was to view the kitchen gardens, a charming *ferme ornée* created by the 1st Earl of Carnarvon following the plans of Mr Lancelot (Capability) Brown. Frederic Rogers and George Verdon as well as Edward, her husband's nephew, kept Lady Carnarvon company. Her husband had also begun to breed pigs to show, which

were kept just behind the dairy yards. The melon houses were sunk half in the ground, with pipes to heat them running through a rectangular pit lined with brick. Another half dozen greenhouses nearby were devoted to raising cucumbers and salads whilst a wide arched gateway led through to the acres of vegetable garden contained within tall mellow brick walls. The garden door at the far end led through to orchards and beyond that to a potato field – altogether a delightful prospect in which to roam.

Since Mary Anne Disraeli had remained

behind, Georgina Cranborne decided to stay as well. Georgina was much closer in age to Evelyn than to Mary Anne but, just like 'Mrs Dizzy', Georgina was devoted to her husband and his career. She hosted many political parties in London or at Hatfield on his behalf since he disliked most social occasions and was very shy. Georgina became involved in the Primrose League and other such organisations, which developed

as forums for political consultation and access. Her advice was often sought and not only by her husband. Just like Mary Anne, however, she used her friendships to support her husband wherever she could.

Georgina was aware of the special relationship between Disraeli and Queen Victoria, who read letters from her ministers and cabinet papers with scrupulous care. The Queen hold Mr Disraeli in high esteem, extending to him both courtesies and preferment. The establishment, then as now, was all about corridors of power and relationships nurtured outside the parliamentary debating chambers.

The following morning, the house party was

finishing breakfast whilst Lady Carnarvon's housekeeper, Mrs Laverick, was kept busy giving directions to the ladies' maids and valets packing trunks and boxes in a flurry of activity, ready for the carriages to arrive and carry the party back to Highclere station.

Upstairs over breakfast, Lord Carnarvon decided to broach one more matter to Disraeli before he left: the granting of a peerage to his friend Sir William Heathcote, but here Carnarvon was to be disappointed as Disraeli said Lord Derby was not likely to agree since he had grown tired of Disraeli advancing his favourites. Perhaps Disraeli had been unable bluntly to refuse the delightful Lady Carnarvon during the dinner. He was, however, rather clearer to her husband.

George Verdon left Highclere having met with more success. Besides securing the warship for his state, he had gained grants for new buildings and instruments for an observatory in Melbourne, with ongoing support for an astronomer and staff. A further project was to initiate work for a national museum. Such cultural endeavours were well received and later Verdon was thrilled to be awarded the 'Companionship of the Bath', an old-established accolade, at a formal Investiture ceremony. Like their employers, the visiting servants would probably have enjoyed the change of scene provided by the days at Highclere: after a later stay Verdon wrote that his servant 'was profoundly impressed with Highclere, but most of all with the kindness of everyone in it, from your Lordship & Lady Carnarvon, to the kitchen maids'.

Inscribe your names — in memory
Of pleasant hours, and days gone bye
A record of each passing year
Which fleeting Time, will more endear.

And if our hospitalities,
You should be pleased to criticize,
Each little hint, we'll gladly take
And Read it for the writers sake

The welcoming verse on the opening page
of the first Visitors' Book at Highclere, 1863

The leftovers from the weekend's dining

would be consumed by the staff, both inside the house and outside, including the grooms and stable lads, who were glad of the generous meals they received. Their quarters were above the stables in the courtyard behind the Castle, not the warmest place during winter.

As the house party dispersed, most of the guests remembered to sign the Visitors' Book laid ready in the Saloon. Lord Carnarvon's diary entry following the weekend was brief and succinct: 'our party all went'. He too returned to London, accompanied by Evelyn, the following day.

POSTSCRIPT

Future developments showed that Disraeli had not been quite so candid about his plans for the Reform Bill as Lord Carnarvon had thought.

Disraeli and Lord Derby brought forward a bill that doubled the existing electorate and was more democratic than most Conservatives had foreseen. The Prime Minister called it 'a leap in the dark'. The ensuing Cabinet arguments led to both Carnarvon and Cranborne resigning, less than six months after they had all gathered for that weekend at Highclere.

Lord Cranborne considered leaving politics. On 12 July 1867 Georgina gave birth to a boy and her husband asked Carnarvon to be godfather and commented humorously:

'both for auld lang syne and political sympathy, shall we call him Benjamin?' He noted that 'the baby was very like Dizzy till he was washed'. He was in fact christened Edward Herbert Cecil.

Six years later, when he formed his own cabinet, Disraeli reappointed both Salisbury and Carnarvon to their former roles. Salisbury later served as Foreign Secretary and would in due course become one of Britain's longest-serving Prime Ministers. He and his wife continued to be regular guests at Highclere.

Benjamin Disraeli did not return although he often dined with Lord Carnarvon in London. Disraeli's career continued its ascendancy and his friendship with Queen Victoria remained constant until he died. She said of him:

> He is very peculiar ... but very clever and sensible ...
> He is full of poetry, romance and chivalry. When he
> knelt down to kiss my hand, he said, 'In loving loyalty
> and faith.'

Mary Anne Disraeli became ill a year later and,

by then aged seventy-five, never properly recovered. Two years after he and his wife had stayed at Highclere, Benjamin Disraeli made a most unusual suggestion to Queen Victoria. 'After 31 years of Parliamentary toil ... with unfaltering devotion ... may he hope that she would be graciously pleased ... to create [his wife] Viscountess Beaconsfield.'

However embarrassing it might have been, Mary Anne Disraeli was indeed created Viscountess Beaconsfield in

Inscribed title pages from a biography of Sir John MacDonald, published in 1883, in the Library at Highclere

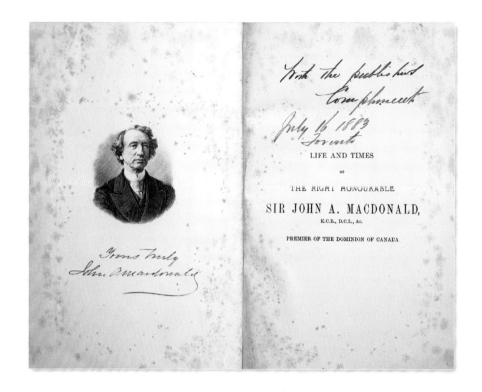

her own right. Her illness was incurable and after her death Disraeli became very depressed, but his friends, including Evelyn Carnarvon's mother Lady Chesterfield, rallied around him. He too was awarded a title: Viscount Beaconsfield.

Lord Carnarvon welcomed John A. Macdonald

to Highclere later in 1866 for the first of several weekends he spent there. Allan the House Steward would have been well briefed to control the accessibility of alcohol. Future weekends were most productive and Macdonald was to forge a lifelong friendship with Lord Carnarvon, who noted in his diary in 1867 that Macdonald 'now appeared with a wife, who I fancy exercises a salutary influence over him so far as his former habits of the bottle are concerned. He was strictly temperate while here and very pleasant.'

Frederic Rogers was at Lord Carnarvon's side, closely observing the drama surrounding the negotiations. 'Macdonald was the ruling genius and spokesman,' Rogers commented:

> I was very greatly struck by his power of management and adroitness. The French delegates were keenly on the watch for anything which weakened their securities.

Lord Carnarvon believed that, without him, the entire Coalition in Canada, and the compromise between the

French and English partisan politicians, would collapse. 'John A.' went on to serve as Prime Minister of Canada for nineteen years. Subsequent visits to England over forthcoming years often began at Highclere. 'John A.' described it as 'a swell place'.

The Canadian Federation was formed

on 1 July 1867 – foretold in a few lines in Highclere's Visitors' Book:

> A Canadian Diplomatist loyal and true
> Comes over to make an agreement with England
> But in nought does he approve that agreement
>   more close
> Than in paying his tribute of homage
> To the beautiful lady of High Clere.

In a letter, 'John A.' wrote to Lord Carnarvon:

> I am glad you like the medal – no one in England has a better right to it than yourself ... I hope you will be able to carry out your half formed intention of visiting Canada. Three months sojourn among us would give you more practical information than you can obtain in any other way. I can assure you of a hearty welcome. We are glad to know that we have in you a friend ...

BREAKFAST

Eggs *Hollandaise* Highclere Castle

SERVES: 6

Whereas Eggs Benedict was created in New York and includes ham, the origin of Eggs Florentine – which includes spinach – is obscure. Nevertheless, both dishes are wonderfully indulgent and therefore my husband disapproves of either for breakfast. One morning, however, when he had left quite early, probably to go shooting, I was left alone, quite content, at the end of the table in the Dining Room, slowly devouring the Eggs *Hollandaise* Highclere Castle that Paul our chef had thought would be a lovely treat for me. They were – Paul's variant features the spinach from Florentine and the ham from Benedict. Occasionally I slip it on to the breakfast menu ...

INGREDIENTS

Hollandaise *sauce*
[**SEE** page 36]

Butter, at room temperature,
for sautéing and spreading

200g (7oz) baby spinach,
washed and sautéed in a pan
with a small knob of butter

3 muffins

6 slices of smoked ham

1 litre (1¾ pints) water

50ml (2fl oz) white wine vinegar

6 eggs

Salt and pepper

Grilled tomatoes, to serve (optional)

METHOD

Make the *Hollandaise* sauce then set it aside somewhere warm until you're ready to serve.

Melt a small knob of butter in a frying pan and sauté the spinach until wilted. Remove from the heat and squeeze excess water from the spinach, if necessary (to avoid making the muffins soggy).

Halve and toast the muffins, spread them with a little butter, top with a slice of ham, then the sautéed spinach, and put to one side.

Bring the water to the boil and add the vinegar. Swirl the water to create a whirlpool then crack the eggs straight into the water (in batches of 2 at a time) and poach them for 4 minutes.

When cooked, remove with a slotted spoon and place on top of the spinach. Season the egg with salt and pepper.

Spoon the *Hollandaise* sauce over the muffins and place them under the grill for 1–2 minutes until brown.

This dish is delicious served with grilled tomatoes sprinkled with a little black pepper.

Devilled Kidneys

SERVES: 3

My brother-in-law, Zed B, delights in cooking devilled kidneys for breakfast on holidays in Cornwall. There is nothing complicated about it, but he begins with buying excellent lambs' kidneys from the butchers in Rock, North Cornwall.

INGREDIENTS

6 lambs' kidneys
(approx. 400g/14oz)

25g (1oz) butter

2 tbsp plain flour

1 tbsp English mustard

1–2 tbsp Worcestershire sauce

Pinch of cayenne pepper

1 tbsp tomato purée

Chunks of bread, to serve (optional)

2 sprigs of watercress, to garnish (optional)

METHOD

Preheat the oven to 190°C/360°F/Gas mark 5, if you don't have an Aga.

Prepare the kidneys by carefully removing the membranes, cutting them in half lengthways and removing the core from each kidney, then rinse them under cold running water.

Melt the butter in a heavy frying pan over a medium heat then add the kidneys and fry for about 2 minutes on each side until browned.

Add the flour, mustard, Worcestershire sauce, cayenne pepper and tomato purée, stirring constantly, then add 2–3 tablespoons of hot water to deglaze the pan. Cook over a medium heat for 2–3 minutes.

Left to keep warm on the hob, we all come along and help ourselves, cutting off chunks of fresh warm bread to mop up the juices. If you wish, transfer the kidneys to serving plates and garnish with watercress.

SAUCE HOLLANDAISE

SERVES: 6

Preparation of *Hollandaise* sauce does require a little practice. The main requirement, however, is to keep gently stirring with a balloon whisk as you add the egg yolks and then the butter.

INGREDIENTS

200g (7oz) unsalted butter

1 bay leaf

6 black peppercorns

2 tbsp white wine vinegar

1 tbsp cold water

4 egg yolks

Salt and freshly ground white pepper

METHOD

Clarify the butter by melting it in a small pan over a low heat until the butter solids separate from the butter fat (do not let the butter brown). Remove and discard the white scum on top and pour the clear butter into a separate heatproof container. Discard the white solids at the bottom of the pan.

Place the bay leaf, peppercorns and vinegar in a small pan over a high heat and let it bubble away for a minute or so, until reduced by two-thirds. Once reduced add the cold water.

In a separate heatproof glass bowl, mix the egg yolks with the strained, reduced vinegar and place the bowl over a pan of gently simmering water, making sure the base of the bowl doesn't touch the water.

Use a balloon whisk to beat the eggs while they are over the heat, for 4–5 minutes, until they are thick and foamy and reach the ribbon stage: ribbon stage is when the egg yolks have started to cook and when you lift the whisk, the sauce makes a 'ribbon' trail that holds in the mixture.

Remove the bowl from the heat and slowly whisk in the melted, clarified butter while it is still warm.

The sauce should now be smooth and creamy. Keep it warm on a very low heat. The sauce will hold for up to 2 hours if it doesn't get too hot (do not refrigerate).

Add salt and white pepper to taste before serving.

Smoked Haddock Kedgeree

SERVES: 6

Originally an Indian dish, this was amended and made popular in Britain during the nineteenth century when the Empire was at its height. The 4th Earl had been appointed Colonial Secretary in 1866 by the then Prime Minister, Benjamin Disraeli. Working closely with Lord Salisbury, Secretary of State for India, he would have eaten many of the new Anglo-Indian dishes as they were introduced into Britain.

Kedgeree can be eaten either hot or cold and was traditionally served as a breakfast dish. Usually made with smoked haddock, this can also be prepared using fresh salmon – Lord Carnarvon's personal favourite.

INGREDIENTS

3 tbsp olive oil

2 medium onions, finely diced

1 small bunch of coriander,
leaves roughly chopped,
stalks roughly chopped

½ tsp turmeric

1 tbsp curry powder

1½ tsp ground cumin

2 bay leaves

750ml (1¼ pints) vegetable stock,
plus an extra 50ml (2fl oz)
[SEE page 160]

700g (1lb 9oz) smoked haddock fillet,
skinned and boned

700ml (1¼ pints) whole milk

Salt and pepper

300g (10½oz) basmati rice, rinsed

4 green cardamom pods

2 cloves

6 eggs, soft-boiled,
peeled and halved

METHOD

Heat the oil in a large saucepan, add the diced onion, chopped coriander stalks, spices and one of the bay leaves and fry over a medium heat for 6–7 minutes until soft. Pour in the stock. Turn up the heat, bring to the boil, then lower the heat and simmer for 15 minutes.

Meanwhile, place the smoked haddock in a large saucepan or wide sauté pan and pour over the milk. Cover and poach over a low heat for 8–10 minutes until the haddock is just cooked.

Remove the fish from the pan with a slotted spoon and place on a large plate or dish. Cover to keep warm, and reserve the milk.

Remove the bay leaf from the stock and add the milk from the haddock to the pan. Bring to the boil and cook, uncovered, until the sauce has reduced by almost half (you want about 850ml/1½ pints after reducing).

Season with salt and pepper then blitz with a hand-held blender until smooth.

Place the rice in a saucepan with the cardamom pods, cloves and remaining bay leaf, cover with boiling water and cook over a medium heat, uncovered, for 15 minutes, or until cooked. Drain and season to taste.

Place the hot rice in warm serving bowls and flake over the haddock fillet. Cover with the curry sauce, garnish with the sliced eggs and sprinkle with the roughly chopped coriander leaves.

Highclere Scrambled Eggs

SERVES: 6

With the help of fourteen Highclere hens, all named after heroines in Jane Austen's novels, my favourite breakfast at the Castle always begins with eggs, preferably scrambled. Everyone makes this and everyone has their own method but the real secret is in getting really good-quality eggs, which is often easier said than done.

Our hens live next door to the bee hives in the old walled kitchen garden. This is now nothing like it used to be in its Victorian heyday when up to twenty-five gardeners lovingly tended it, but it is still a beautiful and peaceful place where I can go for a moment of quiet contemplation and, perhaps, a quick chat with the ladies.

Once you have the right eggs, the next trick is to make sure they are sufficiently yellow and creamy and of just the right consistency. You need to be generous: 2–3 eggs per person and use a heavy pan that does not have too broad a base. This is not an omelette!

INGREDIENTS

150g (5oz) unsalted butter

12 medium eggs (do not beat the eggs before cooking)

Salt and pepper, to taste

50ml (2fl oz) whole milk

50ml (2fl oz) double cream (optional)

Hot buttered toast, to serve

METHOD

Melt the butter in a heavy-based pan over a low heat. Crack in the eggs, season with salt and pepper and add the milk. Stir gently with a wooden spoon, breaking up the yolks and mixing them with the whites, continually moving the egg mixture away from the sides and the bottom of the pan.

After 4–5 minutes, when the mixture is still loose, take the pan off the heat and, if you wish, mix in the double cream. Eat straight away with hot buttered toast.

The SALOON

The Saloon is the heart of Highclere Castle. An amazing space for entertaining, warmed by an immense burnished steel fireplace and dominated by the famous Oak Staircase, it is immediately recognisable to fans of the television series *Downton Abbey*.

Its design may well have been inspired by the original medieval hall that once stood here and was later incorporated into the Georgian remodelling of the house. The ceiling soars to a height of fifty feet and is decorated with intricate stone carving and a vast coat-of-arms at the top of one supporting wall. The grandeur of the decor is reinforced by the rare and splendid Spanish embossed and gilded leather wall coverings. Produced in Córdoba in the mid seventeenth century, they lend richness and warmth to the surrounding stonework.

Designed as a formal reception room, it has always been the most fabulous place for a party. A hundred and fifty guests can assemble here for a reception but it works just as well for weekend house parties when we gather for drinks before lunch or dinner, Scottish reeling or dancing. Brides pause momentarily on the staircase before they carefully descend, brimming over with happiness and excitement; ladies step down lightly in ballgowns and tiaras, ready for the party to begin.

MARGERY GOLDSMITH

Guide

Margery started as a schools' guide at Highclere in March 1993, just before Easter. She had always wanted to guide somewhere interesting and was finishing an Open University history course. Later she became deputy head guide and then in 1998 was offered the job of head guide. Seven years later, she changed tack to work in the office arranging the schools' and group bookings. Of course she admires the grand parklands and historical buildings of Highclere but what she particularly likes is that it is small enough to feel intimate and personal.

'I never get tired of walking into the rooms here: it is a lovely feeling. The Castle has a warmth, a history, and is a lived-in place. My favourite room is the Library because I love books, but my favourite item is the Sèvres plate in the Green Drawing Room that has Madame de Pompadour painted on it, although I am also fond of the spaghetti-eater china figure in there.

'The thing I love doing more than anything else is taking a small group on a tour around the Castle and it does have its funny moments. I was once asked if the paintings in the Smoking Room were genuine "cannellonis" and had to reply with a straight face: "Unfortunately not, they are from the School of Canaletto."

'The schoolchildren just love Egyptology and it amazes me how young children are so interested and get to grips with the complexities of it. A little boy once asked if Lord Carnarvon and his dog were going to be mummified too, whilst another child asked if Tutankhamun still lived in the Castle.

'It is not unusual for Lady Carnarvon to appear spontaneously during a tour and everyone flocks to her for her stories. It causes chaos in small rooms and doorways but is so appreciated by the guests – it creates a sense of fun and warmth. Every day here is different, and flexibility and a sense of humour are essential.'

FISH & SHELLFISH

Beetroot-cured Salmon

SERVES: 6

In November 2007, Paul Brooke-Taylor arrived to cook a trial lunch for my husband, myself and John Gundill, our Castle Manager, as part of his interview to become head chef at Highclere.

I clearly remember this was the first course he chose to cook for us. An excellent, innovative chef, I imagine he hoped at the time that Highclere would be yet another entry on his long CV. I am delighted to say that, besides developing the Castle's reputation as a venue where first-class food is served, like many others he has found a continuing way of life here as well as a career. I appreciate enormously his frankness and passion for cooking.

I love smoked fish and it is so good for us, as is beetroot. The flavour here is subtle and well balanced against the smokiness and oiliness of the salmon. The dish is a wonderful colour and especially eye-catching in the winter months. The salmon is best if it is marinated overnight so make sure you leave plenty of time for preparation.

INGREDIENTS

250g (9oz) table salt

250g (9oz) caster sugar

90g (3¼oz) fresh dill

1kg (2lb 3oz) piece of fresh boneless salmon fillet, skin on and trimmed

400g (14oz) raw red beetroot, peeled and coarsely grated

METHOD

Start by making the lovely green marinade. Blitz the salt, sugar and dill together in a food processor then spread it evenly over the flesh side of the salmon. Cover and refrigerate for 18 hours.

After the marinating time has passed, rinse the fish under cold running water to remove all the salt, sugar and dill.

Once clean, pat the salmon dry and lay it flesh side up on a large baking sheet or board lined with greaseproof paper and cover the top and sides of the fish with the grated beetroot. Wrap the fish and the board in clingfilm and put back in the fridge for a minimum of 4 hours, but longer if possible (up to 48 hours).

Scrape off and discard the beetroot, carefully remove the fish skin, then carve the salmon.

This is great with fresh bread, lemon, *crème fraîche* or just some potato salad.

Seared Scallops

with mussels, clams & crab *bisque*

SERVES: 4

I spent many childhood holidays by the sea in Cornwall. When the spring tides were very low, we would collect mussels from the craggy rocks at the end of the beach and bring them back to the house to clean them.

My father used to drive round to Port Isaac in his beloved Bentley (which was called Boris) and choose crabs and scallops from the fishing boats. We would use the crab to make a *gratin* [SEE page 70], the scallops might well be grilled and served with a cheesy *béchamel* sauce [SEE page 62] and the mussels cooked with white wine, garlic and onions. Here, Paul combines a selection of shellfish with a *bisque*.

FOR THE BISQUE

50g (2oz) unsalted butter

1 onion, chopped

200g (7oz) cooked white and brown crab meat

50ml (2fl oz) white wine

1 tsp peeled and finely chopped fresh root ginger

300ml (10fl oz) fish stock

100g (3½oz) fresh tomatoes, chopped

50ml (2fl oz) single cream

10g (½oz) tarragon, leaves finely chopped

Salt and pepper

FOR THE SHELLFISH

50g (2oz) butter

½ tbsp olive oil

12 medium-sized fresh scallops

100ml (4fl oz) white wine

12 fresh mussels

12 fresh clams

2 garlic cloves, skinned but kept whole

50g (2oz) samphire, to garnish (optional)

METHOD

For the *bisque*, melt the butter in a large saucepan over a medium heat. Add the onion, season with salt and pepper and cook for 6 minutes or until the onion is soft but not coloured.

Add the remaining ingredients to the pan, apart from the cream and tarragon, and simmer gently for 18 minutes, or until the tomatoes are completely soft. Remove the saucepan from the heat and purée the *bisque* in a blender, then stir in the cream and chopped tarragon.

For the shellfish, heat the butter and oil in a large frying pan over a high heat. Start with the scallops and sear them in the pan for 2 minutes on each side until golden brown.

While the scallops cook, pour the white wine into a small pan, add the mussels, clams and garlic, then cover and cook for 4 minutes over a high heat or until all the shells open up. Discard any that remain closed. If you are using the samphire, add it to the pan after the mussels and clams have been cooking for 3 minutes (it only needs a minute to soften). Remove the scallops and the pan of mussels and clams from the heat.

Reheat the crab *bisque* in a pan over a low–medium heat, taking care not to let it boil or the liquid may split. Arrange the scallops, mussels and clams among four shallow bowls then spoon the crab *bisque* around the shellfish. Garnish with the samphire (if using) and serve straight away.

John Dory

with *Sauce Hollandaise*

The Victorian cookery writer Eliza Acton observed that John Dory, 'though of uninviting appearance, is considered by some persons as the most delicious fish that appears at table'. It should either be cooked in a fish kettle or baked very gently in order not to dry it out; hence a buttery *Hollandaise* sauce makes an ideal accompaniment.

The John Dory was also known as St Peter's fish. The Gospel of Matthew (17: 24–27) tells the story of a miracle: a coin in the mouth of a fish. Jesus tells Peter to 'go to the lake and throw out your line. Take the first fish you catch; open its mouth and you will find a four-drachma coin. Take it and give it to them [the tax collectors] for my tax and yours.' Peter picked up the fish and took the coin out, leaving his fingerprints behind the fish's gills. I rather wish we could all pay our tax in this way.

INGREDIENTS

1 John Dory

Sauce Hollandaise
[SEE page 36]

Salt

METHOD

Clean the fish thoroughly and cut off the fins (you may wish to cut off the head, too). Lay it in a fish kettle or a large, shallow pan, cover with cold water, and add a pinch of salt. Slowly bring it to the boil, and simmer gently for 15 minutes.

While the fish is cooking, make the *Hollandaise* sauce.

Serve the fish whole or divide into fillets, place on a warm plate and drizzle the sauce on top.

FISH STOCK

MAKES: approx. 3 litres (5–6 pints)

The key to a fresh fish stock is not to cook it for too long.

INGREDIENTS

1kg (2·2lb) assortment of fresh fish bones and heads, and prawn shells with heads (you can use any fish trimmings, but avoid oily fish, salmon and red mullet, and ask your fishmonger to remove the gills)

1 tbsp olive oil

1 medium leek, washed and roughly chopped

1 celery stalk, roughly chopped

1 fennel bulb, roughly chopped

2–3 sprigs of flat-leaf parsley

1 bay leaf

A few sprigs of tarragon

6 black peppercorns

250ml (8½fl oz) white wine

METHOD

Rinse the fish trimmings in a colander under cold running water to remove any blood, then set to one side.

Heat the oil in a large pan, add the vegetables, black peppercorns and herbs and sauté until they are soft but not brown. Add the white wine and let it come to the boil then simmer for 2 minutes to burn off the alcohol. Add the rinsed fish trimmings and enough water to just cover it all (it's important not to have too much liquid in the pan, as you cannot reduce fish stock). Leave to simmer, uncovered, for 20–25 minutes, then skim any froth off the surface of the stock and pass it through a fine sieve into a heatproof container.

Filets de Sole à l'Italienne

SERVES: 4

We often serve fish rather than meat for dinner at Highclere, as it is easier to digest at that time of day. The photograph opposite shows a whole sole, but our chef at Highclere often uses sole fillets instead. Fillets of sole can be cooked in many different ways but here are served with a traditional *béchamel* sauce. A good vegetable to serve with this would be green beans or roasted baby tomatoes.

INGREDIENTS

2 large shallots, chopped

2 large whole Dover sole or 4 sole fillets (about 175g/6oz each)

200ml (7fl oz) white wine

25g (1oz) unsalted butter, plus extra for greasing

250g (9oz) seasonal mushrooms

1 leek, sliced

75g (3oz) chopped ham

300ml (10fl oz) béchamel sauce [SEE page 62]

Lemon wedges, to serve (optional)

METHOD

Preheat the oven to 190°C/360°F/Gas mark 5.

Grease a large ovenproof dish that is big enough to take both sole, or all four fillets, side by side.

Scatter the shallots in the bottom of the dish and lay the fish (whole or fillets) on top. Pour over the wine. Cook in the oven for 12–15 minutes, or until the fish is just cooked.

While the fish is cooking, melt the butter in a large frying pan and fry the mushrooms and leek until the mushrooms are lightly golden and the leeks still green. If necessary, add a little more butter while frying. Stir in the ham, set aside and keep warm.

Make the *béchamel* sauce.

When the fish is cooked, strain off the cooking liquid and stir it into the sauce (you should have just over 100ml/3½fl oz). Cover the fish with foil to keep it warm.

Gently stir most of the mushroom, leek and ham mixture into the *béchamel* sauce (reserve the rest) and warm through briefly.

To serve, place the whole fish or the fish fillets onto a large warmed serving platter, surround with the *béchamel* sauce and scatter over the reserved mushroom mixture. To serve the whole sole, run a sharp knife along the back of each fish to free from the bones, then peel back the skin to reveal the fillets.

Filets de Sole Mornay

SERVES: 8

In 1903, Auguste Escoffier published a cookbook that remains the bible of the classic cuisine of France, *Le Guide Culinaire*. In it he begins by describing the fundamental techniques of cooking before including well over 2,500 recipes. These include endless ideas for how to cook sole: poaching it, rolling it, stuffing it. But a velvety *béchamel* or white sauce, flavoured with cheese, is a classic and comforting combination that is hard to beat.

INGREDIENTS

675g (1lb 7oz) sole fillets, skin removed (if serving as a starter, slice large fillets in half lengthways)

Juice of 1 medium lemon

25g (1oz) unsalted butter, melted

Béchamel *sauce* [SEE page 62]

2 tbsp grated Parmesan cheese (or more, to taste)

1 tsp English mustard

Salt and pepper

METHOD

Preheat the oven to 180°C/350°F/Gas mark 4.

Wipe each fillet, roll it up and secure by piercing a cocktail stick through the centre. Place the fillets in a shallow rectangular baking dish, season and drizzle with the lemon juice and melted butter.

Cover the dish with foil and bake for 12–15 minutes, until the fish is cooked through.

Meanwhile, make the *béchamel* sauce, adding the grated cheese and mustard to the finished sauce.

Remove the fish from the oven, arrange on a warm serving plate and pour over the *béchamel* sauce.

Sole à la Dugléré

SERVES: 4

Adolphe Dugléré was a *chef de cuisine* to the Rothschild family until 1848 before becoming head chef at the Café Anglais in Paris. It was here in 1867 that he served a famous meal that became known as the Dîner des Trois Empereurs (Dinner of the Three Emperors) for Tsar Alexander II of Russia, his son the Tsarevich (who later became Tsar Alexander III) and King William I of Prussia, the German Emperor. A sauce *à la Dugléré* consists of fish poached in stock (fish *fumet*) with white wine on a bed of tomatoes *concassées* (crushed) with minced onion, shallots and chopped parsley. It is served with a *beurre blanc* consisting of the cooking liquid combined with butter.

INGREDIENTS

2 whole lemon sole,
skinned and filleted so that the two fillets
from the top and bottom of the fish
stay together

75g (2½oz) chilled unsalted butter,
cubed, plus extra for greasing

2 tomatoes, peeled and roughly chopped

15g (½oz) curly-leaf parsley, finely chopped

½ medium onion, finely chopped

Sprig of thyme

1 bay leaf

300ml (10fl oz) dry white wine

2 tbsp double cream

Salt and pepper

METHOD

Preheat the oven
to 180°C/350°F/Gas mark 4.

Season the fish fillets with salt and pepper, lay them on a buttered baking dish, scatter over the tomatoes and sprinkle with the parsley and chopped onion. Add the thyme, bay leaf and the wine and finish with a knob of butter. Cover the dish with foil and bake in the oven for 12 minutes.

Remove the dish from the oven and strain the stock into a pan. Remove the bay leaf and thyme from the fish, then set it aside, covered to keep warm.

Put the pan of stock over a medium heat and let it bubble until it has reduced by half.

Add the cream and bring it back to a simmer for 10 minutes.

Remove from the heat. Whisk the cold cubed butter into the stock to thicken it.

Grill the fish briefly, then coat it with the sauce.

We like to serve this with green beans, wilted spinach and new potatoes.

BÉCHAMEL SAUCE

A *béchamel* saunce was the first sauce my mother taught me to cook. Today it is still considered one of the foundation sauces of French cuisine. It first appeared in a cookbook in 1651 named for Béchamel, the chief steward of Louis XIV of France (the Sun King). Originally it was made with a lot of cream.

INGREDIENTS

25g (1oz) unsalted butter

25g (1oz) plain flour

250ml (9fl oz) milk

Salt and pepper

75ml (2½fl oz) single cream (optional)

METHOD

Melt the butter in a medium pan. Stir in the flour and cook for 1–2 minutes, then remove from the heat and gradually whisk in the milk.

Let it simmer, stirring constantly, until thickened. Season with salt and pepper, then stir in the cream (if using). You can thin it out with a little extra milk if necessary.

Lobster Thermidor

SERVES: 4

This rich dish is nowadays viewed as a great treat, although traditionally lobster was not at all highly prized. Given that lobsters are best bought alive and cooked at home, Paul, our chef at Highclere, prefers to put the live crustaceans into the freezer for two hours before cooking them in boiling-hot fish stock, believing it is the most humane way to deal with them.

INGREDIENTS

23 litres (5½ pints) fish stock
[SEE page 58]

2 live lobsters,
placed in the freezer for 2 hours

50g (2oz) unsalted butter

2 banana shallots, finely diced

100ml (3½fl oz) white wine

250ml (9fl oz) double cream

1 tbsp English mustard

20g (¾ oz) chervil, chopped

20g (¾ oz) tarragon, chopped,
plus extra torn leaves to serve

20g (¾ oz) parsley, chopped

Juice of ½ lemon

75g (2½oz) Parmesan cheese, grated

2 medium egg yolks

Salt and pepper

METHOD

Pour the fish stock into a large pan and bring to the boil. Take the live lobsters from the freezer and place them immediately in the stock. Turn down the heat to a gentle simmer. Depending on the size of the lobsters, it will take 12–20 minutes for them to cook (they will go a nice pink colour). When cooked, use tongs or a slotted spoon to remove from the stock. Transfer the lobsters to a tray and leave to cool a little, then chill. Reserve the lobster stock.

To make the sauce, melt the butter in a saucepan over a medium heat, add the shallots and cook for 3 minutes, until soft but not coloured. Pour in the white wine and simmer until reduced by half, then add the lobster stock and reduce by half again. Add the cream, bring back to the boil and reduce by half. Now add the mustard, herbs, lemon juice, and 25g (1oz) of the Parmesan. Heat briefly, season with salt and pepper, and set aside.

Cut the chilled lobsters in half lengthways and remove the opaque white meat from the tails and claws. Discard the tomalley (the yellow-green substance which serves as the liver and pancreas) and the dead man's fingers (cream/grey-coloured growths in the head). Neither of these are poisonous but just rather unpleasant to eat.

Remove any meat from the heads and set aside. Cut the white meat into bite-sized pieces and place back into the shells, ready to cover with the sauce.

Whisk the egg yolks into the warm sauce and pour the sauce over the lobster meat in the shells. Transfer the shells to a baking sheet.

Sprinkle the remaining Parmesan over the lobsters. Cook under the grill for 10–15 minutes until the sauce is golden.

Scatter with torn tarragon leaves and serve the lobsters with green salad and warm buttered new potatoes.

Potted Shrimps

with malted brown toast & butter

SERVES: *4 people watching Downton Abbey on Sunday evening*

This is a classic dish, a favourite in the London gentlemen's clubs. 'Potting' is actually a traditional way of preserving food and was a commonly used technique in eighteenth-century households. Potted meat or fish from game birds, salmon or shrimps was sealed in a glass jar under a layer of butter. Today potted shrimps are commonly eaten as a starter or Sunday supper, which can be prepared in advance.

Potted shrimps was a favourite dish of author Ian Fleming and his fictional creation James Bond. Ian Fleming and his wife much enjoyed the company of Porchey, 6th Earl of Carnarvon, and they used to holiday abroad together. Back in England I am sure they much enjoyed eating potted shrimps at Highclere together as well.

INGREDIENTS

200g (7oz) unsalted butter

Generous pinch of ground mace

*1–2 pinches of cayenne pepper (to taste),
plus extra to serve*

*Generous pinch of ground white pepper
(or black pepper, for a stronger taste)*

1 tsp thyme leaves, plus 4 sprigs of thyme to serve

Tabasco sauce, to taste

*½ tsp anchovy paste or Gentleman's Relish
(optional)*

200g (7oz) cooked and peeled brown shrimps

1 lemon, quartered, to serve

Malted brown toast and butter, to serve

METHOD

Gently melt the butter in a small saucepan. Carefully pour the clear (clarified) butter into another saucepan, leaving behind the milky solids. Pour 2–3 tablespoons of the clarified butter into a warmed, small jug and set aside.

[**CHEF'S TIP**: You don't need to clarify the butter if you're planning to eat the shrimps within a couple of days. Clarifying the butter just preserves the shrimps for longer.]

Add the mace, cayenne pepper, white or black pepper, thyme leaves, about 6 drops of Tabasco sauce (or to taste) and the anchovy paste (if using) to the clarified butter in the pan and place over a low heat. Cook very gently for 1–2 minutes, then add the cooked, peeled shrimps. Squeeze the juice from one of the lemon quarters into the mixture, stir for a couple of minutes, then remove from the heat.

Divide the mixture between four ramekins, pour on the reserved clarified butter to cover each serving with a thin layer and put into the fridge to set.

Remove the potted shrimps from the fridge 20 minutes or so before you want to serve them. Sprinkle with a little cayenne pepper and garnish each serving with a sprig of thyme.

Serve with lemon quarters and hot buttered toast.

Matelotte d'anguilles

SERVES: 6 as a starter or 4 as a main course

Stewed eels have a long history in British cookery. They are high in protein and very nutritious. They were particularly popular during the nineteenth century when jellied eels were enjoyed in steamy London cafés or pie-and-mash shops. Recipes became highly prized and individual shops fought to keep theirs a secret.

INGREDIENTS

900g (2lb) prepared eels
(ask your fishmonger to remove the heads and skin,
and cut them into chunks)

1 medium onion

4–5 cloves

1 bay leaf

Grated zest and juice of 1 lemon

100ml (3½fl oz) Madeira wine

1·5 litres (2½ pints) chicken or vegetable stock
[SEE page 114 or 160 respectively]

20g (¾oz) butter

1 tbsp plain flour

200ml (8fl oz) double cream

3 tsp cayenne pepper

Salt and pepper

METHOD

Put the chunks of eel in a saucepan, then stud the onion with the cloves and add it to the pan with the bay leaf and lemon zest. Pour in the Madeira and stock and season generously. Bring to the boil then reduce the heat and simmer for 30 minutes, covered, until the eel is tender.

Lift the eel out of the cooking liquor with a slotted spoon and place in a warm serving bowl. Cover and keep warm. Pour the liquor into a heatproof jug.

Melt the butter in the pan and add the flour. Cook, stirring, over a medium heat, for 1 minute to cook the flour and form a roux, then slowly pour in the cooking liquor, stirring all the time.

Once all the cooking liquor has been added, cook the sauce for about 10 minutes until it thickens, then stir in the cream. Season well. Heat to boiling point, add the cayenne pepper and lemon juice, then pour the sauce over the eel chunks and serve.

Crab *au gratin*

by **Almina, 5th Countess of Carnarvon**

SERVES: 4

Almina, like her father, Alfred de Rothschild, was a dedicated hostess. As was common amongst the wealthy at that time, her preferred recipes invariably involved plenty of butter and cream and always the best ingredients.

This crab dish is, however, very practical if you are not blessed with the number of staff who helped Almina at Highclere. You can make up the *gratin* in ramekin dishes a day ahead, chill them and reheat in the oven until the sauce is bubbling, about 15 minutes before serving.

INGREDIENTS

285ml (9½fl oz) whole milk or single cream

Pinch of ground cloves

*25g (1oz) unsalted butter,
plus extra for greasing*

25g (1oz) plain flour

*75g (2½oz) grated cheese
(Gruyère or Parmesan work well)*

Pinch of cayenne pepper

450g (14oz) cooked white crab meat

*1 tsp anchovy essence or anchovy paste,
to taste*

5–6 tbsp fresh white breadcrumbs

*10g (½oz) fresh herbs of choice (such as
tarragon, chives or flat-leaf parsley), chopped*

Salt and pepper

METHOD

To make the white sauce, heat the milk or cream in a pan with the ground cloves until it reaches boiling point. Meanwhile, melt the butter in a separate heavy-based pan over a low heat, then add the flour and cook for 1 minute, stirring, to form a roux. Gradually pour in the hot milk or cream, whisking constantly and making sure it does not catch on the bottom of the pan.

Cook the sauce for about 5 minutes, stirring, until it thickens, then remove from the heat and stir in all but 3 tablespoons of the grated cheese. Season with salt and pepper and add the cayenne pepper.

Mix the herbs into the anchovy paste, reserving some to serve.

Gently stir the crab meat into the sauce and mix in the anchovy essence or anchovy paste, according to taste.

Divide the crab mixture between four 150ml (5fl oz) ramekins, sprinkle each serving with some of the breadcrumbs and the remaining grated cheese. Place the dishes on a baking sheet and grill under a preheated grill for about 4 minutes, until lightly browned and bubbling.

Sprinkle with the reserved herbs and serve with fresh crusty bread.

[**CHEF'S TIP:** For an alternative to cloves, cayenne and anchovies, try adding some Dijon mustard and a glass of sherry to the sauce, or parsley and lemon, which keep the crab flavour simply delicious.]

Saumon Grillé
Sauce aux câpres

SERVES: 4

Capers are the small flower buds of a Mediterranean shrub and are about the size of large peppercorns. Once picked, they are preserved in oil or vinegar or brine. They add a distinctive flavour to many fish or meat dishes. As they are salty, wash them before use and beware of adding further salt to any dish that uses them.

This is a great quick supper dish.

FOR THE SAUCE

175g (6oz) butter

2 tbsp capers, roughly chopped, plus 2 tsp caper brine

1 tbsp anchovy essence

FOR THE SALMON

4 × 140g (5oz) salmon fillets, skin on, pin-boned and trimmed

175g (6oz) butter

1 tbsp oil

Ground pepper

METHOD

For the sauce: melt the butter in a saucepan over a low heat, add the chopped capers, caper brine and anchovy essence, stir, and bring to a simmer to help the flavours infuse (be careful not to burn the butter). After a few minutes, take off the heat but keep warm.

Cook the salmon fillets on a hot griddle pan skin side down with the butter and oil for 3–5 minutes on each side. Season with pepper, remove from the pan, pour over the warm caper sauce and serve.

Poached Whole Salmon

SERVES: 16 as part of a summer buffet

Poaching salmon is one of the easiest and most delicious ways to cook it. The fish is infused with the flavours of the bouillon and the result is moist and tender. You can serve it with *Hollandaise* or just a little lemon and cold-pressed olive oil.

INGREDIENTS

2·5kg (5lb 1oz) whole salmon, scaled, gutted and cleaned (head and tail left on)

1 medium onion, roughly chopped

1 leek, washed, trimmed and roughly chopped

4 celery stalks, roughly chopped

12 black peppercorns

Good pinch of sea salt

1 bay leaf

1 lemon, quartered

2 star anise

250g (9oz) softened unsalted butter, for piping

Caviar, to garnish (optional)

4 cucumbers, peeled and thinly sliced, to garnish

Hollandaise *sauce, to serve*
[**SEE** page 36]

2 bunches of watercress, to serve

Cooked asparagus, to serve

Cooked new potatoes, to serve

METHOD

Place the whole salmon in a fish kettle, gently easing it in and bending it slightly if necessary, to fit. Add the chopped onion, leek, celery, black peppercorns, sea salt, bay leaf, lemon quarters and star anise. Completely cover the fish with cold water and cover the kettle with a lid or foil.

Bring to the boil and as soon as it has come to the boil, turn off the heat and leave the fish to stand in the stock until cool (the fish will continue to cook). To check if the fish is cooked, pull gently on the dorsal fin – it should come away easily. If it doesn't, cook it for a little longer.

Once cool, carefully remove the fish from the kettle (depending on the size of your fish, this might be a two-person job) and place it on a large serving plate or platter, then gently remove the skin by peeling it away from the flesh, leaving the fish whole and intact.

To dress the salmon, you can pipe soft butter (beaten until smooth) in rosettes along the spine, using a piping bag fitted with a small star nozzle, and top each with some caviar (if you wish).

To make cucumber 'scales', lay the peeled cucumber slices all over the top of the fish, slightly overlapping. Pipe an extra star on the head of the salmon to represent its eye.

The salmon is best served with Highclere *Hollandaise*, watercress salad, asparagus and new potatoes.

LES TAYLOR

Head of Security

Les has run Highclere's security office for nearly thirty-five years. His original career was with the Hampshire police force, which he joined in 1952. From there he went into the CID, firstly in Fareham and then the Isle of Wight. In 1964 he was posted to Whitchurch, a town six miles south of Highclere, as section sergeant and, when he retired in 1982, Lord Carnarvon (the current Earl's father) offered him a job organising security at Highclere.

At that time, Lord Carnarvon was the Queen's Racing Manager. Calm and highly discreet, Les was perfect for the job and very much enjoyed driving his new employer to race meetings and stable visits and liaising with the various personal protection officers he came across.

Les also used to load for Lord Carnarvon. In those days the shooting was all private but that began to change after the 6th Earl's death. Les was shoot captain when the first 'let' days began to be offered and he can remember it clearly as a low-key but nevertheless seismic change for the estate.

He loves golf, shooting and sailing and used to keep a family fishing boat and had a 'beach' boat moored at Hillhead. Now he relies on his son and son-in-law to keep him afloat, both of whom have boats near Southampton, and enjoys going out with his grandchildren.

Les is eighty-nine and still going strong. He can remember the current Earl and his brother riding their bikes round Milford Lake when they were six or seven years old. It remains his favourite part of the estate.

'It is a family-run place and in consequence you become part of the family. It is a family job and you are your own boss to some extent, which suits someone like me.'

A WEEKEND
WITH HENRY JAMES

'The whole of anything is never told ... it groups together.'

HENRY JAMES

August 1886

Born in New York in 1843, Henry James was one of the greatest novelists of the nineteenth century. Thanks to his father's inherited wealth James spent much of his early life travelling with his parents to London, Paris and Geneva. Many of his novels are consequently set in Europe and explore the cultural and psychological differences between the Old World and the New. In his books he created memorable archetypal young American women, such as Isabel Archer in *The Portrait of a Lady* or *Daisy Miller* in the novella of the same name, whose innocence is manipulated and destroyed by the bitterness of experience.

The early novels were a tremendous commercial and critical success. James contributed to magazines as well as being an assiduous correspondent. He met other literary figures, both in England and in France, and during the middle years of his career was especially influenced by French writers such as Émile Zola. *The Bostonians* was published as was the custom then in serial form in *The Century Magazine* in 1885-6, and immediately after that in book form. The author had previously visited Highclere and that summer of 1886 he visited again.

ABOVE
Excerpt from Highclere Castle Visitors' Book, August 1886

Elsie, 4th Countess of Carnarvon

Henry James (1843–1916)

Lady Carnarvon and Henry James were sitting under the welcome shade of the spreading branches of the Cedar of Lebanon planted in 1770. Slim and very upright, partly through good deportment and partly from the rigid support of her boned, high-collared dress, Lady Carnarvon was presiding over afternoon tea on this late-summer sunlit afternoon. Her guests had almost all gathered around her after their walks or afternoon rest. She had been delighted that Henry James had once again accepted their invitation to stay at Highclere.

An entry in Lady Carnarvon's diary following the earlier visit by the celebrated novelist, dated 14 December 1884, recorded that: 'We like Mr James, he is very quiet and nice ...' The novelist was a welcome addition to any house party, with his distinguished looks and bearing.

For the past three years he had been entirely engrossed in his writing and had recently dispatched the last instalment of *The Princess Casamassima* to his publishers, commenting that it seemed 'an interminable work'. In the spring of that year he had moved into an airy flat in De Vere Gardens, Kensington, which he liked very much. However, he enjoyed nothing better than receiving an invitation to spend an August weekend in the country. He and Lady Carnarvon had spent the afternoon discussing books and literature, and she had commented that she had greatly enjoyed *The Portrait of a Lady* and suggested how much their present outlook reflected the opening paragraph of his novel:

> Under certain circumstances there are few hours in life more agreeable than the hour dedicated to the ceremony known as afternoon tea ... the situation is in itself delightful ... Disposed upon the lawn of an old English country house in ... the perfect middle of a splendid summer afternoon.

Aged twenty-nine, Lady Carnarvon was an earnest, clever young woman with large grey eyes and a clear complexion. She had been born Elisabeth (Elsie) Howard of Greystoke Castle and had married Lord Carnarvon seven years before when she was around the same age as Isabel Archer when James began exploring her fictional life. By contrast to the American heroine, however, Lady Carnarvon was not an heiress and had a strong sense of belonging to the aristocratic *milieu* in which she lived.

The 4th Earl of Carnarvon with his son Aubrey

In 1886 Henry James was forty-three years old, already balding but with thick dark hair around the lower part of his head and a neatly trimmed beard and moustache as was the fashion. He was always very well dressed. Yet, despite Elsie's best efforts, he felt detached from the house party in myriad small unspoken ways.

His quixotic view of the English class system informed his novels and he had much empathy for those characters who sought to move beyond the confines of the class into which they were born. He was now often invited into the world of the English country house and had met leading figures across British cultural and political society. He was aware that Robert Browning, whom he admired, was a long-standing friend of the Carnarvons.

Elsie revealed that her husband had not long since built a villa above the picturesque fishing village of Portofino in Northern Italy, which they called 'Altachiara' (an Italian version of Highclere). Her husband thought that part of the world 'really divine' and for the first time they had spent from February to April in their new home where the weather had been glorious.

As a well-travelled man and committed Europhile, like the Carnarvons, Henry James knew Italy well and was minded to spend several months there soon.

Lord Carnarvon arrived then and waved to everyone at the tea party to dispense with formalities and sit down. He enjoyed gathering friends from the worlds of literature and politics and engaged them all with his sense of humour and easy manners, creating a marvellously convivial atmosphere.

Lord and Lady Carnarvon were not merely from the same social circles, they were also cousins. His first wife, Evelyn, had tragically died in childbirth in January 1875, leaving behind three small children and their newborn daughter, Victoria, named for Queen Victoria, who had offered to be godmother.

Devastated by his grief, Lord Carnarvon had withdrawn from politics to recover himself and spend time with his children. It was therefore as a widower that he had met Elsie in the autumn of 1878. He had immediately decided she would be the perfect stepmother to his four children. He therefore wrote to her mother, who was also his aunt, about the 'great charm that Elsie has for and over me ... the most beautiful character that I could entirely love ...'

Her mother was not at all sure but Elsie, when finally consulted, decided to accept the offer. She had little time to reflect as they were married on 26 December 1878.

The 4th Earl of Carnarvon at his desk in his Study

Henry Howard Molyneux Herbert, the 4th Earl of Carnarvon, was a slight, bewhiskered figure, one of the foremost classical scholars of his time, a polymath fluent in Ancient Greek and Latin. He had been part of the Victorian political scene in England for nearly thirty years but remained interested in other places and societies. Indeed he had sailed his own yacht the *Marcia* to Australia and Canada during his tenure as Colonial Secretary.

Now that he was no longer in government he had more time for his own work. To that end, he had been diligently working on his correspondence and translation of Homer's *Odyssey* in his study before joining his wife and friends for tea. Just over a year previously, in June 1885, the Prime Minister, Lord Salisbury, had persuaded Lord Carnarvon to serve as Lord Lieutenant of Ireland.

Worried about the danger, given that four bombs had been set off in London in 1885 as well as all the agrarian crime and disturbances in Ireland and the general impossibility of the task, Lord Carnarvon had only accepted the role on the understanding it would be a temporary appointment, something in the nature of a special mission. He wrote to Salisbury: 'I will accept the task, do my best to carry the Government over an acknowledged crisis.'

He noted that his approach would be one of conciliation and his first steps would be to ascertain the facts and opinions on the spot. Therefore he and Elsie had travelled through Ireland, unusually without armed escorts, which created much goodwill. Carnarvon met the Irish Nationalist Charles Parnell and concluded that Ireland needed 'hard cash and kind words'. He also managed to acquire further grants for schools in Ireland because he believed: 'A good education is the best heritage we can give our children.'

Lord Carnarvon judged that Home Rule (government based in Dublin rather than London) would surely please the majority of the Irish and bring peace, but his views were out of kilter with his own Tory Party.

Lord Salisbury's government only survived seven months. In consequence Lord Carnarvon had to resign, leaving Ireland at the end of January 1886. His departure was marked by displays of appreciation for, according to one report, he was a man 'with a heart of gold ... who came with a message of peace ... for a brief space he was the idol of the people'. Public sentiment in England, however, remained opposed to Home Rule. After Salisbury, Gladstone had tried to bring forward a Home Rule Bill but, defeated in its turn, his government fell.

Carte de visite showing Aubrey,
the 4th Earl's and Elsie Carnarvon's eldest son

Drawings by Elsie's children,
Aubrey and Mervyn

Yet again, for the third time in twelve months, a new government would be formed. If Highclere was an oasis of peace, there had been riots in London. The newspapers, meanwhile, were filled with disturbing news of troubles in Ireland and marches and riots in Belfast.

Henry James had been closely following

'the all-overshadowing Irish question'. It remained high on the agenda for house-party discussion this weekend. James commented that he did not know enough about the subject to contribute. However, Lord Carnarvon would surely be the best-informed man to talk about the issues involved.

Lady Carnarvon had stood up to help the footmen rearrange the chairs. She adored her husband and was pleased to see him looking less tired than he had done recently. He was twenty-five years older than she was and the strain he had lived under for the past few years concerned her.

Lord Carnarvon sat down next to Sir George Russell, the MP for Wokingham, whom he noted 'is himself a very nice and pleasant companion' and from whom he gathered

news about the political manoeuvring behind the scenes for a place in Lord Salisbury's new Conservative cabinet. Lord Carnarvon commented that Salisbury 'must have a not very pleasant time. Randolph [Churchill] is already a rival that can compel or thwart, or drive or hold back.'

Lady Russell sat chatting to Lewis Morris, a lawyer but more notably a highly regarded Welsh poet. He was a friend of Lord Tennyson and, at this stage, a possible candidate for Poet Laureate. Listening quietly was Gudbrand Vigfusson, the foremost Icelandic language scholar and a longstanding Oxford friend of Lord Carnarvon.

Elsie smiled as she noticed the little painted

donkey cart, led by Stratton the groom, come into view and proceed slowly across the gravel towards them. It bore her sister-in-law Lady Gwendolen and Elsie's elder son, now six years old. Unmarried and living much of the time in the Castle, Lady Gwendolen was adored by all her nephews and nieces. She was a constant presence in their lives – not very tall but with a twinkling smile and apparently all the time in

Gwendolen in the donkey carriage, drawn in 1854

the world to devote to them. She was very happy to entertain them all, to read to them, to spoil them – and occasionally to remonstrate with them.

Gwendolen had once given her eldest nephew and niece (now in their twenties) some bows and arrows. West the under-butler found them using the Van Dyck painting in the Dining Room for target practice. Lord Carnarvon had been away at the time but Mrs Powell the housekeeper had immediately requested the help of Lady Gwendolen to propose an alternative firing range. Luckily, their aim had been quite poor. Their aunt also tactfully pointed out that it was perhaps not the most suitable location for water fights.

Elsie had added two more young sons to the gang of children at Highclere. Her eldest, Aubrey, was already adept at extracting toys from Aunt Gwendolen. He had begged her for a spear, which soon became embedded in an engraving, leading to early confiscation, whilst a saw had been swiftly purloined and was hanging suspended by a blue ribbon out of reach in the schoolroom after much protest from governesses.

The donkey ground to a halt and the groom opened the door to help out first Aubrey and then Lady Gwendolen. Elsie excused herself and walked happily towards her son, whom she and her husband always called Hereward (they both believed they were descended from Hereward the Wake, the eleventh-century Anglo-Saxon leader). Aubrey ran towards her and then dipped past her, launching himself at his father, laughing with delight. Carnarvon smiled, hugging him and listening as the child chattered about his ride and his books. Lord Carnarvon doted on his little son; Elsie and he took Hereward everywhere, from Ireland during their time there to Portofino.

Whilst in Italy, Carnarvon had become ever-more concerned about Hereward's eyesight. A leading oculist, Dr Leibnitz, was consulted and he recommended that the boy should read for no more than twenty minutes a day. Carnarvon was distraught, but helped his son continue his education by ear, listening and reciting. Undaunted by his near blindness, Hereward's enthusiasm and intelligence would carry him onwards in life.

The ancient Hereward was by legend a hero

and his would turn out to be an apt name for a child who, as
a man, would demonstrate outstanding bravery at Mons and
then Gallipoli. A fluent linguist in over seven languages, an
intelligence officer in the Middle East and Balkans, he was
said to have inspired the character of Sandy Arbuthnot, who
appeared in several of the books in the Richard Hannay series
written by John Buchan.

Hereward's little brother Mervyn was only three years
old and currently up in the Nursery on the top floor of the
Castle with Nurse Osmond. Their half-sister Vera was helping
to look after and amuse him. Unfortunately for Aubrey, he
would soon be collected by an assistant nursemaid and borne
off unwillingly for his tea.

This was served by the nursery footman in Nanny's
domain on the third floor. Mrs Osmond was in charge of
ensuring the children had appropriate food, and tea for them
would have consisted of simple and wholesome things such as
a boiled egg with toast soldiers, bread and jam, and tea buns.
Like every nanny she was full of little rhymes, such as:

Hearts like doors open with ease
To very, very little keys.
And don't forget that two of these
Are 'Yes', I think, and 'if you please'.

Aubrey loved her and raced along the corridor towards
the nursery rooms in which his father before him had spent
his childhood. It had been just as happy, with kind nurses if
a stricter routine.

Gwendolen meanwhile had joined the tea party

on the lawn and sat down next to Henry James. Never short
of conversation, her brother had noted that at the moment she
was 'wonderful in her general health, spirits and her interest
in everything. The greatest change [was] in her voice – altered
by the loss of some teeth. But she was quite delightful, and as
fresh in all her interests now as she was 30 years ago, with
such interest and sympathy with everything.'

Given that her own life had been constrained through
illness, she lived vicariously through her endless interest in
other people's. She confided to Henry James that she had

Rules of 'Golf Croquet'

Croquet was very popular during Queen Victoria's reign. Women enjoyed it particularly as it was a decorous game with the advantage that long skirts allowed the covert manoeuvring of a ball to a better position. It was a game Elsie could enjoy playing with her stepchildren as well as with her guests.

Association Croquet is the older and more complicated form, but Golf Croquet tends to be quicker and more accessible.

Ideally you need four players. Each player chooses one of the four coloured croquet balls (blue, red, black, yellow) and then a partner. Blue and Black make up one team, Red and Yellow the other. The diagram shows you the order in which the hoops are played and the approximate layout of the croquet lawn.

Blue begins, lining up one yard back from the first hoop and, with due control, swings the mallet smartly to hit the ball towards and ideally through the first hoop. Red plays next, then black and finally Yellow.

You win the hoop if you are first through it. Each team member supports their partner, trying to knock the opposition out of the way. Once one of the balls has gone through a hoop, all the players hit the balls following in turn to converge on the next hoop. Therefore, as play continues, either pair may be one hoop up, two up, or all square.

What you must deny doing: accidentally touching the ball – that still constitutes a strike; hitting your ball more than once; touching any ball when it is not your turn; tripping over a ball or moving it surreptitiously with the sole of your foot.

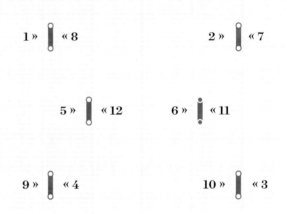

become a vegetarian as she couldn't bear anything being harmed. Her second brother, Auberon, who was an MP and a libertarian philosopher, had also given up eating meat and played a leading role in the passing of an act to protect wild birds.

By comparison with his new companion, Henry James seemed rather silent. Elsie, glancing across, wondered if their literary guest was observing in the silences, manners, habits and customs of the party any telling details that might provide his novels with live historical record, a 'multitude of pictures' of this time.

Lady Carnarvon suggested a game of croquet

and James said he thought he would take the opportunity to go for a further walk as it was one of his favourite recreations, whether in London or the country. He had had doubts about leaving London for Highclere, commenting in a letter that the

> gilded bondage of the country house becomes onerous as one grows older and then the waste of time in vain sitting and strolling about …

James had explored Highclere during his earlier visit, which he had enjoyed. He wrote prior to this one that he would go to:

> Highclere, Lord Carnarvon's, where I shall probably bore myself a great deal in very amiable and very respectable society. But I shall console myself by a ramble in an immense and divine park.

In that occupation he would find a convivial companion in Lord Carnarvon.

Chinese red-lacquered teapoy in the Drawing Room

round to show the way, he was also walking back through centuries of tradition and protocol. This was a world apart from the criminal under-class *The Princess Casamassima* had explored, or indeed from the real-life disturbances in London that year when a 5,000-strong mob had run through Pall Mall, smashing windows and roughing up anyone caught in the mêlée. Returning to the lawns, the sight of tea must have been most reassuring. Despite being an American, Henry James enjoyed tea. It was a moment of companionship with his fellow guests.

Tucked under the window alcove in the gilded

Drawing Room was the painted Chinese tea chest. Inside this very decorative piece were individual lacquered boxes for storing different blends of tea. Lady Carnarvon was more informal than her predecessors and rarely used it. Tea was no longer such a precious commodity since so much was now imported with ease from India and Ceylon. Queen Catherine of Braganza, wife of King Charles II, had introduced the ceremony of taking tea in 1663. Green tea was drunk from delicate bowls of Chinese porcelain. It was fashionable at court and viewed as a luxury.

In 1784, the French essayist and courtier La Rochefoucauld had noted:

> Throughout the whole of England the drinking of tea is general. You have it twice a day and though the expense is considerable the humblest peasant has his tea just like the rich man.

Therefore whilst Lord and Lady Carnarvon were enjoying tea outside or upstairs, so everyone, from the housekeeper Mrs Powell, to the valet Mr Funel, Langton the Groom of Chambers and all the rest of the servants, would pause during

After an engrossing game with loud laughter

and exclamations, it was time for tea. Some of the hoops had led to heated argument, balls were sent hard into the distance and lucky strokes won.

The silver teapots were set on a table in front of Lady Carnarvon, the little sandwiches and cakes prettily arranged on delicate china plates. The women were well shaded by the cedar trees as well as by their fine straw hats, but if they wished to explore the gardens, their cream parasols were propped against the tree. The footmen waited at a discreet distance in case help should be required. It was nearly five o'clock and the relaxed guests watched the flood of light across Highclere's broad lawns begin to wane, the shadows lengthening across the perfectly close-cropped grass and the scent of distant lime trees wafting towards them on the breeze.

If Henry James walked back up the main drive towards the Castle, past the oak tree with its great lower bough bent

The Muniments Room

the day for a cup of tea in their respective sitting rooms. Mrs Talkington, who had really retired as deputy housekeeper, was sitting happily talking to Mrs Powell whilst the Steward's Room Boy brought them buttered bread and slices of cake.

The 7th Duchess of Bedford had found the gap between lunch and a fashionably timed dinner at 8 p.m. too long. In consequence, she would have a tray of cakes and tea delivered to her in the late afternoon and would invite friends to join her. Thus tea, including cakes and sandwiches, became fashionable during Queen Victoria's reign. It was a social event for which ladies would change their dresses and wear hats and gloves.

Offered the opportunity to visit the Muniments

Room with Lord Carnarvon, Henry James's curiosity was aroused. Lord Carnarvon led his guest through into the cool Saloon and along the Red Corridor towards his Sitting Room. His most treasured books were carefully arranged on the bookcases by George Bullock, surmounted by small classical statues. He carefully took down the sixteenth-century edition of the poems of Ariosto to amuse Mr James.

They continued walking. Behind the Study was a narrow winding staircase. Following Lord Carnarvon up this, Henry James found himself standing in front of two huge heavy doors, which swung open into two inter-connected stone-floored rooms. These were packed with labelled metal boxes, each referring to different estates, properties and maps. Lord Carnarvon offered to take his guest to his other Study two floors above, which had some most interesting maps of the New World. Lord Carnarvon laughed as he went up, remarking to his guest that the stairs remained hard work however often he ascended them.

The second-floor Study was lined in gilt-covered leather even more exquisite than that in the Saloon, the blinds

drawn down to protect the remarkable wall covering. A huge desk occupied the middle of the room, with glass-fronted cabinets filled with papers and books ranged along one wall. A large wooden frame on a table held maps the size of small blackboards – a whole world to be explored. With no sense of urgency, the two men conversed about the various travels and tours they had undertaken.

Lord Carnarvon was planning to publish

bound volumes of speeches he had given as well as the translation he was working on. Whilst he shared the same English publishing house, Macmillan, as James, he was not concerned about the number of readers he attracted. Henry James, by contrast, was very concerned and so were his publishers, who were most alarmed to find that the readership for his books had fallen away. *The Bostonians* had not followed on from the success of *The Portrait of a Lady*.

Boxes in the Archive Room

To add to James's woes, his US publisher had just gone bankrupt.

Macmillan also published Lord Carnarvon's literary friends Charles Kingsley and Charles Dodgson (Lewis Carroll). At this time most printing runs were for 1,000 books or less. Macmillan had printed 500 copies of *The Bostonians* and had agreed to print 750 copies of *The Princess Casamassima*, nothing like the earlier successes of Charles Dickens or Mark Twain for example. Each of those authors, however, included illustrations in their books.

Henry James had turned to Frederick Macmillan after the failure of the American publisher James R. Osgood & Co. and he had come to James's aid with good advice about his plight. First and foremost a businessman, however, Macmillan had subsequently written to 'My dear James' about the advance for *The Princess Casamassima*, saying he would like to make 'the preliminary payment on account rather less, say £400 instead of £500'.

In his efforts to find a wider readership, Henry James was now wondering whether he should 'give up the English market' or 'experiment', and later he even considered becoming a playwright.

A wearied Lord Carnarvon thought he might rest before dinner but said his guest was more than welcome to remain in the Study. The author excused himself; he too hoped for a short rest before dinner. His bedroom, Wessex, was on the same floor and he was drawn to the window, to gaze across the park and wooded hills to the arched folly of Heaven's Gate. It stood on the skyline of Siddown Hill, the warm bricks lit by the evening sun, an unforgettable view.

Dinner was served punctually at 8 p.m.

and each man was given a card requesting him to escort one of the ladies. Lady Carnarvon followed the traditional menus of her predecessor, all of which continued to be written in French. Beginning with *consommé* or a vegetable soup, a typical Highclere dinner progressed to fish, meat, and then various vegetable accompaniments before selections of desserts and ice creams, an especial favourite of Lady Gwendolen's.

THE HOUSEHOLD OF THE EARL OF CARNARVON

Numbers for the Week ending Sunday,   19

	DRESSING	LUNCH	DINNER	REMARKS
MONDAY	...			
TUESDAY	...			
WEDNESDAY	...			
THURSDAY	...			
FRIDAY	...			
SATURDAY	...			
SUNDAY	...			
TOTAL				

Will you take in to dinner.

Castle stationery and excerpts from household records

Elsie had proactively asked her husband's cousin Sir John Ogilvy to take her in to dinner. Although eighty-five years old, he was a marvellous conversationalist, 'wonderfully well and of sound memory'. She sought his advice about the party she was organising for the Primrose League Meeting of Highclere & Burghclere Habitations. The League was a new idea, named after the 'favourite flower' of Benjamin Disraeli. In fact, Queen Victoria had sent a wreath of primroses to his funeral in 1881. The association organised social events involving trade unions, involving women as well as men, in order to promote Conservative ideas. She thought there would be about 500 members attending and the Highclere Band would play.

Her husband's idea for the early evening, after the speeches, was to have 'a display of fire-works'. The majority of those attending would never have seen such a thing as a rocket or a squib and Lord Carnarvon thought it would be a very pretty sight against the large cedars and the ruined temple. Elsie did not want there to be a single hitch or difficulty from first to last, but she had never seen fireworks before. Sir John advised her that the crowds should keep their distance as there were always burnings and accidents every year on Guy Fawkes Night.

Lord Carnarvon ate little and Lady Carnarvon ensured that dinner proceeded in a timely fashion because afterwards they intended to enjoy a game of billiards. Elsie had persuaded her husband to buy a billiard table and it became an instant success and after-dinner amusement, both for the family and their house guests. Lady Carnarvon led the way to the Billiard Room whilst other guests opted to retire to the Library. The French windows stood open to the lawns to allow in the evening air.

The conversation quickly turned, however, to the current society scandal. Henry James was intrigued and disapproving. He was drawn back to the 'subject of the moment ... the hideous —— divorce case'. Here James was delicately alluding to the circumstances surrounding the divorce of Sir Charles Dilke, a very able married politician who had had an affair with his sister-in-law but was accused

Carnarvon's brother Auberon was a friend of Dilke's so Henry James was able to glean the gossip from both sides. Dilke had befriended James in his early days in London and James also knew both of the women concerned. He wrote of Dilke: 'for a man who has had such passion for keeping up appearances ... he has in reality been strangely, incredibly reckless.' James further commented that he privately thought the divorce case would 'besmirch exceedingly the already very damaged prestige of the English upper class'.

Lord Carnarvon talked long into the evening and afterwards noted: 'We had some very interesting conversations on many subjects and sat talking in the library till past midnight.' He found Lewis Morris a 'cultivated & agreeable & kindly' man, although in the course of the evening it was clear that Morris rather admired Oscar Wilde who, unfortunately, Henry James could not abide.

James wound his way up the Red Stairs to his bedroom, finding the staircase and corridors lit by candle sconces, the bed turned down and shutters drawn. Lord Carnarvon had explained that Sunday breakfast would be served punctually at 9 a.m. but all the house party was asked to be down beforehand as there were short family prayers, a hymn and a few verses, beforehand. James was not overtly Christian but did feel it was important to do the right thing. He had gathered that later on the Sunday evening, after dinner, one of the clergymen would be invited to officiate at an evening service in the Saloon for the entire household.

Henry James was quite sure he would not be there. He had enjoyed his interlude in the country but was impatient to return to his flat and his writing. Making his excuses, Mr James thanked Lady Carnarvon for her kindnesses and hospitality. Lord Carnarvon sent a message to Brickell the coachman to arrange for the carriage to convey Mr James to Highclere station.

Craving solitude, the novelist wrote that London society

> lingers and dawdles on in a most irritating manner –
> firing off last invitations after one had fondly hoped
> that the peace of God had descended upon this
> distracted city.

also of having one with her daughter Virginia. He was then cited as a co-respondent in the ensuing divorce. He had tried to avoid the witness box in the divorce case so that his affair with Virginia's mother was not revealed in court. Dilke later tried to clear his name but it all went even more horribly wrong. Henry James and everyone in his circle was fascinated by the story. Meanwhile the prosecuting barrister, Henry Matthews, had been catapulted into politics as the new Home Secretary whilst Dilke's career was ruined. Lord Carnarvon had learnt from Sir George Russell that:

> Matthews is said to be able as a speaker – a good
> lawyer – a very good linguist; French, German,
> Italian – an accomplished & agreeable man & a
> Roman Catholic – this is the pleasant side of the
> character – I fancy there is a less agreeable one.

Henry James. Dec. 14th 1884.

Write me a verse, you kindly ask
Before you go away.
Suppress the thought! I dodge the task;
I'll never go — I'll stay!

A little poem in the hand of the author, in the Highclere
Visitors' Book following a later visit in 1884:

> Write me a verse, you kindly ask
>
> Before you go away.
>
> Suppress the thought! I dodge the task;
>
> I'll never go — I'll stay!

POSTSCRIPT

Lord Carnarvon died just four years later.
Elsie and the children were distraught, as were the
downstairs and estate workers at Highclere, bound to him
through ties of trust and affection. He was a man in whom
conscience always prevailed over ambition.

Gwendolen outlived him but not her two other brothers.
Aubrey and Mervyn would, in later life, both include
Gwendolen in their daughters' names and missed their aunt
terribly: 'What a blank is the absence of that little figure in
grey,' said the next Lord Carnarvon.

Henry James found little success during the 1880s:

> My two last novels, *The Bostonians* and the *Princess*,
> from which I expected so much and derived so little.
> They have reduced the desire, and the demand, for
> my productions to zero.

As the century approached its end, however, success
returned to him. He wrote the trilogy of *The Wings of
the Dove*, *The Ambassadors* and *The Golden Bowl* which
are classed as some of the most significant novels of the
nineteenth century, whilst James considered the novella
The Aspern Papers (1888) as one of his best works. The author
continued to live in London for the rest of his life although
he spent part of each year in Italy and also in his house in
Rye, Sussex which he first leased and then bought in 1899.
He remained in contact with Lady Carnarvon and wrote to
her on 1 May 1894, on headed notepaper from his London
flat, the address crossed out:

> ~~34 De Vere Gardens, W~~
> Casa Biondetti, San Vio. Venice
>
> Dear Lady Carnarvon,
>   I very greatly regret that your invitation to dine
> on May 24th should find me so far from England.
> I am making an absence of rather long duration –
> which has already lasted two months. This is my
> habit every spring and it has for its consequence
> that I am nowadays almost never in London after
> March 1st - only in the previous months.
>   Please believe me if this were not the case
> I should, in memory of your kindness to me at
> Highclere, & of Lord Carnarvon's, in times that
> seem already far away, have given myself the great
> pleasure of coming to see you. I shall certainly not
> neglect the occasion the first time it offers.
>   I hope that things are well with you & with your
> children & am, dear Lady Carnarvon,
> most truly yours,
>
> *Henry James*

The LIBRARY

The Library at Highclere Castle is one of my favourite rooms. It conveys an atmosphere of splendid opulence combined with the reassuring comfort of an old-fashioned gentlemen's club.

During Victorian times it was used as a withdrawing room by the 4th Earl of Carnarvon, somewhere to sit quietly while discussing the thorny problems and tricky political characters of the day. However, while it is still used for contemplation and quiet conversation, it can also be an excellent entertaining space, somewhere a string quartet may play or a cabaret act perform for us after dinner.

Nearly 6,000 books line the shelves, from early Bibles to volumes of history, botany, architecture, political speeches, biography, drama, novels and poetry. They are catalogued according to the Dewey Decimal system that divides all knowledge into ten broad classifications. The books date mainly from the eighteenth and nineteenth centuries but the oldest, from 1538, is a comedy by the Italian poet Ariosto.

Two fine pieces of furniture, a George III Carlton House desk and a rent table, are placed at opposite ends of the room, the latter with drawers once carefully labelled to act as a filing system for money received from the estate's tenants.

During the First World War, when the Castle was turned into a hospital for wounded officers and airmen, the Library became the room in which convalescents could rest during the day. They would dine at tables placed in the North Library and play Scrabble or cards or else read in the larger area.

During the Second World War the room was transformed once again: this time the Library was lined with cots and used as a dormitory for young evacuees from London.

The current Earl's father holding
HRH Prince Charles in his arms

MEAT, GAME & FOWL

Beaters' Stew

[a warming beef stew]

SERVES: 4–6

Working behind the scenes of each shoot, head keeper Eddie Hughes relies on the assistance of at least twenty-five beaters and four or five pickers-up. Early in the morning on a shooting day, they all congregate in a hubbub of broad accents, green waterproofs and enthusiastic dogs in the beaters' room at the back of the Castle courtyard.

By lunchtime everyone – guns, loaders and beaters alike – is ready to return from the fields, to dry out or warm up for a spell. The old log fire has already been lit and the trestle tables and chairs set out ready and waiting to welcome the beaters back. Tom, the youngest keeper, and one of the beaters go across to collect a large pot of piping hot beaters' stew from the kitchens and a large saucepan full of mashed potato. Thick tweed jackets are hung on pegs to dry, coffee and tea are set to brew, and lunch is ladled into plates and bowls.

This recipe is very easy to make your own as it is extremely adaptable. Any root vegetable can be added – we tend to use whatever the gardener has brought in that morning. Sometimes, if it is a particularly cold day, we add two tablespoons of pearl barley before we transfer the stew to the oven, which creates a lovely one-pot meal, perfect served with crusty bread. With cabbage and creamed potatoes, this extends to serve at least six hungry beaters!

INGREDIENTS

1kg (2lb 3oz) minced braising steak or good-quality beef mince

2–4 tbsp olive oil

3 small onions, quartered

3 large carrots, cut into chunks

2 garlic cloves, crushed

1 heaped tbsp plain flour

1½ good-quality organic beef stock cubes dissolved in 700ml (1¼ pints) hot water

A few sprigs of fresh thyme

A sprig of rosemary

2 bay leaves

1 heaped tbsp redcurrant jelly

1 leek, washed, trimmed and sliced

Salt and pepper

Cooked green cabbage and creamed potatoes, to serve (optional)

METHOD

Preheat the oven to 150°C/300°F/Gas mark 2.

Season the mince with salt and pepper. Heat one tablespoon of the oil in a large ovenproof casserole dish over a high heat and fry the mince in small batches until brown (if you fry too much in the pan at once, the meat will steam instead of brown). Transfer the browned mince to a plate and set aside.

Once all the mince is browned and removed from the casserole dish, add the remaining oil and the onions and cook for 3–4 minutes over a high heat until they are just beginning to brown at the edges. Turn the heat down and add the carrots and the garlic followed by the browned mince. Add the flour and stir well so that it coats the vegetables and meat, then gradually add the stock, stirring as you go.

Once all the stock has been added, increase the heat to bring the stew up to a simmer, then add the thyme, rosemary, bay leaves and redcurrant jelly, cover and cook in the oven for 2½ hours.

Remove the pan from the oven and add the sliced leek. The meat will be extremely tender and the lovely rich gravy will taste amazing! Serve with fresh greens, such as pointed cabbage, and some comforting creamed potatoes.

Roasted Pork Loin

with onions

SERVES: 6

My son Edward has, at various times, campaigned to increase our animal menagerie here at Highclere. He was hoping for Jersey cows, which I suspected it would fall to me to milk, or pigs for me to keep and look after. I have so far avoided both.

This is a simple method for roast pork. Seasoning the skin with lots of salt produces nice crisp crackling, while cooking it on top of a bed of onions and herbs will give a really good flavour. Just ask your butcher to bone, roll and score the loin first.

INGREDIENTS

50g (2oz) table salt

1kg (2lb 3oz) boned and rolled pork loin, skin scored

3 onions, unpeeled and cut into wedges

4 sprigs each of sage, rosemary and thyme (optional)

50ml (2fl oz) olive oil

Salt and pepper

FOR THE APPLE SAUCE

2 eating apples, peeled, cored, and cut into chunks

2 tbsp water

2 tsp demerara sugar

Knob of unsalted butter

Pinch of ground cinnamon

METHOD

Preheat the oven to 200°C/400°F/Gas mark 6.

For the pork, rub all the table salt and some pepper into the cracks of the skin. Place the onion wedges in a baking tray with the herbs (if using) and put the pork on top. Drizzle over the olive oil, being careful not to wash away the salt.

Cook in the hot oven for 20 minutes. Reduce the temperature to 160°C/325°F/Gas mark 3.

Cook the pork for a further hour (20 minutes per 500g/1lb 2oz plus 20 minutes). Once cooked, remove from the baking tray and leave to rest, uncovered, for a good 20 minutes.

Turn the onions that have captured all the juices from the pork loin into an onion sauce by simply puréeing them, or chop them up to add to a bread stuffing. We do both at Highclere.

To make the apple sauce, place the apple chunks in a pan with the water and the demerara sugar, cover and cook for about 15 minutes, until soft and mushy. Remove from the heat, drain the excess water and beat in the butter and cinnamon. Set aside to cool.

We serve the pork carved at the table with apple sauce and the crackling on the side.

[**CHEF'S TIP**: If the crackling's not done to your liking, remove the skin from the pork and put it back into the oven on a baking tray until crispy.]

Lady Carnarvon's Pheasant Curry

SERVES: 6

No single curry dish of mine is ever quite like another. At any curry's heart is a combination of Indian spices, which can be either mild or strong depending on my mood that day or what I have in the store cupboard.

I was taught to start by cooking the curry powder on a low heat in half butter and half oil. Only after that do I start to add in the other ingredients: first the chopped onions and then the other vegetables and the meat.

The children were always suspicious of curry as I tended to make it using pheasant or partridge, of which there is always a surplus during the shooting season. I, like any other mother, would of course tell them it was chicken but they never quite believed me! Everyone however likes the condiments such as chutney, banana, yoghurt, poppadums and naan bread, which are placed in bowls along the table as accompaniments to the curry and rice.

Somehow the curry always seems to taste better if left for a day then reheated.

INGREDIENTS

40g (1½oz) unsalted butter, plus an extra knob for frying

2 tbsp curry powder

1 tsp turmeric

2 tbsp sunflower oil

1 large red onion, finely chopped

1 tbsp plain flour

1 large sweet potato (about 400g/14oz), peeled and thinly sliced

3 carrots, peeled and thinly sliced

2 parsnips, peeled and thinly sliced

500ml (17fl oz) hot pheasant, chicken or vegetable stock
[SEE page 114 for chicken stock – you can substitute pheasant for chicken – or page 160 for vegetable stock]

1 tbsp demerara sugar

1 tbsp balsamic vinegar

1 tbsp mango chutney

450g (1lb) basmati rice, rinsed

1 clove

1 green cardamom pod

6 pheasant breasts

Salt and pepper

METHOD

Preheat the oven to 150°C/300°F/Gas mark 2.

Melt half the butter in an ovenproof casserole dish over a medium heat, add the curry powder and turmeric and fry for 5 minutes. Add the remaining butter and the sunflower oil along with the onion and cook for about 5 minutes until soft but not coloured, stirring often.

Add the flour, sweet potato, carrots and parsnips and stir well. Gradually pour in the stock, stirring constantly to prevent the flour forming lumps. Stir in the demerara sugar and balsamic vinegar, add the mango chutney and season with salt and pepper.

Cover, transfer to the oven and cook for 45 minutes – 1 hour.

Place the rice in a saucepan with the clove and cardamom pod, cover with boiling water and cook over a medium heat, uncovered, for 15 minutes, or until cooked. Drain and return to the pan to keep warm while you cook the pheasant.

Remove the sauce from the oven. Increase the temperature to 180°C/350°F/Gas mark 4.

Melt the knob of butter in a frying pan over a medium heat. Fry the pheasant breasts in batches, two at a time, skin side down for 2–3 minutes, then turn and fry on the other side for a further 2 minutes. Transfer to a baking tray and place in the oven to cook for 8–10 minutes. Remove from the oven and leave to rest, loosely covered, for 10 minutes.

To serve, put some rice in a bowl with a generous helping of the sauce. Slice the pheasant breasts into strips and lay them on top of the sauce.

[**LADY CARNARVON'S TIP**: Traditionally this curry goes with basmati rice, but I like to mix basmati with wild rice for a bit of extra bite.]

The Official Highclere Chicken Curry

SERVES: 6

Highclere's curry recipe is supposedly derived from a chef whom the 5th Earl brought back with him from his travels in Ceylon (present-day Sri Lanka) just before the turn of the nineteenth century. The story goes that the Sinhalese would cook in the kitchen with a monkey sitting on his shoulder, much to the disapproval of all the other staff.

It is probable that our recipe was influenced by the Malay cooking tradition in which the usual spices are roasted, and coconut cream (or milk) and an additional flavouring such as lemongrass are also used to flavour the curry.

Traditionally the recipe for the Highclere chicken curry was not written down but the mix and balance of ingredients agreed between the chef and the incumbent Earl. Not too spicy, not too hot, the recipe remained a kind of state secret – until now. Like my pheasant curry, it is best served with accompaniments of sliced bananas, yoghurt, mango chutney, poppadums, rice and some mixed green vegetables.

Of all the traditional ingredients in the spice mix, I will always ensure I include turmeric, as it contains an antioxidant called curcumin, which has many healing benefits. I may include a stick of lemongrass in the stock while it is simmering or add some cinnamon, native to Sri Lanka and thought to help regulate insulin and aid digestion.

INGREDIENTS

40g (1½oz) butter

2–3 tbsp medium curry powder (to taste)

60ml (2fl oz) sunflower or vegetable oil

2 red onions, finely chopped

2 garlic cloves, finely chopped

*25g (1oz) piece of fresh ginger,
peeled and finely chopped*

½ tsp turmeric

½ tsp ground coriander

½ tsp mild chilli powder

1 tsp ground cumin

1 tsp black mustard seeds

*5cm (2in) stick of lemongrass, bruised,
or 1 tsp ground cinnamon (optional)*

*900g (2lb) boneless, skinless chicken thighs, cut
into 2.5cm (1in) chunks*

300ml (10fl oz) chicken stock
[**SEE** page 114]

150ml (5fl oz) coconut milk

Salt and pepper

Cooked basmati rice, to serve

METHOD

Melt the butter in a heavy-based pan over a medium heat, add the curry powder and cook for 2 minutes, then add the oil, onion, garlic and ginger and fry gently for 5–7 minutes until soft but not coloured.

Stir in the spices and cook for a further 3 minutes, stirring often.

Add the chicken and sauté for 2–3 minutes, then add the stock and bring to the boil. Turn the heat down, cover and simmer for 1 hour.

Finally, add the coconut milk to enrich the sauce, bring back to the boil and simmer for a further 3 minutes. Remove from the heat, season to taste, and serve with basmati rice.

[**CHEF'S TIP**: Fresh herbs are a fabulous addition to this curry: try adding 20g (¾oz) freshly chopped coriander just before you serve.]

Oie Rôti

[Roast Goose]

with sage and onion stuffing

SERVES: 6

The game larder was an essential room near any kitchen in previous centuries, where meat and fowl could be hung to develop their flavour. At Highclere the room was double-height and had wooden bars and hooks fixed at different levels so that any bird or animal could be stored with ease. The trick was to hang the meat long enough for the flavour to develop but not so long that it became rancid.

During the winter months, geese are fat with plenty of meat on them and are traditionally roasted with stuffing, often with other birds in their cavities. Here we just use a simple sage and onion stuffing.

INGREDIENTS

4–5kg (10lb) goose

1 quantity of Sage and Onion Stuffing
[SEE below]

A few sprigs of rosemary

A few sprigs of thyme

1 peeled whole onion

1 orange, halved

1 heaped tbsp plain flour

Salt and pepper

METHOD

Preheat the oven
to 180°C/350°F/Gas mark 4.

Put the goose on a large board and season with salt and pepper.

Turn the neck end towards you. Lift up the neck flap, then with one hand on the bird and the other tucked under the flap of the neck, use your hands to loosen the skin from the bird. Push the stuffing into the cavity, taking care not to push too hard or break the skin or the stuffing will burst out.

Place the sprigs of rosemary and thyme, the onion and orange inside the bird. Transfer to a large roasting tin and roast for 3 hours, basting every 30 minutes with the juices from the roasting tray, and draining the fat from the roasting tin (reserve it for roast potatoes).

When cooked remove from oven, transfer to a warm platter, cover with foil and a couple of clean tea towels to keep the heat in and let it rest at room temperature for 30 minutes before carving and serving.

While the goose is resting, drain all but 1 tablespoon of the fat from the roasting tin. Stir in the flour and cook over a low heat for 1–2 minutes. Slowly stir in 600ml (1 pint) of the onion cooking water from making the stuffing (or vegetable cooking water/stock) and continue to stir until smooth. Simmer on the hob for 5–10 minutes, until thickened, then taste to check the seasoning and adjust accordingly. Pour into a large warmed jug to serve.

Sage and Onion Stuffing

This stuffing can be used for turkey as well as goose.

INGREDIENTS

3–4 large onions, quartered

10 sage leaves

200g (7oz) stale bread, blitzed to form
breadcrumbs

100g (3½oz) softened butter

1 egg yolk

Salt and pepper

METHOD

Put the onions in a pan of boiling water. After a minute, turn the heat down and let them simmer for 5 minutes, until tender. Add the sage leaves to blanch for a minute.

Use a slotted spoon to remove the onions and leaves from the water and set aside to cool. Reserve the water to use later for gravy [SEE above].

Finely chop the onions and sage on a board and put into a bowl. Add the breadcrumbs and butter and season well. Add the egg yolk, then use a spoon to bind the mixture together.

Poulet Maryland

Chicken Maryland is historically associated with the Eastern Seaboard of the United States and many families there liked to use their own secret combination of ingredients to make the dish their own. However, it was also served in nineteenth-century Europe as it is mentioned in Escoffier's menus, where it is paired with a garnish of banana. It was also served on the *Titanic* on 14 April, the day before it sank in the early hours – which is, of course, the point at which the TV series *Downton Abbey* began, with the death of the Earl of Grantham's nearest heir.

This recipe is for the version of the dish we serve today.

INGREDIENTS

4 tbsp plain flour

1 tbsp hot paprika

1 medium egg, beaten

*100g (3½oz) breadcrumbs
(homemade if possible)*

*4 × 125g (4½oz) skinless,
boneless chicken breasts
or 8 chicken drumsticks and thighs*

50g (2oz) butter

*½ red pepper, deseeded
and roughly chopped*

300ml (10fl oz) double cream

8 slices of streaky bacon

Salt and pepper

*Sprigs of watercress,
to garnish*

*Mashed potatoes
and green beans, to serve*

METHOD

Preheat the oven
to 200°C/400°F/Gas mark 6.

Grease a baking tray.

Combine the flour, paprika and some seasoning in one bowl, place the beaten egg in another bowl, and the breadcrumbs in a third bowl. Remove a tablespoon of the seasoned flour and set aside in a small bowl for later. Coat each piece of chicken with the rest of the flour mixture. Dip the floured chicken pieces into the beaten egg, then coat in the breadcrumbs. Place on the baking tray and bake for approximately 45 minutes until the chicken is cooked through.

While the chicken is cooking, melt the butter in a saucepan over a low heat. Add the chopped pepper and cook for about 5 minutes until soft, then stir in the reserved tablespoon of seasoned flour and take off the heat. Gradually stir in the cream and return to a low heat for 2–3 minutes, stirring all the time (do not let the sauce boil or it will split), until thickened.

Roll up each rasher of bacon and secure them with cocktail sticks. Place on the baking tray with the chicken and cook for 8 minutes, until crispy.

Garnish the chicken with watercress sprigs and serve with the creamy pepper sauce, streaky bacon rolls, mashed potatoes and green beans.

Perdreaux à Highclere

with *Pommes Anna* & braised red cabbage

SERVES: 4

Looking through some old papers, I found a recipe for partridge from Almina, the 5th Countess of Carnarvon, and it was without doubt on the menu during the time of her predecessors. I like to use our own produce and partridge is low in fat. I always used to tell the children it was chicken and I'd roast it, or turn the breast meat into a stew or curry. I roast partridge upside down so all the juices run down into the breasts, then if I slightly forget about them in the hurly-burly of cooking a weekend lunch they will still taste delicious. Paul, our chef, tends to roast them the right way up, however, as he is better at watching the timing than I am.

INGREDIENTS

2–4 partridges, depending on size (one per serving if small, or 2 to share if larger)

1 tbsp olive oil

15g (½oz) butter

4 sprigs of rosemary

FOR THE SAUCE

25g (1oz) unsalted butter

1 tbsp olive oil

1 shallot, finely chopped

2 tbsp fresh breadcrumbs

250ml (9fl oz) hot chicken stock

2 tbsp fresh orange juice

Salt and pepper

METHOD

Preheat the oven to 220°C/425°F/Gas mark 7.

Brush each partridge with olive oil, put half the butter inside each partridge (or quarter of the butter inside each, if cooking 4), and a sprig of rosemary under each leg (or under each bird, if cooking 4) and put them in a roasting tin.

Roast in the oven for 25 minutes then remove from the oven, cover with foil and set aside to rest for 5 minutes.

To make the sauce, put the butter and olive oil in a heavy-based saucepan over a medium heat. Add the shallot and cook for around 10 minutes until softened, turning the heat down slightly if the shallots are browning too much.

When they are soft, add the breadcrumbs and stock to the pan, season well and stir everything together. Bring to the boil, turn down the heat and simmer for 4–5 minutes, then stir in the orange juice.

Pass any meat juices from the rested partridge through a sieve into the pan, stir the sauce again, then taste for seasoning and adjust accordingly. Strain the sauce through a muslin-lined sieve and serve it with the partridges.

If you are serving 1 partridge per person, simply put each partridge on a warm plate, or – if serving 2 between 4 people – carve off each breast and allow one breast per guest.

Serve with *Pommes Anna* [SEE below] and braised red cabbage [SEE page 114]. It also goes well with parsnip crisps.

Pommes Anna

SERVES: 4

This celebrated simple dish of potatoes baked in melted butter was the creation of Adolphe Dugléré and possibly named for the celebrated Parisian courtesan Anna Desilion. It became a new and more glamorous way to present that most basic of vegetables: the *pomme de terre* (potato).

INGREDIENTS

1kg (2lb 3oz) waxy potatoes

75g (2½oz) unsalted butter, melted, plus extra for greasing

Salt and pepper

METHOD

Preheat the oven to to 200°C/400°F/Gas mark 6.

Grease a 24cm (9in) cake tin.

Peel and slice the potatoes into thin rounds (cut them as thinly as possible, or use a mandoline), then arrange a layer of overlapping slices of potato in the base of the round cake tin. Drizzle over a little melted butter and season with salt and pepper.

Continue with layers of potato, butter and seasoning until all the potatoes have been used up. Drizzle any remaining melted butter over the top of the potato cake.

Cook in the oven for 40–50 minutes, until the top is crispy and golden. Cut the 'cake' into wedges and serve with a roast, such as partridge [SEE above].

Braised Red Cabbage

SERVES: 8 as a side dish

Officially there are fourteen ingredients needed to make this recipe. I almost never remember all of them but as long as you have at least eight or nine it will be fine. None of my family or guests have ever pointed out that it tastes slightly different each time they have it! The outer skins of the red onions are supposed to be good for asthmatics. I have two in the family, which is an excellent excuse to get someone else to start peeling.

INGREDIENTS

2 tbsp sunflower oil

50g (2oz) butter

1 medium red onion, sliced

1 large red cabbage, finely sliced

3 tbsp red wine

6 cloves

½–1 tsp ground allspice

½–1 tsp ground cinnamon

4 tbsp balsamic vinegar

2 tbsp demerara sugar

2 tbsp mango chutney

500ml (17fl oz) chicken stock
[**SEE** below]

1 apple, peeled and chopped or grated

Salt and pepper

METHOD

Put the oil and butter in a deep heavy-based pan over a low heat, add the onion and cook gently for 4–5 minutes until soft but not coloured, stirring often.

Add the cabbage to the pan and stir, then add the red wine, cloves, allspice, cinnamon, balsamic vinegar and demerara sugar and stir again. Finally, add the mango chutney and chicken stock and give it a final stir. Season generously with salt and plenty of freshly ground black pepper. Cook gently for 45 minutes, being careful that the cabbage does not catch on the bottom of the pan. You are looking for a gentle simmer. If the stock is evaporating too quickly, cover and stir every 5 minutes.

Add the chopped or grated apple to the pan, stir again, and cook for a further 15 minutes. Remove from the heat.

This dish can be prepared up to 3 days in advance and reheated, or frozen for up to a month. To thaw, defrost overnight in the fridge and reheat in a pan until hot.

CHICKEN STOCK

MAKES: 1 litre (2 pints)

INGREDIENTS

Bones from 1 large 1·8kg (4lb) chicken that you have roasted for some other purpose

2 onions

2 celery stalks

1 carrot

Blade of mace

Sprig of thyme

1 bay leaf

METHOD

Put the bones, vegetables and herbs in a stock pan and cover with water. Bring to the boil and then simmer for a minimum of 4 hours (keep topping up the water so it just covers the bones).

When done, skim the surface to remove the fat and strain.

Let the stock cool before covering and put in the fridge. It will keep for 3–4 days. Alternatively, you could also put the stock into a plastic container and freeze for up to 3 months.

Rack of Lamb

with *Pommes dauphinoise*, baby vegetables, rosemary *jus*

SERVES: 6

Highclere remains a working farm with 1,800 ewes and a small herd of rams. Each year around 3,500 lambs are born in the pens underneath the Iron Age fort on Beacon Hill. Once they are old enough they spend the spring and summer grazing the 1,000 acres of Capability Brown parkland around the Castle, keeping the grass short and the view suitably pastoral.

It is believed that sheep have grazed here since Roman times. There are old vellum records dating from 749 AD showing the fields designated for grazing. During medieval times, the wool trade became such an integral part of the English economy that the Crown derived one-third of its total revenue from it.

Those days are long-gone but sheep are still very much a feature of Highclere's estate and lamb remains a classic dish on our menus here today.

You may wish to just use a selection of the baby vegetables, depending on what's in season.

INGREDIENTS

10 garlic cloves, crushed

2·5kg (5lb 1oz) large potatoes, peeled and cut into 1cm- (½in-) thick slices

1·5 litres (2½ pints) double cream

4 racks of lamb (6–7 bones each)

3 sprigs of rosemary

2–3 tbsp red wine

1 tsp sugar

12 baby carrots, trimmed

6 courgette flowers (optional)

12 baby leeks, trimmed

6 baby aubergines

18 asparagus spears, trimmed (optional)

200ml (7fl oz) rosemary jus, to serve (optional)

Sea salt and pepper

METHOD

Preheat the oven to 160°C/300°F/Gas mark 3.

Place the crushed garlic in a bowl with 1 teaspoon of salt and stir to make a paste.

To prepare the *Pommes dauphinoise*, we line an ovenproof dish with non-stick baking parchment so we can turn it out at the end, but if you are serving it straight from the dish you don't need to do this. Start by layering the sliced potato evenly in the dish, seasoning each layer with salt, pepper and crushed garlic. Do this at least six times to give you a nice height to the potato dish.

Pour the double cream over the potatoes, pushing the potatoes down with the flat of your hand until you can see the cream seeping through your fingers. Cover with foil and bake in the oven for at least 1 hour, removing the foil for the final 15 minutes of cooking time to allow for the top to brown, then remove from the oven, set aside and keep warm.

Increase the oven temperature to 180°C/350°F/ Gas mark 4.

Score the back of the lamb racks (the fatty side) with a sharp knife and season with salt and pepper. Put them fat side down in a cold frying pan and place over a medium heat to render the fat. When the fat side is a nice golden colour, turn the racks to seal all sides.

Create a bed of the rosemary sprigs in an ovenproof dish, lay the lamb on top fat side up and cook in the oven for 20 minutes. Transfer the lamb racks onto a plate, cover with foil and leave to rest for 10 minutes.

Deglaze the roasting tray with the red wine and strain the cooking juices into a warm jug to create your *jus*.

While the meat is resting, cook the vegetables.

Bring a pan of salted water to the boil and add the sugar. Add the baby carrots and cook for 4–6 minutes.

Place the courgette flowers (if using) on an ovenproof tray, drizzle with a little oil and roast for 4 minutes.

Boil the baby leeks in a pan of salted water for 3 minutes.

Halve the baby aubergines, score them with a cross-hatch pattern using the tip of a sharp knife and pan-fry with a little butter for about 5 minutes until golden and soft.

Cook the asparagus (if using) in the same way as the aubergine over a low heat.

Carve the rested cutlets and serve with the baby vegetables and *Pommes dauphinoise*, and a drizzle of the rosemary *jus*.

[**CHEF'S TIP**: the *dauphinoise* can be finished under a grill with some grated cheese – Parmesan, Cheddar or Gruyère all work well.]

Le Gigot de Mouton

with *sauce piquante*

SERVES: 8

Previous generations were a lot more robust about food than we are today, and virtually every part of an animal would have been used for something. Each part would have been destined for the kitchen and cooked appropriately.

Strictly speaking, the meat from sheep is subdivided into three types: lamb, hogget and mutton. Meat sold as lamb should be from an animal less than one year old, hogget is typically one to two years old and mutton is the meat from older ewes. As a general guide, lamb is less strong in flavour and requires less cooking time, while mutton is best cooked slowly and for longer.

The *gigot* or leg is one of the tastier joints and, having been hung, washed and dried, it is simply roasted in the oven, basted and left to rest before serving.

INGREDIENTS

Approx. 2kg (4lb 9oz) leg of lamb

Butter, for rubbing

FOR THE *SAUCE PIQUANTE*

50g (2oz) butter

1 small carrot, finely chopped

4–5 shallots, finely chopped

3 sprigs of thyme

1 bay leaf

2 sprigs of rosemary

20g (¾ oz) curly-leaf parsley, chopped

2 cloves

6 black peppercorns

5g (⅛oz) mace

1–2 tsp cayenne pepper

2 slices of lean ham, finely chopped

4 tbsp red wine vinegar

300ml (10fl oz) stock
made with 1 good-quality beef stock cube

10g (⅛oz) demerara sugar, or to taste

Salt

METHOD

Preheat the oven
to 200°C/400°F/Gas mark 6.

Wipe the meat with a clean tea towel and pat it dry. Rub it all over with a little butter and place in a roasting dish. Season with salt and cook in the oven for 20 minutes.

Reduce the oven temperature to 180°C/350°F/Gas mark 4.

Cook for 50 minutes per kilo of meat (for medium doneness), which in this case would mean a total of 2 hours.

While the lamb is cooking, make the *sauce piquante*. Melt the butter in a large saucepan over a medium heat. Add the carrot and shallots and cook for 3–4 minutes, then add all the herbs, the spices, the ham, vinegar and stock. Bring to a simmer and cook for about 10 minutes, until the vegetables are very soft, stirring occasionally.

Add the sugar to taste (you want to keep the sharpness from the vinegar) and season with salt.

Skim several times, to remove any impurities or scum from the surface of the sauce, then strain the sauce through a sieve into a heatproof jug or bowl.

Serve very hot with the lamb.

Filet de Boeuf à la Maître d'Hôtel

The name refers to the fact that this dish was often cooked at the table in a restaurant or hotel by the head waiter or *maître d'*. It relies completely on the quality of the meat used. Any good cut of steak will do but, as usual when searing or grilling, the most important consideration is the relative thickness of the meat and the length of time it is cooked. This is best served simply with green beans cooked *al dente* or wilted spinach.

You can scale up the quantity of parsley butter, roll it into a sausage shape and chill it, so rounds can be sliced off when needed. It is delicious served with fish, too.

INGREDIENTS

Olive or vegetable oil, for frying

*4 × 175g (6oz) fillet steaks
(rib eye or sirloin work equally well)*

Salt and pepper

FOR THE PARSLEY BUTTER

50g (2oz) softened unsalted butter

*10g (½oz) curly-leaf parsley,
leaves finely chopped*

½ lemon, for squeezing

METHOD

To make the herb butter, put the butter in a bowl and add the chopped parsley, a pinch of salt and pepper and a generous squeeze of lemon juice, then mash everything together using a fork.

Divide the flavoured butter into four equal portions, press each into a small flat round, transfer to a plate and chill.

Heat a pan over a high heat, then add a drizzle of oil. Fry the steaks.

For meat that is over 1 inch/2cm thick:

2¼ minutes each side for rare,
3¼ minutes each side for medium rare,
4½ minutes each side
for medium to well done.

For steaks less than 1 inch/2cm thick:

1½ minutes each side for rare,
2 minutes each side for medium rare,
2¼ minutes each side
for medium to well done.

Once cooked to your liking, transfer the steaks to a plate, cover and leave to rest for no longer than 5 minutes at room temperature.

Serve each steak on a plate and with a round of the parsley butter on top to melt.

[**CHEF'S TIP**: To test doneness, press your fingers onto the steak: a rare piece should feel soft, a medium-rare piece will have some give, and if it's well done it will feel firm.]

Haggis

with swede, turnip & potato mash

SERVES: 20 for a Burns Night party

Haggis is a savoury pudding containing sheep's pluck (heart, liver and lungs) minced up with onion, oatmeal, suet, spices and salt, mixed with stock, which is traditionally spooned into a sheep stomach (though that is not often done today and sausage casing is used instead).

Although the name 'hagese' was first used in England in c.1430, haggis has come to be almost the national dish in Scotland, largely as the result of Robert Burns's 'Address to a Haggis', first printed in *The Caledonian Mercury* in 1786.

It is the main constituent of a Burns Night supper. We hold one each year at the Castle – it is a splendid excuse for a party at an otherwise fairly bleak time of year and I was at a Scottish university! After some reeling, we all go into the Dining Room for a formal dinner. The haggis is piped in, held aloft by chef Paul, and I ask an old friend and fellow St Andrew's student to recite the eponymous poem.

Making a haggis at home should only be attempted if you are feeling adventurous and needs to be started the day before. It is best served with a nice dark game jus, flavoured with a good red wine.

INGREDIENTS

1 lamb's stomach, washed and cleaned, or sausage casing

1kg (2lb 3oz) lamb's liver

1kg (2lb 3oz) lamb's heart

1kg (2lb 3oz) lamb's lungs

4 large onions, finely diced

250g (9oz) oatmeal

250g (9oz) dried shredded suet

100ml (3½fl oz) lemon juice (from about 4 juicy lemons)

36g (1¼oz) cayenne pepper

50g (2oz) rosemary, leaves stripped from stalks and chopped

75g (3oz) thyme, leaves stripped from stalks and chopped

75g (3oz) curly-leaf parsley, leaves chopped

40g (1½oz) ground allspice

300ml (10fl oz) cold game stock
[**SEE** page 125; if you can't get hold of game stock, use beef or chicken stock, page 125 or 114 respectively]

Salt and pepper

Wholegrain mustard, to serve (optional)

FOR THE MASH

1kg (2lb 3oz) each of swede, turnips and potatoes, peeled, washed and cut into cubes

250g (9oz) butter

METHOD

If you're making a single large haggis, soak the washed and cleaned stomach in a bowl filled with water, to which you've added a pinch of salt. Leave it for 8–10 hours or overnight. If you're making smaller haggis, with sausage casings, skip this step.

Simmer the pluck (the liver, heart and lungs) in a pan of water, covered, for around 2 hours, making sure to keep the windpipe hanging over the side of the pan.

Drain the pluck, leave to cool, then mince or chop it finely. Place the minced or chopped pluck in a bowl, add the onion, oatmeal, suet, lemon juice, cayenne, chopped herbs and allspice, season and mix thoroughly. Add the stock.

For a large haggis, place the mixture loosely inside the soaked lamb's stomach, making sure you leave enough room for the oatmeal to expand. Push out any air from the stomach and sew up the haggis with a needle and butcher's string. Prick it a few times so that the hot air can escape, place the 'bag' in a large pan of boiling water and simmer for 3 hours.

To make smaller haggis, divide the mixture into roughly equal portions, then spoon into the sausage casings, tying off after each portion. Prick each small haggis, place them in a large pan of boiling water and simmer for 1½ hours.

To make the mash, cook the swede in salted boiling water for about 40 minutes, or until very soft. Drain, leave to cool slightly, then purée with a hand blender. Season to taste and add a third of the butter. Keep warm. Repeat the process with the turnip and the potatoes and the remaining butter. Taste and adjust the seasoning accordingly.

Serve spoonfuls of each mash on each plate, then scoop out a spoonful of haggis. We often serve it with some wholegrain mustard.

Highclere Loin of Venison

with fondant potato, parsnip purée, wild mushrooms & juniper berry *jus*

SERVES: 6

The earliest records of the deer park at Highclere date from about 750 years ago. Deer parks were a recognised part of the medieval landscape for aristocratic and royal households as venison was very much prized by them. By establishing parks and, in some cases, whole new forests for the deer, as well as creating ferocious anti-poaching laws to protect them, supplies of venison were made available all year round.

Deer are still 'managed' at Highclere but they are effectively wild and not confined. As a result they eat a natural and varied diet, free from antibiotics for example. The resulting meat has high levels of iron and a very low fat content. To preserve its nutritional value and to make the most of its rich flavour, our chef Paul sears the meat before cooking it as slowly as possible, to tenderise it without making it tough and chewy.

With all good wild mushrooms there will be a coating of grit and dirt. It is a time-consuming process but it is always better to brush this dirt away rather than to wash the mushrooms as their gills work like sponges and soak in water, impairing the flavour. Paul's tip is to use a small pastry brush.

Neither he nor I feel sufficiently qualified to forage for our own mushrooms around the estate although I am assured that there are some good crops at certain times of the year. We can and do, however, collect our own juniper berries. Sprawling juniper trees grow all over Beacon Hill just to the south of the Castle. Not only can they be used to add flavour to various meat dishes like ham, duck and venison, as they are here, they can also be used to flavour gin or vodka.

This dish is fabulous with a selection of vegetables. We at Highclere Castle are big fans of baby vegetables such as carrots and leeks.

INGREDIENTS

50g (2oz) butter

2 tbsp olive oil

1–1·2kg (2lb 3oz–2lb 11oz) loin of venison
(170–200g/6–7oz raw weight per person),
trimmed

Large handful of thyme sprigs

6 garlic cloves

5 banana shallots, finely diced

300g (10½oz) seasonal wild mushrooms,
cleaned

75ml (3fl oz) Madeira wine

12 juniper berries

1 litre (1¾ pints) dark game stock
[SEE page 125]

Salt and pepper

FOR THE FONDANT POTATO

6 large potatoes, peeled

200g (7oz) salted butter, melted,
plus a knob for frying

Olive oil, for frying

15g (1oz) thyme sprigs

15g (1oz) rosemary sprigs

½ garlic clove, crushed

FOR THE PARSNIP PURÉE

25g (1oz) butter

2kg (4lb 9oz) parsnips,
peeled, cored and cut into 2cm (¾in) dice

1 tsp Highclere honey
(or runny honey of choice), or to taste

1 litre (1¾ pints) whole milk

Salt and pepper

METHOD

Preheat the oven
to 150°C/300°F/Gas mark 2.

To make the fondant potatoes, shape them into equal-sized cylinders (we use a circular cutter similar to a hockey puck).

Melt the knob of butter in a pan with a splash of oil and add the thyme, rosemary and garlic. Fry the potatoes in the pan in batches until they are browned on all sides.

When they are all browned, transfer them to an ovenproof dish, submerge them in the melted butter, and cook in the oven for 1–1½ hours, until tender when pierced with a sharp knife.

Remove the fondant potatoes from the cooking butter and drain off the excess fat. Set aside to keep warm while you cook the parsnips and venison.

To make the parsnip purée, melt the butter in a large saucepan, add the parsnips and sauté gently for 5 minutes (without burning the butter), then season with salt and pepper and add the honey. This will caramelise quickly, so keep the parsnips moving in the pan.

Add the milk and simmer for 20–25 minutes until the parsnips are cooked through and very soft.

Remove the parsnips from the milk with a slotted spoon and blend in a food processor until smooth. To help make the mixture smooth, add a little of the cooking milk to the blender but be careful not to add too much. Remember you are making a purée, not a sauce. Set aside and keep warm.

Turn the oven temperature up to 180°C/350°F/ Gas mark 4.

For the venison, melt half the butter with 1 tablespoon of the oil in a clean pan over a high heat, add the venison loin and seal the meat on all sides. Take your time to colour it a nice even dark brown, then add the thyme sprigs and garlic, and season with salt and pepper.

Transfer the venison with the thyme and garlic to a roasting tin and cook in the oven for 20 minutes. Remove from the oven, cover with foil, and leave to rest for 20 minutes before serving.

Meanwhile, in the same pan you sealed the venison in, melt the remaining butter with the rest of the oil and add the shallots and wild mushrooms. Sauté over a medium-high heat for about 3 minutes until they are cooked, then set aside. Add the Madeira and juniper berries to the pan and simmer until the liquid is reduced to half. Add the game stock and simmer for up to 15 minutes, until you have a reduced and 'sticky' *jus*.

To serve, place a fondant potato in the centre of each plate. Carve the venison into equal slices with a sharp knife, and arrange slices on each plate. Spoon some parsnip purée onto each plate and scatter the wild mushrooms over each serving before drizzling with the venison *jus*.

Venaison Braisée à la Forestière

Venison or chicken served *à la Forestière* should always include mushrooms, but given that the name also indicates ingredients that can be gathered from the forest, juniper berries and herbs such as thyme give added interest and depth.

INGREDIENTS

100ml (3½fl oz) olive oil

100g (3½oz) unsalted butter

2–3 onions, finely chopped

1kg (2lb 3oz) boned shoulder or leg of venison, cut into 2·5cm (1in) chunks

2 tbsp plain flour, seasoned with salt and pepper

2 celery stalks, finely chopped

300g (10½oz) selection of seasonal mushrooms, quartered

250ml (8½fl oz) red wine

1 litre (1¾ pints) beef stock, made with a good-quality beef stock cube

3 juniper berries

3 sprigs of thyme

2 bay leaves

1 tbsp redcurrant jelly

Salt and pepper

METHOD

Preheat the oven to 150°C/300°F/Gas mark 2.

Heat half the oil with half the butter in a pan over a low heat. Add the chopped onion and cook gently for 15 minutes until just starting to brown.

Meanwhile, put the venison chunks in a large bowl with the seasoned flour, and toss to ensure the chunks are evenly dusted in the flour.

Melt the remaining butter with the rest of the oil in a large ovenproof casserole dish over a medium heat, then turn up the heat, and sear the venison in batches until brown on all sides (transferring the venison to a plate once browned).

When all the venison has been browned, add the celery and mushrooms to the casserole dish, stir, and cook for 3 minutes, then return the venison to the pan. Add the cooked onion and red wine to the pan and simmer for 5 minutes or so until the wine has reduced by half.

When the red wine is reduced, add the beef stock, juniper berries, herbs and redcurrant jelly. Season well, cover with a lid and cook in the oven for about 2 hours. Check the braise every 30 minutes or so and add extra stock if necessary. It's ready when a piece of meat can be pulled apart easily with two forks.

This is great with freshly baked bread or mashed potatoes.

GAME STOCK

INGREDIENTS

1·5kg (3½lb) assortment of raw bones (beef or venison bones, or pheasant/partridge/grouse carcasses)

2 tbsp plain flour

2–3 tbsp olive oil

2 red onions, quartered

2 celery stalks, each cut into 2–3 large pieces

2 large carrots, roughly chopped

2–3 garlic cloves, whole and unpeeled

Assortment of herbs (a few fresh thyme, marjoram, rosemary and parsley sprigs work well)

1 bay leaf

Black pepper

250ml (8½fl oz) port

METHOD

Preheat the oven to 200°C/400°F/Gas mark 6.

Place all the bones on a baking tray. Grind over plenty of black pepper, sprinkle them with the flour, drizzle over some of the olive oil and bake for about 45 minutes, until they turn a nice golden colour.

Meanwhile, place all the vegetables, including the garlic, on another baking tray. Again, grind over some black pepper and drizzle with some olive oil. Place the tray on another shelf in the oven about halfway through the cooking time and roast at the same time as the bones for the remaining 20 minutes.

Remove from the oven and tip all the bones and vegetables into a large stock pan. Add the herbs, the port, and cover all the bones with water so that the pan is nearly full. Bring to the boil, then turn down the heat and simmer uncovered for a minimum of 4 hours. Make sure the pan remains fairly full of water for the first 2 hours (top it up occasionally, if necessary). Do not stir. Paul, the chef, leaves the stock pans simmering on the hob all day, but I tend just to simmer them for an afternoon.

You do not have to roast the bones and vegetables first but this does make a difference to the stock, giving it a deeper colour and flavour.

Skim the surface of the stock to remove the fat during the cooking and at the end strain it through a fine sieve into a heatproof container. The cool, strained stock will keep in the fridge for 2–3 days or in the freezer in an airtight container for up to 3 months.

EDDIE HUGHES

Keeper

One morning in 1957, as fourteen-year-old Eddie Hughes was cutting firewood in the fields, the 6th Earl of Carnarvon and his agent came towards him. Lord Carnarvon commented that Eddie was doing such a good job he would like to offer him a more permanent position. Eddie thought nothing of it – after all, he had only just finished school – but three days later the agent returned and offered him a job assisting the keepers in rearing pheasants.

At that time the estate employed eight keepers. Their day began at 4 a.m., working through to nightfall. The old keepers were very strict and once, when Eddie had an accident and thought he had cracked a rib, he was told, 'That don't give you no reason to go home!'

When the keepers were shutting up the chicks at night, the broody hens used to hatch and rear them, would hear the noise of the grass against the men's Wellington boots. To avoid raising the alarm, on a rainy night the under-keepers would have to take off their boots and walk through the wet grass in their socks so that the hens would not hear them coming and the chicks would not do a runner! Today, Eddie has two under-keepers and they care for the young birds in sheds and pens strategically placed throughout the woods.

Eddie met his wife here at Highclere where she was a lady's maid. She looked after the ladies each evening before helping Robert Taylor the butler in

the Dining Room. Just as in *Downton Abbey*, all the staff would stand up when the butler entered the staff rooms.

Since starting at Highclere, Eddie has worked for three generations of the family. He recalls: 'Lord Carnarvon [the 6th Earl] was a smashing man: good company, a real gentleman and a Victorian eccentric. I went all over the country loading for him. The 7th Earl loved life – any excuse and he would have a party. You could not work for a better employer than Geordie [the 8th and current Earl], very fair and honourable, a lovely bloke. I have been very lucky. It is a lovely place to work and I would not get a better office than this.'

Eddie lives in a cottage under the Iron Age fort at Beacon Hill. He comments: 'My only regret is that Ivory Farm Cottage is not quite big enough for my love of cooking and parties. But Highclere is about tradition. It's in my blood and I could not do anything else.'

ROYALTY & RICHES

A Visit from the Prince of Wales

December 1895

His Royal Highness the Prince of Wales was named Albert in honour of his father and Edward in honour of his maternal grandfather, Prince Edward, Duke of Kent. He was related to royal families throughout Europe and stood as heir apparent to the largest empire in the world at that time. As Queen Victoria's eldest son he would become King Edward VII on her death in 1901.

In 1895 he was fifty-four years old, yet deprived of any involvement in affairs of state by his mother. The Queen approved neither of his fashionable lifestyle, nor his friends. Her own self-imposed isolation following the death of her beloved husband Albert in 1861 had compromised the popularity of the monarchy and encouraged the growth of the republican movement. This sentiment gained ground in Britain after the establishment of the French Third Republic in 1870 and a subsequent republican rally in Trafalgar Square demanded Queen Victoria's removal.

The Prince of Wales, however, created a public role for himself: he became adept at putting on a show, pioneering the idea of royal public appearances, keeping royalty foremost and present in his subjects' minds. He was the very essence of a charming prince.

Queen Victoria nevertheless considered her son profligate and consistently refused to loosen her purse strings. The Queen's Keeper of the Privy Purse commented that part of the Prince of Wales's character was such that 'it makes it impossible for him to deny himself anything'. In response, the Prince of Wales commented that: 'I don't mind praying to the eternal father, but I must be the only man in the country afflicted with an eternal mother.' Fortunately, wealthy friends such as Alfred de Rothschild often gave discreet financial support to the extravagant if beleaguered Prince.

and the Ephrussis – many of the great financiers of the day, well known for being connoisseurs of art among diverse other intellectual interests. The reception was held in the elegant eighteenth-century Lansdowne House in Berkeley Square, just a short carriage ride away. Each and every room was themed with different flowers and the celebrated Gottlieb's Orchestra played in the central Saloon.

At the front of the church stood Almina's mother Marie, accompanied by Alfred de Rothschild. Marie Wombwell had been a long-standing companion of his and was currently living in a house in Bruton Street in the heart of Mayfair, which he had given her. Rothschild himself owned a large house nearby: number one Seamore Place. Its gilded walls were hung with his fabulous art collection; French furniture, antiques and ceramics adorned every room, setting the stage for the exquisite dinner parties he threw to amuse his friends.

Alfred regularly entertained the Prince of Wales at his brilliant supper parties where entertainment was provided by charming artistes including the actress Lily Langtry and opera diva Nellie Melba, who would, unusually for her, sing in private for Alfred and his guests – perhaps because Alfred looked after her money for her. Later, she was to achieve worldwide acclaim: the Australian heroine with a golden voice, beloved in New York, at La Scala in Milan and Covent Garden in London. Like his father-in-law Alfred de Rothschild, the bridegroom Lord Carnarvon thoroughly enjoyed opera and played the piano passably well.

In June 1895, amidst much pomp and circumstance, Almina Wombwell, the illegitimate only daughter of Alfred de Rothschild, married George Edward Stanhope Molyneux Herbert, 5th Earl of Carnarvon. She arrived at the doors of the ancient St Margaret's Church, adjacent to the Houses of Parliament in Westminster, on the arm of her 'uncle' Sir George Wombwell. He was from a most respected Yorkshire family, a famous and very brave cavalryman who in 1854 had taken part in the Charge of the Light Brigade in the Crimean War. The pews were crowded with society figures and the church was overflowing with gorgeous flowers, from tall potted palm trees to white lilies, orchids, peonies and roses.

The list of wedding guests included all the great and the good of the day, from Lord Rosebery, who had just resigned as Prime Minister, to Lord Salisbury who had succeeded him. The bride's side of the aisle included Rothschilds, Sassoons

Nothing was too much trouble for Alfred when entertaining guests, from the excellence of his chefs, to the rare wines served and the calibre of the entertainment provided. At his country home, Halton House, he had his own orchestra, which he conducted with a diamond-encrusted baton. He arranged for a circus to perform and, remarkably, managed to drive a pair of zebras harnessed to a carriage. He maintained his own private railway carriage and even his own fire service.

Lady Dorothy Nevill wrote in her reminiscences that in her view Alfred was 'the finest amateur judge in England of eighteenth-century French art'. He was a meticulous and insatiable collector, who indulged his passions with no expense spared. Disraeli had declared Seamore Place 'the most charming house in London, the magnificence of its decorations and furniture equalled by their good taste'. In return, Alfred ensured a suite of rooms in Seamore Place was kept at Disraeli's disposal towards the end of his life. Disraeli died in 1881 and it was his dear friend Alfred who helped to organise his funeral procession.

Alfred was highly intelligent and had been made a director of the Bank of England at just twenty-six years of age. He was also a flamboyant bon vivant and was said to have attended a conference abroad accompanied by no fewer than four valets. To round off his famously idiosyncratic personality, he was also a renowned hypochondriac.

If the bridegroom's sisters privately wondered about the propriety of the marriage, they nevertheless loyally supported Lord Carnarvon's choice of bride. His brother-in-law Lord Burghclere noted that Almina was very much in love with the dashing young Earl, but commented that he did hope Carnarvon felt the same way. Almina was 'very pretty, with an immaculate figure and tiny waist'. She was tiny, just over five foot tall, known as the 'Dresden Doll', always beautifully dressed and adorned with exquisite jewels given to her by her father on the occasion of her marriage.

Apart from the ties of love, however, there was the marriage contract. The settlement was made between Alfred de Rothschild, Almina and Lord Carnarvon, and provided a dowry of some £500,000 (towards £30 million today). Lord Carnarvon had perhaps followed Jane Austen's adage, that whilst you should never marry for money it might be foolish to marry without money.

He was far from impecunious, owning five estates, farmland, coal mines and a house in London. However, agricultural revenue was no longer enough to maintain the estates and his lifestyle. During a time of increasing global trade, cheaper wheat from America and Canada, the commodities market had begun irrevocably to change and farming revenues continued to decline in England for the next fifty years. He had run up significant debts and Alfred de Rothschild kindly gave him a further £150,000 to resolve his 'challenges'.

Six months after their marriage, Alfred wished to signal Almina's arrival in society. He therefore arranged for His Royal Highness, the Prince of Wales, to be invited to a three-day shooting party at Highclere Castle. Almina and her father were determined to make sure the Prince of Wales's visit was a great success and Almina's generous instinct was to over-order everything.

December 1895 may have been inclement, requiring fortitude to make outside excursions, but most of the activity at Highclere that month was concentrated inside the Castle. Almina had been very busy – under the expert guidance of her father she was preparing to welcome one of the most important men in the world. Much planning was required for such an event. But there was an added anxiety: her new relatives and her husband would be observing how, or indeed if, she could carry off the forthcoming occasion.

Preparation for the shooting party had begun shortly after her wedding, the date arranged with her father's help.

Although the new young Lady Carnarvon was only twenty years old, she seemed utterly undaunted by the task ahead of her and entirely unconcerned by any considerations of economy. With her father's approval, she updated the hangings and furnishings at Highclere. Almina's father and uncle had both built their houses, Halton House and Waddesdon, in a very short time and had all the required craftsmen on hand. Meanwhile Almina accompanied her husband to Scotland and Devon on various expeditions throughout the autumn of 1895 and managed to fit in some sixty days' shooting. Lord Carnarvon was regarded as one of the finest shots in England.

Following consultation with Almina's husband, Stanhope was deemed the grandest bedroom suite, looking east over the pleasure gardens to the folly, Jackdaw's Castle. Deep-red damask silks were immediately procured for the walls as well as further fabric to be made into curtains. A huge new bed was purchased, a rich red carpet laid, and furnishings

RIGHT
Stanhope bedroom where HRH The Prince of Wales stayed
in December 1895, with a view to the temple folly known as
Jackdaw's Castle

BELOW
The Countess of Carnarvon's accounts book for the visit of
the Prince of Wales

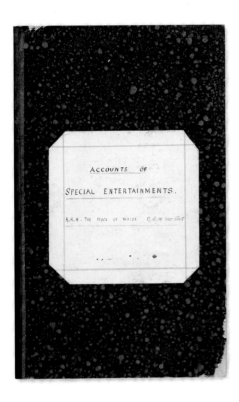

including a beautiful rug, French clock, ornate mirrors and lamps began to dress the bedroom. The charming detail of the plasterwork on the ceiling was picked out in fresh paint. Finally the bedchamber and its accompanying dressing room were deemed fit for a prince.

In early December, Streatfield, the House Steward, had been dispatched to London to hire extra chefs from the Savoy and to purchase an excess of provisions and flowers. His habitual calm and eye for organisation, both above and below stairs, belied the frenzied preparations going on behind the scenes. He had also made sure that all the railway guards and policemen at every station between Highclere and London Paddington received gifts of pheasant and partridge, to ensure the trains ran to time and supplies arrived in good order for the royal stay.

On the afternoon of 17 December Almina returned upstairs once more. She walked around the Gallery to Stanhope and stood by the desk, nervously rearranging

the leather blotting album and brass ink roller lying to one side. Nothing that could ensure the prince's comfort and convenience was to be omitted from the bedroom. She had observed and learnt much from her father and mother, but until recently had never been mistress of a house or responsible for the seamless running of an elegant and successful weekend house party.

Glancing out of the tall windows, framed by yards of draped and tasselled deep-red silk, she could see the line of carriages disappearing down the drive. Her husband had set off in the first, wrapped up against the very windy December weather. He was being driven by the head coachman, Brickell, to meet their esteemed guest at Highclere railway station.

The backs of the carriage horses gleamed in front of the coachmen, the cold day rendering their breath visible as they trotted smartly over Live Arch Bridge, up towards

London Lodge, build by the 1st Earl of Carnarvon in 1793

the Temple of Diana. They passed the grey cold expanse of Dunsmere Lake before carrying on out through London Lodge Gates and covering the last two miles to the station.

Brickell could still smell the oil used on the harnesses. He had made sure his stable lads had not missed any speck of dirt whatsoever. The inside of the carriage was furnished with rugs and hot bricks, to ensure the royal party's comfort on the return journey to Highclere. Further carriages and pairs of horses had been hired and followed behind to collect other guests, including the valets and private detectives. There were luggage carriages to carry trunks and cases full of clothes for day, for tea, for breakfast, for evening – capes, jackets, hats and shoes – no need for these guests to economise on anything.

The station platform was as immaculate as it could be in the gales that were battering southern England. Everyone waited expectantly for the Royal Train.

Almina Carnarvon could not find anything
missing from their principal guest's room. She knew of one fellow hostess who had enquired after a royal visit whether everything had been to the liking of her guest. Apparently the Prince of Wales had paused for thought and then suggested she was missing hooks for his dressing gowns. The unfortunate hostess had been mortified. Almina had provided dressing-gown hooks.

She returned downstairs to the Saloon, where the fire had been lit. Despite its double height, the Gothic-style Saloon felt warm and welcoming. Almina's father had just given her the most exceptional new Steinway grand. The piano's rich sustaining tone was quite beautiful. After some thought, she had positioned it in the Saloon, well away from the fireplace. There were plenty of chairs arranged near the fire, as well as desks and console tables, and a wonderful tall fern that was another gift from her father.

James Veitch & Sons had created an extravagantly large floral arrangement for the table at the back of the Saloon near the Drawing Room doors, and had sent yet more exotic ferns. Veitch were the foremost nursery and flower business in England and indeed the world, founded by John Veitch and his son James, who had come to prominence in the world of horticulture whilst working as gardeners to Sir Thomas Dyke

Highclere staff, including Fernside the valet holding Lord Carnarvon's dog, and housekeeper Mrs Bridgeland, immaculately dressed, sitting in the centre.

The Castle's complement of servants during this period amounted to at least fifty people. They were led by House Steward Streatfield, a butler, under-butler, fourteen footmen, Lady Carnarvon's maid, the Groom of the Bedchamber, valet, housekeeper and housemaids, chef, cook, kitchen porters, kitchen maids, stillroom maids, hall boy, and steward's room boy. There were many more serving in the outside departments of grooms, keepers, maintenance and forestry, etc.

During a shooting party the numbers downstairs would increase as every gentleman would bring a valet cum loader, every lady a maid.

The Highclere servants prided themselves on the hospitality offered to their visiting counterparts. They had coal fires in their bedrooms, excellent and plentiful food, and would amuse themselves in their leisure time by dancing around the piano in the staff dining room.

Acland, grandfather of Lord Carnarvon's great-grandmother Kitty Acland, 2nd Countess of Carnarvon, at Killerton in Devon. The Veitches had founded the Royal Horticultural Great Spring Show, which would eventually become the Chelsea Flower Show. Almina wondered if her sister-in-law Winifred would think it all too much.

Footmen in dark blue livery, silk stockings, shoes blackened and polished, buttons burnished, were standing ready to assist with luggage and tea for the anticipated cavalcade. The Room List had been memorised. Streatfield stood, tall and magisterial, managing the staff as a conductor would an orchestra. The hall boy kept lookout, ready to give the alert that carriages were approaching through the descending dusk. Soon they heard the sound of wheels crunching across the gravel and the horses' rhythmic trotting just audible above the eddying winds.

Relieved of his mantles, His Royal Highness

entered the Saloon. Almina dipped into a curtsey. Winifred Burghclere, waiting beside her, followed suit. The Prince of Wales was not very tall but of 'magnificent girth', testament to his love of excellent dinners. He was renowned for his enjoyment of life and could make himself extremely agreeable when he chose.

Lord Carnarvon had invited a collection of his friends to make up the shooting party who, whilst known to the Prince

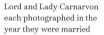
Lord and Lady Carnarvon
each photographed in the
year they were married

of Wales, were nearer Carnarvon's own age. Sir Edward and
Lady Colebrooke, friends of Winifred, were both easy and
charming guests. Sir Edward was a Liberal politician and
courtier, as was another guest, Earl Howe. Lord Westmorland
would later serve in the Northamptonshire Regiment in
South Africa and, like others in the party, was appointed an
aide-de-camp to King George V. As the old-fashioned name
might suggest, Lancelot Lowther was a keen hunting man, and
would ride to hounds whenever he could.

The following day Lord Ashburton, a renowned shot,
would also join the guns for the shoot. Mr Boulatzell was
attached to the Russian Legation in London and, whilst he did
not shoot, was charming company for the ladies of the party,
willingly escorting them out to lunch in the field, with endless
entertaining conversation and gossip.

The house party made for a young, amusing collection
of guests, if not quite as racy as the 'Marlborough House Set'
from the Prince of Wales's London life.

The redoubtable Lady Dorothy Nevill moved forward,
leaning on her silver-topped cane, to curtsey to the Prince of
Wales. Ever elegant, a horticulturalist and hostess of note, she
had been a regular weekend guest at Highclere for over thirty
years. Captain the Honourable Sir Seymour Fortescue was on
duty as the Prince of Wales's Equerry-in-Waiting. Fortescue
continued as ADC when the Prince became King Edward VII
and then served his son, King George V, from 1910 to 1921.

Almina led the Prince and the rest of the party
through to the Drawing Room where tea was set out. It was
now nearly dark outside, but electric lights as well as candles
in wall sconces shed warmth and light. All the fires had been
lit well in advance and were generously blazing in the winter's
afternoon. New electric lighting had recently been introduced
into the Castle. A small battery house was built behind the
stables to produce the alternating current. The electric
lights at Highclere made a tremendous difference, not just
to Lord and Lady Carnarvon but to all the downstairs staff
looking after them. The oil-lamp man would shortly be out of
a job but an electrician's team was soon employed full-time.
The light was better and clearer and there would be no more
everlasting soot for the housemaids to sweep up. It was also
front-page news that the US President, Grover Cleveland,
had arranged for the White House Christmas tree to be lit
with Edison electric bulbs. Almina thought she would also try
that at Highclere, but not this year.

The Drawing Room had been charmingly redecorated by
her in the French style. Like her father, she enjoyed collecting
eighteenth-century furniture and antiques from France, and
had bought an Aubusson rug, a dazzling chandelier from
Bohemia, desks, chairs and a vast French Louis XV marble
chimney mantel.

The walls were hung with new green silks copied from
Marie Antoinette's boudoir at Versailles, another wedding

The chandelier in the Drawing Room is from Bohemia and has 365 pieces of glass

LEFT
The Robing Room

RIGHT
Today's butler Luis sets the table to
the same exacting standards as has
been done for generations at Highclere

gift from Alfred to his daughter. It was a huge change for
Winifred from the more restrained decoration she had
lived with during her childhood at Highclere. She could not,
however, say anything because now it was Almina's house.

Streatfield marshalled the butler and footmen to bring in
the little tables and trays for tea. Almina had suggested using
the dark blue Meissen china her father had given her. The
guests soon retired to rest and change for dinner.

Formal weekends entailed endless changes of

clothes: for the morning, for shooting or riding, for tea and
then for dinner. Clothes were extravagant but underneath any
ladies' oufit was a tightly boned corset designed to emphasise

the waist. All ladies' clothes had numerous hooks and clasps.
The bodices and evening dresses had intricate fastenings
and tiny buttons, calling for deft-fingered ladies' maids,
whether to dress or undress. Daytime jackets had ever-more
extravagant leg o' mutton sleeves, a style that influenced
Almina's choice in clothes for a further ten years. Fashion
suggested that her hair should be curled and arranged high on
her head, all of which took further time every evening.

Each male guest had his own valet and it was their job
to be just as punctilious with their master's dress. By now
they would be casting a final eye over the gentlemen's evening
wear, checking the nap of the cloth was perfect, the tie
symmetrical and collar studs secure.

Dinner was at 8.30 p.m. A few of the men were already
down and playing cards in the Library. Almina looked
stunning in the exquisite diamonds and emeralds her father
had given her. The Prince of Wales was punctilious about
time-keeping and walked around the Gallery to the Oak
Staircase promptly. The assembled guests were all waiting
downstairs and turned to face him, either to bow or curtsey,
until he was amongst them and genially nodding and waving
at them to stand up. He noticed what the ladies wore, their
jewellery and gowns, and no woman would dare to wear the
same outfit twice. The Prince of Wales was regarded as the
arbiter of fashion and now preferred black tie to white for
dinner. White tie was complex to assemble as it required a
precise construction of the shirt, collars, waistcoat, jacket
and accessories. The guests may well have been delighted to
follow his lead.

Streatfield had reviewed the tables, each place setting perfectly measured, the flowers spectacular and the crystal and silver sparkling. A little menu card in front of each guest set out the courses, thereby allowing them to pace their appetite if they wished. Streatfield would station himself behind Lady Carnarvon, any instructions to him during dinner relayed with a whisper or a gesture that remained almost imperceptible. *Service à la Russe* was now the fashion for formal dining: it required far more footmen passing around the dishes so the guests were indeed waited on 'hand and foot'. The blue-coated, bewigged and powdered footmen stood behind the chairs as the ladies sat down, with the Prince of Wales to the right of his hostess.

If the first challenge for Almina had been to create an array of interesting menus to amuse the Prince of Wales, the subsequent test during each dinner was to keep the conversation flowing so that the Prince could listen and interject his own comments. He liked to hear the babble of conversation even if he himself was not the easiest conversationalist. He could switch from English to French, which was something Almina found relatively easy to cope with since her mother was half-French.

It was both an honour and a strain for Almina and the other house-party guests to ensure they were always doing the 'right thing', but of course, for all the Prince of Wales's apparent *bonhomie*, woe betide anyone who returned his

tolerance with familiarity. Lady Nevill sat to the other side of him as she was a noted conversationalist. She observed:

> The real art of conversation is not only to say the right thing at the right place, but to leave unsaid the wrong thing at the tempting moment.

Streatfield had earlier carefully opened several bottles of Château Lafite, which was the only wine the Prince of Wales drank. Alfred was delighted to be able to offer a rare 1875 vintage. Château Lafite was managed by his three cousins, who continued the centuries-old tradition of producing superb, full-bodied, delicious Bordeaux.

Dinner concluded with ices: ice cream *à la Napolitaine*, a fashion exported across the Atlantic, originating from Italian immigrants to New York, where American manufacturers had begun to produce early fridges. Highclere had used an ice house in the south-west gardens for generations. It stored ice, collected each winter, which could be retrieved and packed round metal dishes or cold boxes. The kitchens, however, would also soon trial the more modern machines.

Following dinner, as was the custom, Almina retired to the Drawing Room with the ladies, whilst her husband remained with the men in the Dining Room, a cold buffet arranged to one side in case anyone should feel in need of further sustenance. After dinner the Prince of Wales enjoyed a glass of Napoleon brandy as well as a short cigar. He was a heavy smoker and a line of cigars was created and named for him. He did not however linger long at the table, preferring to join the ladies without much delay.

Card tables had been set around the fireplace in the Saloon in case they should be needed. The fire was lit in the Billiard Room. Alfred had also provided vintage Champagne to enjoy with the card games and other entertainments. Almina knew that the Prince of Wales was a keen bridge player, and whilst his bids could be daring, his temper was short if he was losing.

When the Prince of Wales withdrew to his room, which fortunately was not too late, the remainder of the household could retire. Some cold meats were taken to his room in case he felt hungry in the night.

Streatfield and his staff now set to work to clear the dining tables, opening the windows briefly to air the room, and carrying the elaborate silver wine coolers and candlesticks back down to the strongroom until the following evening. The silver cutlery was carefully washed and polished dry before finally one longer table was re-laid for breakfast and the footmen could retire to bed.

The next morning, at 8 a.m., dressed in warm shooting tweeds and spats, the guns appeared promptly in the Dining Room. They enjoyed a hearty breakfast of eggs, potted meats, game pie, hams, tongues, devilled kidneys, grilled mushrooms, kippers with toast, tea, coffee, hot cocoa and even tankards of beer, before gathering in the Front Hall to set off for the day's shoot. The Prince of Wales wore tweeds and a Norfolk jacket sufficiently loose to be suitable for the shooting field, a waistcoat with the bottom button left undone supposedly because of his large girth, which then became a general fashionable habit, and a homburg hat.

Woe betide anyone infringing the prescribed dress code! Apparently the Prince had rebuked the Prime Minister, Lord Salisbury, one morning for inappropriate dress. Ever tactful, despite being deep in an international crisis, Salisbury's response to the Prince of Wales was that it had been a dark morning and 'my mind must have been occupied by some subject of less importance'.

The ladies took breakfast in bed, with a little porridge and toast brought up to them on pretty china and trays. The hour after breakfast with the men off at the shoot was an excellent time to sit down and write letters, a task taken seriously in those days, or to chat to one another. Given the inclement weather, they planned to join the guns at lunchtime. Almina did not actually shoot herself, but some women were beginning to take up the sport in the 1890s. The Duchess of Bedford and Mrs Willie James, one of the great hostesses of the period, were notably good shots. Queen Victoria naturally considered such activity very 'fast' and unsatisfactory.

The day began with the team of guns making their way to Biggs and Warrens, fields and woods to the west of the Castle. Each gentleman would shoot with two guns, which required the assistance of two loaders and a young lad. Henry Maber, the head keeper, ensured there were plenty of beaters and was in the thick of them to make sure they kept the line. At this time of year, as well as the under-keepers, Maber would use farm labourers and gardening boys for the day. They had already flanked in the first drive and older, more experienced but perhaps less mobile beaters stood at the corners of the woods, ready to raise their white flags as the drive progressed.

The drives for the day had been planned by
Lord Carnarvon and his head keeper with military precision.
Indeed, no one had been allowed to disturb the fields and
woodland during the previous few days. There was always
banter from Lord Ashburton, a keen observer and shot, with
strong opinions on where his host should best place the guns
and the teams of beaters. The Prince of Wales liked clouds
of pheasants, not too high, in order to precisely select a bird.
Fellow guns tried to avoid poaching any birds that flew near
the Prince and nor did they wish to drop any near him.

During the previous fifteen years the traditional English
approach to shooting had fundamentally changed. Instead
of walking through woodland and shooting pheasants or
partridge as a pair of dogs put them up, the great estates
had now been laid out for driven shoots. One of the men
responsible for this development was in fact the Prince of
Wales himself. His figure and temperament were admirably
suited to the extravagance and comfort of this type of shoot.

Instead of hunting or walking across fields, he could find
his peg at two or three drives and enjoy a very pleasurable
day's sport without having to undertake too much exercise.
Highclere was one of the best sporting shoots in the country
and Lord Carnarvon one of the best shots in company with
Lord de Grey, Lord Walsingham, Prince Victor Duleep
Singh, his brother Prince Frederick Duleep Singh and Lord
Ashburton. Prince Victor Duleep Singh remained a close
friend of Lord Carnarvon and became godfather to his son,
one of whose names was Victor in his honour.

In addition to the preferences of the Prince of Wales,
another reason why driven shoots had developed was
innovation in shotgun mechanics. The advent of breech-
loaders in the 1850s, with hammerless guns and later ejectors,
allowed for consistent and regular firing. In the 1880s Colonel
Shultz invented a smokeless powder – the black powder used
until then could be unreliable and also obscured sightlines,
thus slowing down competitive shots such as Lord de Grey.

The Maber dynasty: head keepers at Highclere

Three generations of Mabers have worked and lived at Highclere. Head gamekeeper was an important role; he was given his own house, a cob to pull his cart or to ride, and twenty-five staff under him. They had their own tweed uniforms, made by the local tailor Dodds.

The 6th Earl of Carnarvon wrote this warm obituary appreciation of Charles Maber (1891–1972), successor to Henry Maber [LEFT] who had served at the time of the Prince of Wales's visit:

Charles came from a long line of dedicated gamekeepers; his father, Henry Maber, was a great character and I was happy in his company when he was my father's head keeper.

Charles took over his job in 1923 and considering that he was badly gassed in the First World War, he did his duties marvellously well, in an age when keepers walked many miles daily and bicycles were their only other means of transport. We never had a cross word in fifty years and I learned much from him about wildlife.

He was the Churchill of his profession and his wise counsel was frequently sought during World War Two by the Ministry of Agriculture concerning the many problems connected with the preservation of game and the production of food for the nation. He was greatly respected and loved by all who knew him.

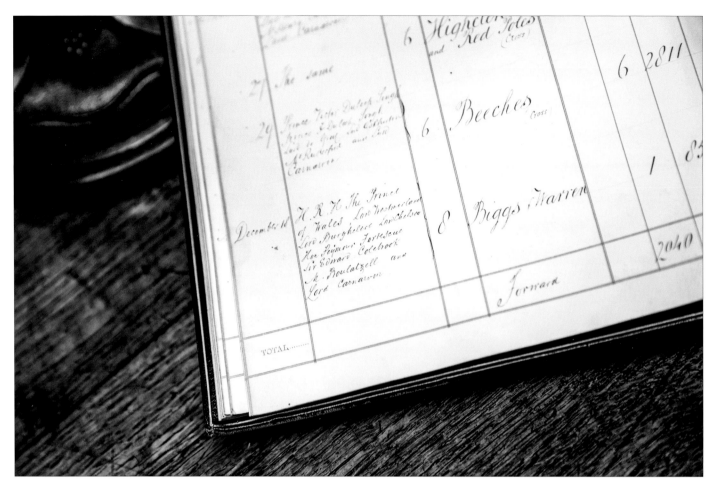

Highclere Castle Game Book, December 1895

Lunch took place out of doors in the field, in a strategically placed lodge to give some protection and relief from the weather. Almina travelled out with the ladies by barouche. Five courses for lunch would be expected and must be promptly served as the daylight hours were short. Oysters were an especial favourite of the Prince of Wales's, so Almina had ensured they were offered as a first course. The vintage Champagne was produced again although the Prince was abstemious with alcohol at lunchtime.

The day's sport was excellent and the bag totalled one partridge, 855 pheasants and 2,168 rabbits before the party returned to the Castle for tea at 4 p.m. Almina and the other ladies hastened upstairs to change their dresses, but by the time they returned downstairs, some of the men had retired exhausted and would not be seen again until dinner. Shooting was tiring, not least because of the deafening noise produced by such a huge number of shots, and splitting headaches as a result were not uncommon.

Dinner followed the extravagant length and form of the previous night's. It was a veritable cavalcade of dishes served on silver platters. 'No age since that of Nero can show such unlimited addiction to food,' commented the diarist Harold Nicolson. Beginning with soups, and then fish dishes, followed by medleys of sweet and savoury dishes, delicately prepared vegetables followed by meats, then fruits and ice creams. The chefs in the kitchens were busy creating works of art with delicately garnished jellies, whilst the final roasts were carefully carried out along the corridors towards the backstairs and the Dining Room.

The Prince of Wales was generally good-natured and considerate but did require amusement after dinner, thus Almina had organised a small concert and entertainment. He had given up dancing, but he enjoyed opera and music. The chairs were arranged in rows in the Library because Almina had engaged Ashton's, the Prince's favoured theatrical agency, as recommended by her father.

Season 1895-6.

GAME KILLED.

DATE.	By whom Killed.	Where Killed.	Pheasants	Partridges	Hares.	Rabbits.	Various.	TOTAL.	REMARKS.
1895	Brought Forward		45	8442	2033	401	8638	91	19650	
December 13	Mr. Wentworth's party	Weir Copse	"	50	"	"	"	"	50	
16	Picked up on Warren		"	"	"	"	64	"	64	
"	Warreners	Highclere Wood	"	"	"	"	69	"	69	
18	H.R.H. Prince of Wales		"	"	"	"	"	"	"	
	Lord Chelsea, Lord		"	"	"	"	"	"	"	
	Burghclere, Lord		"	"	"	"	"	"	"	
	Westmorland, Honble F	Biggs & Warren	"	855	1	"	2165	2	3023	
	Fortescue, Mr. Bouletgell,		"	"	"	"	"	"	"	
	Sir Edward Colebrook,		"	"	"	"	"	"	"	
	Lord Carnarvon.		"	"	"	"	"	"	"	
20	Warreners	Park	"	"	"	"	220		220	
"	Keepers	Warren	"	"	"	"	225		225	
"	—— do ——	—— do ——	"	4	"	"	50		50	
24	Warreners	Park	"	"	"	"	16		16	
26	—— do ——	—— " ——	"	"	"	"	140		140	
27	—— do ——	Woodhay Common	"	"	"	"	42		42	
30	—— do ——	Park.	"	"	"	"	106		106	
31	Prince V. Duleep Singh,		"	"	"	"	"	"	"	
	Lord Carnarvon, Dr.									
	Cooper, Mr. Uhde	Easton Park & Grotto	wcock 1	214	4	26	287	4	536	
	Mr. Rutherford									
		Carry Forward	46	9565	2038	427	12028	97	24201	

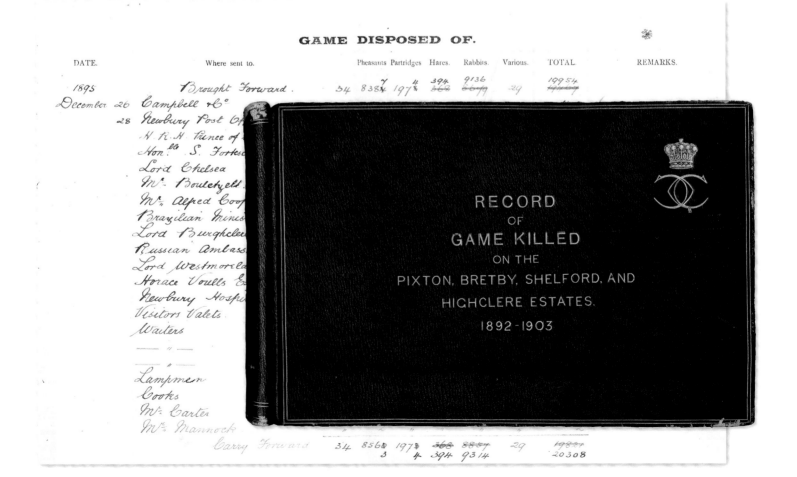

GAME DISPOSED OF.

DATE.	Where sent to.	Pheasants	Partridges	Hares.	Rabbits.	Various.	TOTAL.	REMARKS.
1895	Brought Forward.	34	8384 7	1973 4	394 368	9136 8619	29	19954
December 26	Campbell & Co							
28	Newbury Post Off							
	H.R.H. Prince of							
	Honble S. Fortesc							
	Lord Chelsea							
	Mr. Bouletgell							
	Mr. Alfred Coop							
	Brazilian Mines							
	Lord Burghclere							
	Russian Ambass							
	Lord Westmorla							
	Horace Voules E							
	Newbury Hospi							
	Visitors Valets							
	Waiters							
	"							
	Lampmen							
	Cooks							
	Mr. Carter							
	Mr. Mannock							
	Carry Forward	34	8560 3	1973 4	366 394	8867 9314	29	19801 20308

From THE EARL OF CARNARVON

PARTRIDGES

PHEASANTS

HARES

RECORD OF GAME KILLED ON THE PIXTON, BRETBY, SHELFORD, AND HIGHCLERE ESTATES. 1892-1903

colt then went on to a successful stud career, a lucrative and helpful addendum for his owner.

After all the preparations, the visit by the Prince had passed very quickly. Breakfast on the final day was set again in the Dining Room. Rows of lamps warmed silver chafing dishes containing porridge, devilled kidneys, lamb cutlets, omelettes, kedgeree; alongside were laid the cold hams and pheasants, toast, marmalade and pots of tea, chocolate and coffee. Breakfast was never hurried and thus the ladies were dressed and waiting downstairs in the Saloon with Almina and Winifred to curtsey to the Prince as they all bade farewell.

The Visitors' Book was laid out for all the guests to sign. Streatfield stood near the front door, footmen lined up outside as the carriages drew up to make the return journey back to Highclere station and thence by the Royal Train to London.

The chefs and back-of-house staff remained invisible, although the housemaids had run up to the top-floor windows at the front of the house to catch a glimpse of the Prince of Wales as he left. They would all be thoroughly entertained by Streatfield's descriptions later that day below stairs.

George Ashton ran Ashton's Drawing-room Entertainment Agency offering artistes for at homes, dinner parties, etc. He advertised his services as being 'By Special Appointment to HRH the Prince and Princess of Wales'. Almina could choose between Ashton's Blue Hungarian Band, Yvette Guilbert, or the Neapolitan Troupe of Mandolinists and Guitarists.

Carnarvon sat towards the back with his sister Winifred. Reserved by nature, he always remained very close to his elder sister. They had clung together following their mother's death, when they were just nine and ten years old. Lord Carnarvon had, however, every confidence in his new young wife, seated at the front next to their distinguished guest. She had indeed organised a resoundingly successful occasion.

With their guest of honour in a mellow mood after the music, the conversation turned to horses and racing. This year had been a good one for the Prince. He had bred the two-year-old racehorse Persimmon, a beautiful bay colt with exciting prospects, which over the next two years would go on to exceed all expectation by winning seven prestigious races including the Epsom Derby, St Leger and the Epsom Gold Cup. The prize money would amount to some £35,000, before the

POSTSCRIPT

A few days later the Carnarvons would set off for Halton House, to spend Christmas with Alfred de Rothschild. His friendship with the Prince of Wales continued whilst the Prince remained heir in waiting at the same time as his young cousins were Emperor of Germany and Tsar of Russia. It would be another five years before the Prince of Wales succeeded as King Edward VII.

In 1896 Persimmon won the Derby as well as other races in fine style and the Prince of Wales's finances and ability to enjoy life continued unabated.

Almina's Rothschild inheritance was essential to Highclere's survival over the next fifty years.

Menu du

Prawn Cocktail

___

Perdreau Roti
See Pan
Legumes

___

Chocolat Menche
Soufflé.
Patisserie

___

Café

A NOTE ON MENUS

Menus at Highclere Castle were designed to reflect prestige on the house and its owners. They also demonstrated the virtuosity of the chefs as well as the organisational skills of the hostess. They still followed an order familiar from the previous century:

POTAGES
Soups

POISSONS
Fish

ENTRÉES
formerly known in England as 'made dishes'

RELEVÉS
Substantial *entrées*

RÔTS
Roasts

ENTREMETS
A medley of sweet dishes and dishes
of delicately prepared vegetables

Huîtres

POTAGES

Consommé clair

Cock-a-leekie   PAGE 176

POISSONS

Saumon grillé aux câpres   PAGE 72

Sole à la Dugléré   PAGE 62

Filets de merlans frits   PAGE 68

ENTRÉES

Timbale à la Milanese

Ris de veau panés

Soufflé de volaille

RELEVÉS

Aloyau de boeuf rôti

Le gigot de mouton,
sauce piquante   PAGE 118

RÔTS

Perdreaux à Highclere   PAGE 112

Oie rôtie   PAGE 109

Pommes Anna   PAGE 112

Venaison braisée à la Forestière PAGE 125

avec salade de choux-fleurs   PAGE 168

ENTREMETS

Artichauts à la crème   PAGE 168

Compôte de poires à la Chantilly PAGE 231

Profiteroles au chocolat

Rissoles au fromage

Glace à la Napolitaine

BUFFET

Cold roast beef

Hot and cold roasted fowls

Tongue

Cold beef salad

The DRAWING ROOM

The Drawing Room reflects the style and taste of Almina, 5th Countess of Carnarvon. Her father gave her enough fine turquoise silk to cover the walls of this charming south-facing room. After the original silk became faded and torn it was replaced in 1999 with new fabric as close as possible to the original colour.

Rococo Revival was a very fashionable decorative style in Almina's day and she filled this room with exquisite French furniture and *objets de vertu*, some of which still remain in place. The eighteenth-century Bohemian crystal chandelier that lights the room has 365 pieces of glass. The French marble fireplace with mantelshelf is very different in style from those in the other State rooms and the sheer size of it always makes me wonder how it was ever carried in and fitted into place.

The concert-sized black-lacquered Steinway piano stands diagonally across one corner of the room and after a few glasses of Champagne guests are often encouraged to play upon it. One New Year my sister Penny, an accomplished pianist, retired early, leaving her music behind with friends, who proceeded to struggle very, very slowly through some well-known songs. I still cannot listen to them being played today without smiling at the memory. One girlfriend laughed so much at the excruciating performance that tears ran down her face – an unforgettable evening.

PAT WITHERS

Painter & Decorator

One spring morning in 1960 Miss Stubbings, Lord Carnarvon's agent, arrived outside Ivory Farm Cottages to ask if Pat and her father would like to paint the windows on the outside of the Castle. Neither of them had seen the Castle until then and they were somewhat stunned when they arrived in front of it. Pat clearly remembers Miss Stubbings's attempts to reassure them that it would not be too bad because all the windows opened inward except of course for the little square windows at the top of the Castle, which didn't open at all.

One of her best memories of her time at Highclere is of being presented to the Queen by Lord and Lady Carnarvon (the current Earl's parents) when the Castle was first opened to the public in 1989. Pat had not wanted to go to the opening as it was going to be attended by 800 people, which she thought was not her thing, but was persuaded to attend. Stan the furniture restorer was standing with her when she realised the Queen was coming their way. Stan just had time to grab Pat's large handbag and thrust it out of sight, hoping that it wouldn't catch the priceless china behind them and send it crashing to the ground. The Queen said she had heard that Pat had painted the Castle three times and might be painting it a fourth, at which point Pat told her she would need a Zimmer frame by then. Lord Carnarvon promptly agreed, offering to get her one and to help her push it.

Pat first met her husband Mike at a dance near Highclere. She had just lost her father and been stood up by her *fiancé*. Mike stood out like a sore thumb, dressed in a suit when everyone else was wearing jeans. They were married in 1973 in Highclere Church. Mike's hobby is bee-keeping and he now collects the estate honey, which is used in the kitchens and sold in the gift shop. Occasionally his hobby gets him into trouble: on the morning of their wedding, Mike was side-tracked when he found and collected a swarm of bees from an apple tree near his mother's home.

Pat's hobby is keeping ferrets. She currently has about twenty of them and their names include Gert, Daisy, Elsie, Doris, Boris, Sam and Crackers.

Pat has now worked for three generations of Carnarvons, doing many other odd jobs as well as painting. She's helped in the house during the shooting season and likes to tiptoe up the stone staff stairs in the Castle to look through the balustrade of the Gallery at the dancing below in the Saloon. She says: 'You couldn't get nicer people to work for than the Carnarvons.'

Each of the three Earls was totally different and absolutely brilliant, in Pat's opinion. The 6th Earl called every woman 'my love' and every man 'my friend'. However, Pat loves the current Earl even more because she has known him since he was born. She has no favourite place on the estate; there is always something beautiful and something different to see every day. 'I love working here otherwise I would have been gone a long time ago.' She reckons she is the longest-serving member of staff, working at the Castle for even longer than Eddie Hughes the keeper with whom she went to school.

Pat is still painting the Castle.

VEGETABLES, SOUPS & SAVOURIES

Pea & Mint Risotto

SERVES: 6

Risotto rice is an excellent standby to keep in the pantry or store cupboard. The unusual and colourful secret to this recipe is that our chef Paul makes a little pea purée, which gives the dish its vibrant colour.

INGREDIENTS

400g (14oz) frozen garden peas (or 1kg/2lb 3oz fresh peas, podded), plus 100g (4oz) podded fresh or frozen peas, cooked, to serve

*1·75 litres (3 pints) good-quality vegetable stock (preferably homemade) [**SEE** right]*

100g (3½oz) unsalted butter

1 large onion, diced

1 garlic clove, crushed

400g (14oz) risotto rice (such as Arborio)

1 bay leaf

100ml (3½fl oz) white wine

50g (2oz) Parmesan, grated, plus shavings to serve (optional)

1–2 tbsp finely chopped fresh mint (tender leaf tips only)

Salt and pepper

Finely grated lemon zest, to garnish

Crème fraîche, to serve (optional)

METHOD

To make the pea purée, add the 400g (14oz) peas to about 400ml (13fl oz) of the vegetable stock, purée in a blender, then pass through a sieve.

Pour the purée into a large saucepan and stir in the rest of the stock. You will need about 1·75 litres (3 pints) of this bright green pea-flavoured stock. Keep it warm on the hob over a very low heat.

Melt the butter in a pan over a low heat, add the onion and sauté for 2–3 minutes, then add the garlic and sauté for another 2–3 minutes until the onion is soft but not coloured.

Add the rice and the bay leaf to the pan and cook for 1–2 minutes, stirring, then add the white wine and let it reduce by half.

Stir in the hot pea stock, a little at a time, letting it be absorbed at each addition before you add more.

Cook the rice for 15–18 minutes or until *al dente* (you may have some stock left over). Remove the bay leaf.

Stir in the grated Parmesan, then finish with the 100g (4oz) cooked peas and mint tips.

Remove from the heat, season with salt and pepper, garnish with lemon zest and top each serving with a spoonful of *crème fraîche* and shavings of Parmesan, if you wish.

VEGETABLE STOCK

MAKES: 2 litres (3½ pints)

INGREDIENTS

50ml (2fl oz) vegetable oil

200g (7oz) celery stalks, diced

1 fennel bulb, diced

200g (7oz) onions, diced

200g (7oz) carrots, diced

200g (7oz) leeks, finely sliced

2 tbsp tomato purée

2 bay leaves

10 black peppercorns

50g (2oz) bunch of rosemary

50g (2oz) bunch of thyme

2 sprigs of tarragon

8 garlic cloves (whole)

4 litres (7 pints) cold water

METHOD

Heat the vegetable oil in a very large saucepan, add the vegetables and fry gently for 5 minutes, then stir in the tomato purée followed by the rest of the ingredients, including the water. Simmer for 2 hours, uncovered, skimming off any scum that forms on the surface.

When the stock has reduced by half, strain it through a sieve into a large clean pan and bring it to a rapid boil. Let it reduce for a further 20 minutes. Remove from heat, leave to cool and refrigerate.

The stock will keep in the fridge for up to a week, or can be frozen.

Roasted Beetroots

SERVES: 6

We grow beetroots from seed in the vegetable garden. Within three months they are between the size of a golf ball and tennis ball and perfect to pick. Beetroots have been used in cooking for over 1,000 years. They are believed to stimulate the liver's detoxification process, are supposed to help suppress cancers as they contain betacyanins, and also to support the heart. Whatever the truth of these claims, they are definitely low in fat and full of vitamins and minerals.

Despite all this, they remain one of the less popular vegetables with many claiming not to like them at all. Personally, they are one of my favourites. Delicious in a soup (borscht), they are very simple to roast as here. The fun comes from using different-coloured beetroots but you must be careful not to put them together to cook or all the colours run into each other and spoil the effect.

INGREDIENTS

50g (2oz) butter

50ml (2fl oz) olive oil

3 sprigs of rosemary, leaves chopped

6 sprigs of thyme, leaves chopped

3 garlic cloves, chopped

200g (7oz) golden beetroots, peeled and cut into wedges

200g (7oz) candy beetroots, peeled and cut into wedges

200g (7oz) red beetroots, peeled and cut into wedges

Salt and pepper

METHOD

Preheat the oven to 180°C/350°F/Gas mark 4.

Melt the butter with the oil in a pan. Remove from heat and add the chopped herbs and garlic. Divide the mixture between three separate bowls.

If you don't want to stain your hands, wear rubber gloves. Starting with the golden beetroots, tip the wedges into one of the bowls of garlic-herb mixture and toss, adding some salt and pepper. Repeat with the other beetroot wedges. Transfer the seasoned wedges to a baking tray.

Roast in the oven until cooked. The cooking time will depend on how big the beetroot wedges are (up to 45 minutes). After the first 20 minutes, turn the beetroots over to help cook them more evenly.

Take out of the oven, season again with salt and pepper and enjoy! They are delicious with roasted beef, venison or on their own as a warm salad.

Asparagus Mousse & Spears

SERVES: 10

Ihave very clear memories of my mother frequently making mousses, as they could be prepared well ahead of time. My sister Sarah and I liked to run our fingers round the mixing bowl, after our mother had made a mousse either of fish or, as here, asparagus and cream.

A mousse is simply a purée of fish, poultry or, as in this case, vegetables. The purée is then bound with cream or eggs and cooked. It can be served as a first course or as a Sunday supper after a big lunch. Asparagus mousse is best made the day before it is needed so that it has time to set properly. Serve with crackers, bread or French toast.

INGREDIENTS

100g (3½oz) unsalted butter, plus extra for frying

50ml (2fl oz) olive oil, plus extra for frying

3 banana shallots, diced

2 garlic cloves, crushed

5 celery stalks, chopped

500g (1lb 2oz) asparagus spears, top 5cm (2in) of each spear reserved for the centrepiece, remaining asparagus trimmed and chopped

100ml (3½fl oz) vegetable stock
[**SEE** page 160]

400ml (13fl oz) double cream

100ml (3½fl oz) whole milk

100g (3½oz) spinach

20 mint leaves

7 leaves of gelatine or agar agar

Grated zest and juice of 1 lemon

10g (½oz) pea shoots, washed, to serve (optional)

Sea salt and pepper

METHOD

Melt 75g (2½oz) of the butter with the oil in a pan over a low heat. Add the shallots, garlic, celery and chopped bottoms of the asparagus spears, season, and cook for about 5 minutes until soft but not coloured.

Add the vegetable stock, turn up the heat and simmer for up to 10 minutes, until the liquid is reduced by half.

Pour in the cream and milk and continue to simmer for up to 5 minutes, until the asparagus is tender.

Remove from the heat and allow to cool slightly, then blitz with a stick blender until smooth and season to taste.

Add the spinach and mint and blitz again. Pass the mixture through a sieve to ensure it is completely smooth. It will be a lovely green colour. Season to taste.

Soak the gelatine in cold water for 3–5 minutes until soft, then remove it from the water and add it to the vegetable mixture and stir well. Pour the mixture into a 20cm (8in) *rhum baba* mould (base measurement) or individual moulds or pots and leave to cool, then cover with clingfilm and refrigerate for at least 8 hours until set.

When the mousse is set, hold the mould briefly over hot running water to free the edge and carefully turn it out onto a plate.

Pan-fry the asparagus tips in the remaining butter for about 3 minutes. Once browned, add the lemon juice and zest and reduce until evaporated.

Garnish the mousse with the asparagus tips and serve. If liked, top with some pea shoots for a final flourish.

Baked Parmesan Baskets

filled with roasted vegetables

SERVES: 6

Parmigiano-Reggiano (Parmesan) is a delicious hard cheese, which is called 'the king of cheeses' according to the Italians, who have otherwise got rid of all their royalty. It should have a nutty, gritty texture and in this recipe is used to create a baked cup into which you can spoon different roasted vegetables depending on the time of year and your preference. It is a way of jazzing up even quite uninteresting vegetables and therefore excellent for more formal dinners. The vegetables become sweet and delicious when roasted but retain some of the enyzmes we need – thus I can convince my husband that this is still nominally 'healthy' despite the inclusion of cheese.

INGREDIENTS

240g (8¾oz) Parmesan cheese, grated

*50–75ml (2–2½fl oz) olive oil,
plus extra for drizzling*

6 baby fennel, roughly sliced

6 baby carrots, sliced diagonally

6 baby aubergines, quartered

*6 baby leeks
(or 6 baby courgettes, if in season)*

20g (¾oz) butter, plus extra for greasing

1 garlic clove, crushed

Finely grated zest and juice of ½ lemon

Salt and pepper

Salad and herb leaves, to serve

METHOD

Preheat the oven to 180°C/350°F/Gas mark 4 and turn off the fan if your oven is fan-assisted (a fan setting will cause the Parmesan to splash when melting).

Line a large baking sheet with baking parchment or a silicone sheet and grease the exterior of 6 small ramekins or dariole moulds.

It is so simple to make the baskets: place the grated Parmesan in six roughly circular 8cm (3in) diameter piles of 40g (1½oz) on the lined baking sheet. Bake for 8 minutes. When the cheese turns golden brown and starts to look crisp, remove from the oven and quickly shape each piece over the upturned greased ramekins or dariole moulds while they are still hot and pliable. Set aside to cool.

Increase the oven temperature to 190°C/360°F/Gas mark 5.

Season all the vegetables and drizzle over a little oil, keeping them separate (they require different roasting times). Put the butter and crushed garlic in a heavy baking tray and place it in the hot oven for about 3 minutes or until the butter just starts to brown. Add the baby fennel. After 2–3 minutes add the baby carrots, then 3 minutes later the aubergine and, after a further 3 minutes, the baby leeks or courgettes. Roast all the vegetables together for a final 3–5 minutes, until all the vegetables are just tender.

Each time you add a different vegetable to the tray, toss them with the butter and oil to coat. To serve, dress all the roasted vegetables with lemon juice, lemon zest and extra olive oil, divide them between the 6 Parmesan baskets and scatter a few salad and herb leaves over each.

Bread

MAKES: 1 loaf

Highclere remains a mixed working farm growing wheat, oats, barley, linseed or other break crops. In the old days the wheat was turned into flour by being fed into a chute, from which it was ground between great milling stones and then sieved. The finest flour was used to form bread, the coarser separated for wholemeal flour and the rougher stuff used in cattle feed. The principles are the same today, although flour may subsequently be bleached or have additives incorporated into it.

Many bought breads now rely on the 'Chorleywood' bread process, which adds various enzymes and preservatives to the basic ingredients, to allow the dough to be made faster and the bread to last longer, which may or may not be an advantage for consumers. However, it is very easy to make bread yourself. Basic bread needs just four ingredients: flour, yeast, water and salt.

INGREDIENTS

500g (1lb 2oz) strong white bread flour, plus extra for dusting

1 tsp coarse salt

325–350ml (11–12fl oz) lukewarm water

7g (¼oz) sachet easy-blend dried yeast

METHOD

Preheat the oven to 220°C/425°F/Gas mark 7.

Pour the flour and salt in a large mixing bowl and form a well in the centre. Mix the lukewarm water and yeast together in a jug, then pour most of it into the well and mix it into the flour to form a soft dough (you may not need all the water).

Knead the dough on a floured worktop for about 10 minutes until smooth and no longer sticky, then place it in a large bowl, cover the bowl with a clean, damp cloth or clingfilm and set aside at room temperature for 45 minutes – 1 hour until the dough has doubled in size.

Pour a cup of water into an oven tray and put the tray at the bottom of the oven to create some steam. This helps the bread to form a lovely crust.

Tip the dough out of the bowl, lightly knead it and mould it into your desired shape, then place on a greased baking sheet and set aside at room temperature for a further 20 minutes or a bit longer, covered with a clean damp cloth, until well risen and doubled in size.

Bake in the oven for 30–40 minutes until golden brown and the base of the loaf sounds hollow when you tap it underneath. Remove from the oven and transfer to a wire rack to cool.

Artichauts à la Crème

SERVES: 10 as a side dish

Jerusalem artichokes are knobbly brown tubers that you can use in much the same way as parsnips. It is an odd name, as there is no connection to the Middle East: they were originally collected and used by Native Americans. The flower looks like a sunflower, known to American Italian settlers as *girasole*, which sounds a little like 'Jerusalem', proving that no one nation ever quite understands another.

In this recipe, the artichokes are combined with mashed potato to give the dish a little more substance. The hazelnuts are optional but give an additional layer of flavour. If any guest has a nut allergy then it still tastes delicious if you omit the hazelnuts.

INGREDIENTS

10 Jerusalem artichokes, scrubbed, trimmed and chopped

6 large potatoes, peeled and diced (we like to use red-skinned potatoes)

100g (3½oz) unsalted butter

50ml (2fl oz) double cream

150g (5oz) finely ground hazelnuts

Salt and pepper

METHOD

Bring a pan of salted water to the boil, add the artichokes, reduce the heat to a simmer and cook for up to 40 minutes, until tender. Drain.

While the artichokes are cooking, cook the diced potato in a pan of simmering salted water over a medium heat for 15–20 minutes, until tender. Drain and mash the potato.

Melt the butter in a large saucepan, add the artichokes and cook for a few minutes in the butter. Remove from the pan with a slotted spoon and rub them through a sieve into a bowl, reserving the cooking butter, then pour the reserved butter over the sieved mixture.

Add the mashed potato to the artichoke purée and mix them together, then add the double cream. Season and add the ground hazelnuts followed by a little more cream if you like (the mash should have the consistency of whipped cream).

Serve in small side dishes or a large bowl so guests can take as much or as little as desired.

Salade de Choux-fleur

SERVES: 4

In the past this salad would have been made from plain boiled cauliflower, left to cool and then simply tossed in an olive oil and vinegar dressing and decorated with parsley. Today, however, I much prefer to break up the cauliflower florets and toss them in oil to cook in a roasting pan in the oven for 15–20 minutes.

INGREDIENTS

1 cauliflower, broken into small florets

2 tbsp olive oil

3 tbsp grated Parmesan cheese

100g (3½oz) roasted almonds, chopped

Small bunch of parsley, leaves chopped

FOR THE DRESSING

1 tbsp olive oil

2 tbsp white wine vinegar

1 tsp Dijon mustard

1 tbsp honey

Salt and pepper

METHOD

Preheat the oven to 200°C/400°F/Gas mark 6.

Toss the cauliflower florets in a bowl with the olive oil. Transfer to a roasting tin and roast for 15 minutes. Remove and sprinkle the Parmesan over the dish, then return to the oven for a further 4–5 minutes.

In the meantime, make the dressing by mixing the oil, vinegar, mustard and honey in a bowl with some seasoning.

When the cauliflower florets are cooked, remove from the oven, mix with dressing and sprinkle with roasted almonds.

Finish by sprinkling with parsley and serve while the cauliflower is still warm.

Watercress & Nutmeg Soup

SERVES: 4

Today's supermarkets provide us with a huge choice of salads and vegetables but I consciously choose foods that are versatile and full of health-giving nutrients. Watercress contains phytonutrients and antioxidants and has, apparently, a reputation for preventing diseases as well as inhibiting carcinogens.

INGREDIENTS

50g (2oz) butter, plus an extra large knob or 80ml (3fl oz) olive oil

2 medium onions, finely chopped

2 leeks, washed and trimmed

250g (9oz) potatoes, peeled and thinly sliced

1 litre (1¾ pints) chicken stock [SEE page 114]

½ small carrot, cut into thin strips

3 bunches of watercress (about 400g/14oz in total), washed, tough stems discarded and leaves roughly chopped

1 tsp ground nutmeg

Salt and pepper

METHOD

Melt the 50g (2oz) of butter in a large saucepan over a low–medium heat and add the chopped onion. Cook gently for 6–8 minutes until soft but not coloured, stirring often.

Cut the green part of each leek from the white part. Reserve the white part from one (keep the other for another dish) and half the green part of the other to garnish. Chop the rest of the green part and add to the pan with the onions. Cook for 2 minutes over a low heat then stir in the potatoes. Pour in the stock and season with salt and pepper.

Increase the heat, bring to the boil and skim off any foam that forms on the surface, then reduce the heat to low and simmer, covered, for about 20 minutes, or until the potatoes are tender (the cooking time will depend on how thick the potato slices are).

Meanwhile, cut the reserved white and green bits of leek into very thin strips. Heat the knob of butter or the oil in a non-stick frying pan over a medium heat, add the carrot and leek, season with salt and pepper and sauté for 3 minutes, until softened. Transfer to a plate and set aside.

Stir the chopped watercress into the soup pan, replace the lid and simmer over a low heat for 4–5 minutes (no more or you will lose the bright green colour). Stir in the nutmeg and remove from the heat. Leave to cool slightly, then blitz the mixture with a stick blender until smooth. If you want the soup a bit thinner, stir in a little more stock.

Season to taste and serve hot, garnishing each serving with a pile of the sautéed vegetables.

DARK MEAT STOCK

MAKES: about 2·25 litres (4 pints)

The essence of a good soup is a good stock. Stock is regularly made in some quantity in Highclere's large domed kitchens. Today it can then be frozen in batches for future use. In Victorian times they would also have included trimmings from chickens, which you can do, too.

INGREDIENTS

2kg (4lb 9oz) beef and veal bones, washed

1 tbsp goose fat

2 red onions, quartered

3 cloves (optional)

About 500g (1lb 2oz) selection of root vegetables, such as turnip, carrots, leeks and celery (or whatever vegetables you have to hand), roughly chopped

A handful of mixed herbs such as thyme, rosemary, bay and parsley

METHOD

Preheat your oven to 180°C/350°F/Gas mark 4.

Roast the bones in a roasting tray with the goose fat in a medium oven for about 30 minutes until they are caramelised and a deep golden colour.

Put the roasted bones into a deep pan on the hob and cover the bones with water. Add the onions, cloves (if using), root vegetables and herbs. Heat the stock until it reaches simmering point then simmer (do not boil) for 8–10 hours. Do not stir the stock as it cooks, but do carefully skim off any scum that settles on the surface.

Leave to cool, then skim off any grease or fat and strain the stock through a fine sieve.

Potage à la Julienne

MAKES: 6 hearty portions

This recipe has appeared time and again in the menus at Highclere throughout the last 150 years, and is a firm favourite.

INGREDIENTS

75g (3oz) unsalted butter

500g (1lb 2oz) each of carrots,
turnips and leeks, and 5 celery stalks,
cut into thin strips (julienned)

2 onions, finely chopped

2 litres (3½ pints) dark meat stock
[SEE page 170]

10g (½oz) sorrel, leaves chopped

10g (½oz) tarragon, leaves chopped

Salt and pepper

French baguette,
sliced into rounds, to serve

METHOD

Melt the butter in a pan over a medium heat, add the vegetables and sauté for about 4 minutes until softened.

Pour over sufficient stock to cover the vegetables, then bring to a simmer and season with salt and pepper.

Leave to simmer for about 15 minutes, add the herbs and simmer for a further 5 minutes.

Serve the *potage* in bowls, poured over a slice of round white bread.

Consommé Madrilene

SERVES: 6

The key to making a good *consommé* is to let it simmer over a low heat. In this recipe, flavoured with tomato and best served cold, the acid within the tomatoes helps draw out the impurities from the stock, which will collect on the surface. The egg whites then bind them together and they can be discarded. Given it is best served cold, if you can, plan to make the *consommé* the day before you serve it, so that it can properly chill.

Consommés have been an essential part of cooking since medieval times and this is how it is done at Highclere today.

INGREDIENTS

8 egg whites, lightly beaten

1 leek, washed, trimmed
and cut into thin strips

6 celery stalks, roughly chopped

2 large carrots, peeled and cut into thin strips

200g (7oz) lean minced chicken breast

2·25 litres (4 pints) cold chicken stock

6 large tomatoes,
4 roughly chopped and 2 whole

2 green bell peppers,
deseeded and quartered

40g (1½oz) chives, finely chopped

50g (2oz) red bell pepper,
deseeded and finely chopped

Salt and pepper

METHOD

Whisk the egg whites in a spotlessly clean bowl until they form soft peaks.

Mix the vegetable strips together. Gently fold the minced chicken breast and the strips of vegetables into the egg whites (this is called a 'clarify').

Pour the cold chicken stock into a large pan and add the tomatoes and green bell peppers.

Now, mix the 'clarify' into the pan, place over a low heat and start to bring up to the boil, keeping this mixture moving (gently stirring it with a wooden spoon) until the clarify starts to firm up like a set foam. Once the stock has come to the boil turn down the heat to a gentle simmer.

Once the 'clarify' has firmed up, break a hole in it while it's still in the pan so the stock simmers gently over the set foam. This is how the stock clarifies and becomes clear. Do not allow the stock to reboil.

When you can see the stock is clear, remove the pan from the heat and set aside. Ladle out the stock with great care, without disturbing the impurities from the clarify.

Pass the clear stock through a muslin or fine sieve then chill (it's best chilled overnight) before using.

Peel, deseed and finely dice the remaining 2 tomatoes, then mix with the chives and the red pepper.

Place 2 spoonfuls of the tomato, chive and pepper mixture in the bottom of each soup bowl, and pour the chilled *consommé* over to serve.

Roasted Butternut Squash, Coconut & Coriander Soup

SERVES: 6

Butternut squash makes a colourful autumnal soup. It has a sweet, rich flavour and a wonderful texture. It is full of nutrients such as beta carotene and minerals such as potassium and magnesium.

INGREDIENTS

1 butternut squash (about 1·5kg/3lb)

2 medium onions, each cut into 8 wedges

4 garlic cloves, left whole in their skins

40g (1½oz) butter

3 tbsp olive oil

1 litre (1¾ pints) vegetable stock
[**SEE** page 160]

2 large handfuls of fresh coriander, leaves roughly chopped, plus extra to garnish (optional)

200–250ml (7–8½fl oz) coconut milk

Salt and pepper

METHOD

Preheat the oven
to 180°C/350°F/Gas mark 4.

Cut the butternut squash lengthways into four wedges. Remove and discard all the seeds. Cut the squash into about 16 smaller wedges and place them in a large roasting tray. Add the onions, garlic, butter (in knobs) and oil, toss together, season with salt and pepper and roast in the oven for about 1 hour, or until the squash is soft and tender.

When cooked, remove from the oven and leave until the squash is cool enough to handle, then use a spoon to remove the flesh of the squash, leaving the skin in the tray.

Squeeze the garlic flesh out of the skins and discard the skins. Purée half the roasted vegetables (squash, onions and garlic) in a blender or food processor with about 350ml (12fl oz) of the stock until smooth.

Pour into a large saucepan and repeat with the rest of the vegetables and more stock, along with the fresh coriander. Add this to the first batch of soup. Pour the rest of the stock into the pan and stir in, along with coconut milk (to taste).

Reheat, season to taste, and serve piping hot with a garnish of extra chopped coriander if you wish.

Potage à la Reine

SERVES: 8

The 4th Countess of Carnarvon offered an alternative soup, *Potage à la Reine*. This is a white soup based on Charles Elmé Francatelli's recipe of 1861 of boiled fowl and rice cooked in a mix of veal stock and chicken broth which is then finished with cream.

INGREDIENTS

*1·8kg (just over 4lb)
whole free-range chicken*

85g (3¼oz) long-grain white rice

150ml (5fl oz) single cream

Flat-leaf parsley, to garnish

FOR THE STOCK

2 onions, chopped

2 celery stalks, chopped

1 carrot, chopped

Blade of mace

Sprig of thyme

1 bay leaf

2·5 litres (4½ pints) cold water

METHOD

Preheat the oven
to 180°C/350°F/Gas mark 4.

Roast the whole chicken in a roasting tin for 1 hour 20 minutes, then leave to rest for 20 minutes at room temperature. When cooled, remove all the meat from the bones, discarding the skin, fat and any gristly bits, put the meat in a bowl and set aside. Chill once cooled.

To make the stock, break down the chicken carcass and put the bones in a stock pan with the vegetables, herbs and the cold water. Cover with a lid, then bring to the boil and cook at a very low simmer, still covered, for 4 hours. When the 4 hours are up, skim the surface to remove the fat and strain the stock into a large pan.

Now, make the soup. Add the chicken meat and rice to the stock broth and simmer for up to 20 minutes (until the rice is cooked). Remove from the heat and allow to cool a little, then transfer the soup to a blender or food processor and blend to a smooth consistency. Return the soup to the pan and place over a low heat for 10 minutes (do not let it boil).

Gently stir in the cream and serve with a garnish of parsley.

Carrot, Coriander, Ginger & Coconut Soup

SERVES: 4

This soup is a popular vegan, gluten- and dairy-free soup option at Highclere. Coconuts are a type of fruit seed or drupe. Their milk, oil and fruit are good sources of electrolytes and minerals. Root ginger is traditionally renowned for its health-bringing properties.

INGREDIENTS

2 tbsp vegetable oil

1 large onion, chopped

50g (2oz) fresh root ginger, peeled and diced

1 large potato, peeled and diced

450g (1lb) carrots, peeled and roughly chopped

1 litre (1¾ pints) vegetable stock
[**SEE** page 160]

Medium bunch of coriander, leaves and stems roughly chopped

400ml (14fl oz) tin of coconut milk

Salt and white pepper

METHOD

Heat the oil in a large saucepan over a medium heat. Add the onion and ginger and sauté for around 4 minutes until softened. Stir in the diced potato and cook for 2 minutes, then add the carrots and vegetable stock, bring to the boil and simmer for 20 minutes, or until the carrots are cooked. Remove from the heat.

Place in a food processor and blend with the coriander and coconut milk until smooth, in batches if necessary (alternatively, add the coriander and coconut to the pan and blitz with a stick blender). Season with salt and white pepper to taste.

Cock-a-leekie Soup

SERVES: 8–10

This is a simple but traditional winter soup where the first ingredient is an older chicken – a cock – which is boiled, hence the name.

INGREDIENTS

1 medium chicken

1 large onion, finely diced

2·25 litres (4 pints) fresh chicken stock (not from a cube)
[**SEE** page 114]

1·4kg (3lb) leeks, trimmed, washed and cut into 2·5cm (1in) lengths

8 presoaked prunes, chopped (optional)

Small bunch of tarragon, stalks removed and leaves chopped

Salt and pepper

METHOD

Put the chicken and onion into a large pan with the stock and half the chopped leeks. Place over a medium heat, bring to the boil then simmer gently for 30 minutes.

Add the remaining leeks and simmer for 3–4 hours. Every now and again, skim off any scum that forms on the surface of the soup.

Add the prunes once the 3–4 hours are up (if using) and simmer for 10–15 minutes. Season to taste.

To serve, remove the chicken from the pan, discard the bones and skin, and place the meat in a tureen or serving dish, then pour over the soup and leeks. Scatter over the chopped tarragon.

Gazpacho

Talking about the weather is the quintessential British pastime, and invariably 'the weather is like the government – always in the wrong' (Jerome K. Jerome). Given our climate, soups are usually served hot – but occasional glorious outbreaks of sunshine call for a more refreshing alternative. *Gazpacho* is a cold Spanish soup best made a day ahead so that the flavours can develop. So, if the weather forecast appears hopeful, quickly gather the ingredients to make this delicious and easy recipe.

The most important ingredient, to my mind, is the olive oil so proper cold-pressed olive oil is worth using for this dish.

INGREDIENTS

6 slices of stale white bread, crust intact

12 ripe plum tomatoes, cored and sliced (juice reserved)

3 red peppers, deseeded and chopped

6 spring onions, washed, trimmed and chopped

4 garlic cloves, roughly chopped

Leaves from 1 medium bunch of basil

1 cucumber, peeled, deseeded and chopped

200ml (7fl oz) good-quality cold-pressed olive oil

150ml (5fl oz) red wine vinegar

Tomato juice, if needed (from a carton)

Sea salt and pepper

Fresh red chilli, deseeded and chopped, to serve (optional)

Ice cubes, to serve

METHOD

Take a large bowl into which the ingredients can be layered. Start at the bottom with a slice of bread, some sliced tomatoes, some chopped red peppers, some spring onions, some of the garlic, the whole basil leaves and chopped cucumber.

Repeat the layering process until all the bread, tomatoes, peppers, spring onions, garlic, basil and cucumber have been used up, retaining a few basil leaves for a garnish.

Pour over the olive oil, reserved juice from chopping the tomatoes and red wine vinegar, cover and refrigerate overnight.

The next day, blitz the mixture with a stick blender until smooth. If you feel it's too thick, add a splash of tomato juice until you are happy with the consistency. Season with salt and pepper, add a little chilli to taste, if you like, or a splash more vinegar or olive oil.

Shred the reserved basil leaves and garnish each serving with a sprinkling of shredded basil and some ice cubes.

Goats' Cheese & Spinach Soup

SERVES: 8

Goats' cheese has been made for thousands of years and was probably one of the earliest dairy products. We have never kept goats at Highclere, instead buying goats' cheese from small award-winning producers near the Castle.

Goats' cheese softens when it is exposed to heat rather than melting in the way many cows'-milk cheeses do. The spinach gives the soup a fabulous flavour and a vibrant green colour.

INGREDIENTS

100g (3½oz) butter

6 banana shallots, roughly chopped

2 garlic cloves, roughly chopped

6 celery stalks, roughly chopped

*1 leek, white part only,
washed and roughly chopped*

1 litre (1¾ pints) vegetable stock

1 floury potato, peeled and cut into 12 chunks

1kg (2lb 3½oz) baby spinach, washed

2 x 150g (5oz) rolls of goats' cheese

Sea salt and pepper

METHOD

Preheat the oven
to 180°C/350°F/Gas mark 4.

Melt 75g (2½oz) of the butter in a large pan, add the vegetables and sauté for 5 minutes until soft but not coloured. Add the vegetable stock and potato, bring to the boil and simmer for about 20 minutes, until the potatoes are very soft.

Remove from the heat, add 750g (1lb 10 oz) of the spinach to the soup and blitz with a stick blender until smooth. Season with salt and pepper to taste, set aside and keep warm.

Slice each roll of goats' cheese into 4 even rounds to make 8 rounds. Place them on a baking sheet and cook in the oven for 9 minutes.

In a separate pan, sauté the remaining spinach with the rest of the butter for about 1 minute, until just wilted.

To serve, divide the sautéed spinach between warmed serving bowls and place the goats' cheese rounds on top. Spoon the spinach soup around the spinach and goats' cheese.

[**CHEF'S TIP**: If you have one, you can use a blowtorch to lightly brown the goats' cheese before serving.]

Oeufs en cocotte

SERVES: 4

'Have you ever seen a man, woman, or child who wasn't eating an egg
or just going to eat an egg or just coming away from eating an egg?'

P.G. WODEHOUSE

Oeufs en cocotte or baked eggs is a family favourite and a very appealing dish served perfectly plain. However, it can be easily varied: put some chopped cooked spinach into each individual ramekin before you crack the egg into it; alternatively some ham or cooked bacon. Another possibility is to layer a mixture of cooked vegetables, such as sautéed courgettes and mushrooms, into a larger oval dish, and crack six eggs on top followed by 4–6 tablespoons of cream, according to taste, before seasoning. Bake in the oven for 15–20 minutes. Guests can then help themselves from the dish.

INGREDIENTS

Butter
(a knob for each ramekin dish)

4 large eggs

4 tbsp double cream

Salt and pepper

Focaccia, toasted, to serve

METHOD

Preheat the oven
to 180°C/350°F/Gas mark 4.

Drop a knob of butter into each of 4 ramekin dishes. Put the dishes in a baking tray filled with sufficient water to come halfway up each one. Place in the oven for 2–3 minutes until the butter has melted and the water is getting hot.

Remove the tray of ramekins from the oven and break one egg into each ramekin. Pour a tablespoon of cream over each egg and season with salt and pepper. Place the tray of ramekins back in the oven and bake for 12–15 minutes.

Alternatively, place the knobs of butter in one ovenproof dish and follow the method as above, but break all the eggs into the one dish and bake for 14–15 minutes.

Serve with toasted focaccia.

Sausage Rolls

MAKES: 16 rolls

The then Chancellor of the Exchequer, George Osborne, threatened to impose VAT on sausage rolls and pasties in his 2012 Budget. However, there was such an outcry from outraged, sausage-roll-loving members of the public that revolution seemed just days away. The proposal was swiftly dropped.

Sausage rolls are not often home-made but are well worth the effort for a special occasion. Paul, our chef, prefers to use sage to flavour his sausage rolls but you can use any herb you like. You could also add a little grated apple to the sausage mix.

INGREDIENTS

25g (1oz) butter

1 small onion, finely diced

Sprig of sage (or your preferred herb), leaves chopped

450g (1lb) sausage meat

1 x 375g (13oz) packet ready-rolled all-butter puff pastry

2 medium egg yolks, beaten

Sea salt and cracked black pepper

Chutney, to serve (optional)

METHOD

Preheat the oven to 200°C/400°F/Gas mark 6.

Melt the butter in a pan over a low heat, add the onion and cook for 10–15 minutes, stirring occasionally, until soft but not coloured. Remove from the heat and add the sage leaves. Leave to cool.

Put the sausage meat in a bowl then mix in the cooked onion and sage, and season with a little salt and pepper.

Unroll the puff pastry on a board. It should be around 25 × 37cm (10 × 15in). Cut the pastry in half lengthways to create two long rectangles measuring 12·5 × 37cm (5 × 15in). Set aside one piece of pastry.

Divide the sausage meat in half and roll one piece into a long thin sausage to fit the length of the puff pastry (you may need to do this in two pieces then fit them together in the middle). Lay the sausage meat in the middle of one piece of pastry then brush one edge with a little egg yolk. Roll the pastry over and press down lightly to secure. Carefully slice the roll in half, then slice each half again into four even-sized sausage rolls to make eight in total. Brush the rolls with beaten egg.

Do the same again with the remaining pastry, sausage meat and beaten egg to make 16 rolls in total. Place on a baking sheet, making sure you put the sealed edges on the bottom – this will help make sure they don't burst open when cooking.

Sprinkle on a little sea salt and cracked black pepper and bake in the hot oven for about 25 minutes, or until the pastry is golden and crisp. Serve warm with a spoonful of chutney (if you wish).

The Highclere Scotch Egg

SERVES: 6

The London department store Fortnum & Mason claims to have invented Scotch eggs in the eighteenth century. By the next century recipes for them were appearing in Victorian cookbooks, although at this time they would have been served hot with gravy. These days most English supermarkets sell a version of them and they have become a ubiquitous picnic food.

However, a homemade Scotch egg is something quite different, though equally good for a picnic. The most important thing is to feel free to flavour the sausage meat. We sometimes use leeks (chopped then softened in a little butter and oil), but you can use anything you like, from chilli powder to cumin to fennel seed.

INGREDIENTS

10 medium eggs

100g (3½oz) dry breadcrumbs

100g (3½oz) plain flour, plus extra for dusting

600g (1lb 5oz) sausage meat, flavoured to taste

Vegetable oil, for frying

Salt and pepper

METHOD

Cook 6 of the eggs for 8 minutes in a pan of salted boiling water. Cool as quickly as possible under cold running water to prevent discoloration of the egg white, then peel them and set to one side.

Crack the remaining eggs into a shallow bowl and beat well. Season and set aside. Place the breadcrumbs in a separate bowl, and the flour in a third bowl with some seasoning.

Divide the sausage meat into 6 even-sized portions, then roll each one out on a lightly floured board until around 1cm (½in) thick. Place the cooked eggs on top of each sausage-meat portion and wrap the sausage meat around them until each egg is evenly and completely covered.

Roll a sausage-meat-covered egg in the flour, then dip the ball in the beaten egg and finally roll it through the breadcrumbs. (Sometimes we give the Scotch eggs a second coat of beaten egg and breadcrumbs for greater thickness, but that is up to you.) Repeat with the remaining 5 eggs.

Heat a large pan of vegetable oil to 180°C/350°F or use a deep-fat fryer. Fry the balls in batches for 6–10 minutes until golden brown, carefully remove from the hot oil, and drain on kitchen towel.

Enjoy hot or cold but please eat on the same day as making.

MUSIC & DISCORD

Sir Malcolm Sargent and the London Set

Easter 1935

In 1930s London the composer and conductor Malcolm Sargent was a huge celebrity, known as much for his presence in society drawing rooms as he was for his work with the English National Opera and the phenomenally successful D'Oyly Carte Opera Company at the Savoy.

On 24 November 1934 he was one of 2,000 great and good invited to the ball of the year, perhaps even the decade, at Buckingham Palace, to celebrate the forthcoming marriage of HRH Prince George and Princess Marina of Greece. Naturally the equally glamorous Lord and Lady Carnarvon also featured on the guest list. It was a spectacular evening – and was to lead to new friendships and a bitter parting.

ABOVE
Excerpt from Highclere Castle Visitors' Book, April 1935

Catherine, 6th Countess of Carnarvon,
painted by Simon Elwes in 1929

Swathed in warm furs against the winter cold, Lady Catherine Carnarvon sat beside her husband in the Bentley as they left the Ritz Hotel in London's fashionable West End. November 1934 had been a dull and foggy month, but on this particular evening the street lamps revealed streets brightened by ingenious displays of garlands and arches made from brightly coloured paper flowers. Entwined monograms and portraits of Prince George and Princess Marina were prominently displayed in shop windows. The chauffeur negotiated the turning into the Mall, drove round the impressive marble memorial to Queen Victoria, completed just a decade before, and slowed to make way through the small crowd of onlookers clustered around the imposing black iron gates of Buckingham Palace.

Cars waited their turn to draw up under the portico entrance to the Palace, where liveried and gold-braided footmen glided forward to open the doors. Catherine carefully stepped out, grateful of a helping hand to keep her pale

silk dress immaculate, whilst her husband, Porchey, true to form, leapt out after her, as eager as always to get to the party. HRH Prince George had been guest of honour at the Carnarvons' wedding twelve years previously and two years later, in 1924, had stood as godfather to their first-born, Henry.

The roar of conversation and laughter filled the crimson-and-gold-hung State Rooms where imposing oil paintings presided over the gilded and white walls. Ladies sparkled in their magnificent dresses, jewels and tiaras under the rose-tinted crystal chandeliers. Taking the proffered glasses of Champagne, Catherine and Porchey set off through the first rooms, following the other guests towards the sound of an orchestra playing in the distance.

It was not long before they encountered Prince George, who was in high spirits. He had commented eight weeks earlier to his future brother-in-law Prince Paul of Yugoslavia: 'It's all so lovely and I am so happy that I can hardly believe it.' Catherine had been in Salzburg in August with Prince George and Princess Marina during the first few days of their engagement. A much-trusted friend, she divulged nothing until their forthcoming marriage was officially announced in the Court Circular on 29 August. Porchey bowed formally to Prince George whilst Catherine curtseyed gracefully before the Prince took her hand affectionately. He and his *fiancée*, a dazzling pair, then moved on to greet other eager guests and receive their heartfelt congratulations. It was the love story of the decade. King George V and Queen Mary found Princess Marina utterly charming and were delighted by their son's choice.

Sir Malcolm Sargent (1924–1967)

Amongst the throng, Lady Carnarvon caught a glimpse of Dr Malcolm Sargent, the dashing and distinguished conductor. She knew of him, of course; who didn't? The urbane musical genius had made a name for himself as one of the country's finest conductors as well as a composer of some note and a pianist who could have performed to concert standard had he not chosen to stand in the orchestra pit instead.

He had been out of the limelight since October 1932 due to a near fatal illness. He had begun to suffer from a recurring high temperature and at times was doubled over in agony. Although alarmingly thin, he had continued working to his packed schedule until tuberculosis was eventually diagnosed. He survived a difficult operation early in 1933, but it was by no means certain he would ever be able to resume his former hectic lifestyle as a conductor and celebrity.

However, he followed the traditional English path of recuperation, travelling to the mountains of Switzerland where sanatoria offered clear air and complete relaxation, although Sargent had found the enforced boredom nearly as hard to bear as the illness itself. A restless, gregarious man, he thrived on the company of friends and the adulation of an audience.

Sargent was an ambitious, driven man who had come a long way from the small terraced cottage in Stamford, Lincolnshire, where he had lived as a child. His ascent to the zenith of English music could be attributed in equal measure to his self-discipline, innate talent, and the patronage of the great conductor Sir Henry Wood, founder of the Promenade Concerts. An eccentric figure, Wood gave Sargent his first chance with the Queen's Hall Orchestra in 1921. Sargent always acknowledged this debt and, just like his patron, would also create for himself a reputation for flamboyance as well as sheer musical ability.

Lady Carnarvon could see why he was nicknamed 'Flash Harry': he looked exceedingly debonair and was impeccably dressed. By now fully recovered, he was clearly relieved to be back amongst fashionable society. He had plainly noticed her too, delighted to renew their acquaintanceship from previous encounters. He crossed the room to join her and was soon making Catherine laugh with stories about his riding misadventures in Hyde Park. She found him excellent company and he found her not merely stylish and fascinating but a great conversationalist.

As celebrated as he was, Sargent was eclipsed by the intense interest directed towards a certain slim, dark-haired lady, Mrs Simpson, dressed in violet lamé worn with a vivid green sash and exquisite jewels. Everyone knew these had been given to her by the Prince of Wales and the latest, most exquisite, Cartier bracelet was triumphantly flaunted on one white-gloved arm. Society, and indeed the whole of Europe, was agog at the Prince of Wales's relationship with this married woman. Mrs Simpson's acquiescent (cuckolded) husband Ernest stood awkwardly at the side of the room for much of the evening.

Malcolm Sargent and Catherine Carnarvon threaded their way through to the ballroom to join the dancing.

RIGHT
A recipe book from the archives

FAR LEFT
Catherine and Porchey

LEFT
Christening picture of Catherine
holding her son Henry, the future
7th Earl of Carnarvon

The band was playing a foxtrot. Catherine's husband Porchey was dancing with a *soignée* brunette, whom Catherine thought she recognised. In any case, Porchey had a habit of refusing to dance with his wife as he said he had spent all day with her. Half an hour later, having greeted Catherine's sister-in-law Eve and her husband Brograve Beauchamp and been reunited with Porchey, they decided to find supper, settling down at a large round table which presently filled up with old friends. The centre was laden with delicious cold food, from partridge to quail, beef fillet and lamb cutlets, pâtés and ham, to lobster salad. Teams of liveried footmen wearing powdered wigs relayed further dishes to the diners at their tables.

Catherine was caught up in the warmth and glamour of the evening, smiling and laughing, and Malcolm Sargent enthusiastically accepted her invitation to come and stay at Highclere Castle in between forthcoming professional engagements. It was the start of a close friendship, which lasted the rest of their lives.

That same year, Catherine's husband Porchey

followed in his father's footsteps and spent a few months in Egypt. His father, the 5th Earl of Carnarvon, and Howard

Carter had become close to overnight global celebrities when they discovered the tomb of Tutankhamun in November 1922. After nearly twenty years of excavation, persevering in the inhospitable desert, the two men had uncovered the royal tomb of the boy king, filled with 'wonderful things' that would rewrite historians' understanding of Ancient Egypt and fascinate people for generations to come.

Exhausted by the extraordinary events that had overtaken his investigations in the Valley of the Kings, the 5th Earl of Carnarvon fell dangerously ill and Porchey had hurried by ship and train to Cairo, reaching his father's bedside hours before he died in April 1923. At that saddest of times, all the lights in Cairo went out and Lord Carnarvon's dog Susie at Highclere howled and died at exactly the same moment as her master two thousand miles away. Superstitious about the so-called 'Curse of the Pharaohs', it was eleven years before Porchey returned.

Back in Cairo in 1934, the new Earl simply enjoyed the good life. As a well-known amateur jockey, he was riding five times a week with 'unrivalled enthusiasm' as quoted in the newspaper, and was the life and soul of the evening parties held at Cairo's Gezira Club. He eventually returned

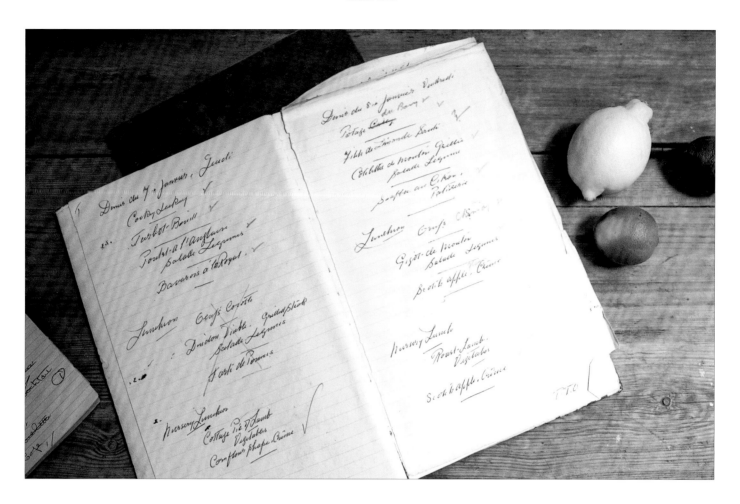

to England looking tanned and well, just in time to join Catherine in entertaining the Prince of Wales at Newbury Racecourse in early April.

Catherine had diverted herself during her

husband's absence by asking a few close friends to stay for weekends. The young Newmarket trainer Jack Clayton was an admirer and Catherine shared his interest in the racing world. Her great friend Lady Sibell Lygon was, rather dashingly, writing articles for magazines such as *Harper's Bazaar*. She and her siblings had recently befriended a novelist called Evelyn Waugh, who proved somewhat more successful at writing than she was. Of course, Malcolm Sargent had also stayed many times although only once with his wife Eileen, and again just once with his son Peter.

Catherine and Porchey, however, had decided to organise a larger house party over the long Easter weekend in 1935. They thought they might also include some children, who would be good company for their own two, Henry and Penelope. Porchey's sister Eve and her husband Brograve

would assume they were invited anyway, along with their daughter Patricia. Catherine adored them more than if they were her own siblings. She decided she would ask Malcolm Sargent and Porchey asked two army and racing cronies, Captain Armstrong and the Hon. Lionel Montagu. Finally Colin and Gladys Buist accepted the invitation to spend Easter with them and Fernside the butler was given the list of guests' names.

On Monday, 15 April, Mrs Lloyd, Highclere's tall and stately housekeeper, knocked on the door of Lady Carnarvon's pretty pink sitting room, curtseyed and stood in front of her whilst they agreed the list of bedrooms to be prepared. Mrs Mackie the cook was requested to suggest some suitable menus, which Lady Carnarvon could then consider; she thought nothing too complicated was needed. With her cook and housekeeper fully briefed, Lady Carnarvon could devote her own efforts to ensuring that her friends spent a memorable and relaxing weekend. It was the hostess's subtlest art to suggest suitable activities for her guests without imposing a rigid programme.

Arundel bedroom today

VISITORS' ROOMS

Mercia	.	.	.	.
Queen Caroline's Room	.		.	
East Anglia .	.	.	.	
East Anglia Dressing Room	.			
Stanhope	.	.	.	.
Stanhope Dressing Room	.		.	
Herbert	.	.	.	.
Herbert Dressing Room	.		.	
Portico	.	.	.	.
Arundel	.	.	.	.
Arundel Dressing Room	.		.	
Wessex	.	.	.	.
Wessex Dressing Room	.		.	

Room List

On Good Friday, 19 April, Catherine was on her own, walking back up the ochre-coloured gravel path from the Monks' Garden towards the cedar trees. She found peace under their evergreen branches, enjoying the landscape around her, the promise of spring, the tiny buds forming on the roses she had planted in her own garden. It was an hour to herself before the guests were due to arrive. She saw a long black car approaching along the gravelled drive and hastened towards it.

When she arrived at the front entrance to the Castle, Malcolm Sargent was stepping out of the car before turning to assist his twelve-year-old son Peter. Malcolm had already greeted Arthur the footman by name – he had, after all, been rather a frequent guest at Highclere since Christmas. Despite being married, Malcolm conducted his social life on his own terms. His son Peter was much the same age as Catherine's children and as it was Easter Weekend, and a school holiday, both father and son were staying.

Arthur, as always dressed in smart navy livery, stood to one side of the front door; he would deal with the luggage later. Catherine greeted both her guests and walked with them back into the Hall. She waited whilst Malcolm gave his coat and hat to another footman, George, and his son did likewise. They were hung on the tall, polished wood and brass stand next to

the impossibly smooth and white marble bust of the 2nd Earl of Carnarvon. Peter could not help but run his hands over the carving. It was displayed on a marble pedestal, framed between two elegant pale stone Gothic arches culminating in decorative scrolls. Catherine led the way into the galleried Saloon, with its soaring, fan-vaulted ceiling.

The impression of perspective and space was counterbalanced by the carefully considered placing of sofas, chairs and tables, large and small, so as to create a welcoming impression.

The Room List – on which Mrs Lloyd had carefully written and matched the names of guests to bedrooms – lay on the green-leather-topped table just inside the Saloon. Catherine led Malcolm up the grand Oak Staircase and along the Gallery towards the Arundel bedroom, which she had recently had redecorated in pale colours. It enjoyed far-ranging views across the cedars, towards the Temple of Diana and surrounding woodlands. Peter would share the children's bedrooms and nurseries on the floor above.

The nurseries and schoolroom were the domain of Mademoiselle Huc, beloved French governess to Henry and Penelope. They all called her 'Doll' and, like many nannies, she remained part of the Carnarvons' lives for decades, becoming their confidante and an honorary member of the family. Peter would be in her care over the weekend.

Fernside the butler would soon be announcing

tea and the members of the house party would gather. It was impossible to imagine not having tea, the most informal and relaxed way of introducing house guests to one another. It allowed time for perfect idleness or stimulating conversation, gourmandising on the irresistible combination of tea and hot toast with plenty of butter, or high-minded abstinence with a single cup of Earl Grey. Everyone would gather in the Library as the footmen brought in the warmed silver teapots.

Porchey's sister Eve and her husband Sir Brograve Beauchamp had arrived the day before from London with nine-year-old Patricia. The large figure of Captain the Hon. Lionel Montagu was happily ensconced in a deep-red leather armchair, pipe in hand. An extraordinarily brave man who had fought right through the First World War, he had been awarded a DSO for his actions during the Battle of the Somme.

Now, like his host Porchey, he was very keen on the world of horse racing. Commander Colin Buist and his wife Gladys were much the same age as the Carnarvons. Colin had served in the Royal Navy and seen action at the Battle of Jutland, serving with Lord Louis Mountbatten. He then became Equerry to the Duke and Duchess of York, continuing in the role when they became King George VI and Queen Elizabeth,

the unanticipated new royal couple after Edward VIII's short-lived reign.

During the last ten years, Porchey and Catherine's house parties had gained a reputation for always being enormous fun, bringing together amusing people from the worlds of royalty, aristocracy, and increasingly the stage. Catherine much enjoyed making sure that the domestic details were attended to scrupulously. Brograve was partial to ginger cake and so slices were presented alongside the silver teapots on the Library table.

As usual the children would arrive at teatime

and Catherine looked forward to the familiar clatter of running feet. Her two and their cousin had been out on their ponies with their groom Shuff. However, on arriving back at the stables, they had jumped straight off their mounts and, rather than go upstairs to change, run in through the kitchen door to see if Mrs Mackie had any treats for them. They loved spending time in her huge kitchen, with its amazing smells of bread baking or, later in the day, meat roasting for dinner.

however, a complete phobia about some of the stern-looking figures in the paintings she saw there. The Red Staircase, leading all the way up to the Nursery floor, was lined with portraits of early ancestors.

The huge old study of Sir William Herbert was terrifyingly dark and ten times as big as she was. She would quickly run up the stairs and, if she did catch sight of the painting out of the corner of her eye by mistake, would comfort herself by concentrating on the little white dog shown by Sir William's feet as he reminded her of her own much-cuddled terrier, Tom Thumb. She was especially terrified of the Dining Room with its enormous equestrian painting of King Charles I on a white charger. Her timid progress around the Castle was considered somewhat eccentric by her cousins.

The nurseries and the children's bedrooms lay at one end of a very long corridor on the top floor and the various other rooms and large cupboards there were considered perfect for playing hide and seek. Peter found wind-up cars and a train set to while away the time while the grown-ups socialised downstairs. His mother Eileen had promised him a train set when he had won a scholarship to the Royal Choir of St George's Chapel, Windsor. He had come second out of three hundred boys. Thrilled, Peter had run straight away to tell his father, who simply asked why he had not come first. A train set had not been forthcoming – his father rewarded him with books instead. The scholarship was not merely prestigious but very useful as the Sargent family were short of money: the last few years had been financially very lean due to Malcolm's illness.

Doll had, needless to say, found them there and borne them upstairs to change and meet Peter before tea.

The children's weekend ran to a different schedule from the adults'. They took their meals on the top floor and, depending on how strict Doll was feeling, would either have a lesson or play tennis, go fishing in Dunsmere Lake or explore their own gardens outside. Children always found Highclere packed with interest and excitement.

Hands and faces scrubbed, they went down to the Library to find their mother and reported that they had had a marvellous ride up to the woods on Siddown Hill. As tea in the Library was ending, Doll appeared to gather them all together to return to the Nursery floor in the upper part of the Castle.

Patricia Beauchamp spent nearly as much time at Highclere as her cousins Henry and Penelope did. She had,

RIGHT
Electric bellboard in the downstairs
corridor, to alert the footmen to the room
where they were required

BELOW
Henry and Penelope in the 'Red Bug' car

Patricia promised Peter a trip around the grounds in their small electric car, 'The Red Bug'. (Porchey had bought this vehicle, known in the USA where it was made as a 'Country Club', for the children as a toy.) Patricia and her cousins had a particular favourite trick, which was to offer a ride to an unsuspecting guest such as Peter. If they turned the car hard away from the passenger side, the door flew open and the passenger tumbled out – until they got wise to the manoeuvre.

If the weekend offered time for convivial

conversation and leisure pursuits for the house party, the staff downstairs worked to a schedule.

The hours between tea and dinner were very busy for Gladys and Jessie, two of the housemaids, who hurried round the State Rooms straightening chairs and plumping cushions, removing ashtrays, teacups and glasses. Gladys was trying

hard to please Mrs Lloyd as she had recently got into serious trouble for playing with the children's train set instead of cleaning the Nursery and had nearly lost her job.

The footmen were carefully setting the Dining Room table in gloved hands, overseen by Fernside.

Catherine and her guests would rest and

change before dinner each evening. Lady Carnarvon was considered one of the best-dressed women of her generation; her slim figure admirably suited the fluid silk evening dresses which were so in vogue in the thirties. At eight o'clock all the guests started gathering downstairs but before she joined them she went up to the Nursery to bid the children goodnight.

The shutters were closed and the thick curtains drawn, the cosy bedrooms peaceful. She bent over Henry and Penelope to kiss them goodnight, wafting the familiar

Martini

There is no mystery to the classic Martini, except that it involves two decisions: do you use gin or vodka, and is it shaken or stirred.

Martinis are an integral part of films and books: James Bond drank them shaken, not stirred; Ernest Hemingway's Gin Martinis were very strong; they were aphrodisiacs in Scott Fitzgerald's novels; and were enjoyed nonchalantly in Evelyn Waugh's *Brideshead Revisited*.

This is how it is done at Highclere …

INGREDIENTS FOR ONE COCKTAIL

Ice cubes

70ml (2½fl oz) gin or vodka

15ml (½fl oz) dry vermouth

Strip of lemon rind, to garnish

METHOD

Combine the gin or vodka with the dry vermouth in a mixing glass or cocktail shaker filled with ice cubes. Stir for 30 seconds, then strain into a chilled cocktail glass.

Twist and squeeze the oil from the lemon rind over the drink before garnishing it with the lemon twist.

comforting scent of her perfume and whispering words of love. Walking along the dimly lit corridor, she looked in on Peter and Patricia too and told them to sleep well.

Porchey was by then already downstairs in the Saloon, ever punctual and ensuring that every little detail was attended to so as to make their guests' stay at Highclere perfect. In letters to Nancy Mitford, Evelyn Waugh would describe part of a weekend as 'very Highclere', if that weekend had been exceptionally comfortable and amusing.

Malcolm Sargent's preferred drink was a

Champagne Cocktail, but Fernside was ready to convert him to his speciality, the Martini. 'A perfect Martini should be made by filling a glass with gin then waving it in the general direction of Italy,' according to Noël Coward. And Dorothy Parker declared: 'I like Martinis, two at the most, three I am under the table, four I am under the host.' Fernside would certainly have preferred Noël Coward's more decorous sentiments.

Lord Carnarvon never knowingly deprived himself of any enjoyment and Catherine had thought the Friday menu should include lobster following the *consommé* and knew that lamb cutlets were always a favourite as the meat course. With excellent wines chosen also, perhaps she was instinctively observing Oscar Wilde's *bon mot*: 'After a good dinner one can forgive anybody, even one's own relations.'

Like Porchey, Lionel Montagu, the Buists and the Beauchamps were all very keen race-goers, and conversation would inevitably and swiftly turn to a discussion of the merits of past and future prospects. Porchey had bred a colt named Blenheim, but had unfortunately sold him as a yearling to the Aga Khan for 4,100 guineas. Blenheim went on to win the Derby and subsequently became an extremely successful stallion, in America as well as England. Left out of the money entirely, Porchey had no other recourse than to try his luck, regaling his friends with this story of his own bravado in approaching the horse's new owner:

'Now one thing, my dear Aga, before you forget about this great achievement. As I bred this horse, I hope you will give me a free nomination for every year that he stands at stud?' After a fractional pause, the Aga Khan had replied: 'Certainly not.'

Unbelievably the Aga Khan had another outstanding three-year-old prospect this year: Bahram, a half-brother to Blenheim. He was entered for the 2,000 Guineas the following month and then the Derby. Lionel Montagu happily argued with Porchey about whether Bahram would ever be as good as Windsor Lad, who had carried all before him the previous year.

Malcolm Sargent had no interest in the racing

world but like most of society – male and female – was agog at the *on dit* about the Prince of Wales and Mrs Simpson. It was all anyone was talking about that year. After the racing at Newbury two weeks earlier, the Buists had returned with the Prince of Wales to Fort Belvedere, his weekend retreat near Windsor where Mrs Simpson was ensconced.

Colin told everyone gathered at Highclere that he had been informed that the Prince of Wales had not long before met the King to discuss the forthcoming Royal Jubilee celebrations. At that meeting he had sworn to his father that Wallis and he were not lovers. Reluctantly, the King had to take his word for it and therefore George V had agreed that Mrs Simpson could come (with her husband) to a court ball in two weeks' time. Colin and the other equerries were horrified by the outright lie and by the complicated chain of cover-ups that would ensue.

The consensus was that the Prince of Wales was blindly besotted. Colin and Gladys, however, tried to steer a careful course through all the interest and gossip. As courtiers and long-standing friends of the Duke and Duchess of York, they knew more than most about the situation – and certainly more than King George V and Queen Mary. They were also genuine friends of the Prince of Wales, who had occasionally stayed with them.

During the weekend Catherine and Porchey balanced their own everyday tasks against the need to look after and amuse their guests. In the early morning around 6.30 a.m. Porchey left the Castle to ride out at Dick Dawson's yard in Lambourn seventeen miles from Highclere. Lincoln the hall boy was waiting, ready to jump up and open the front door for him. Gibbins the chauffeur had the engine of the Bentley already humming. Lord Carnarvon would be back by nine. His guests would never know he had gone.

From 8.30 a.m. the footmen were kept busy carrying up breakfast trays of fresh fruit and toast and marmalade to all the ladies who preferred to take breakfast in bed. Catherine took the opportunity to write letters and answer invitations. The men would enjoy breakfast in the Dining Room, joined by their host towards 9.30 a.m. after he'd returned from the gallops and dressed for the morning. Chafing dishes were set out on the side table in the

Dining Room. Breakfast was no longer as substantial as it had been in Edwardian times, but nevertheless porridge and platters of eggs, kidneys and sausages were on offer, plus cold meats, as well as coffee and tea. A favourite morning occupation was to drive up to see the horses at Highclere's stud farm, to inspect any potential winners bred by the 6th Earl.

Catherine had also developed a passion for racing following her marriage to Porchey, but with it, unfortunately, an expensive predilection for gambling. It began rather well for her but almost inevitably ended very badly. After various betting disasters she had to sell her jewellery to settle her debts – something her husband was not necessarily aware of. She had confided everything to Eve and had by now managed to cease betting entirely.

If not shooting or racing, everyone played golf. Naturally Highclere had its own course. Porchey's father had built nine holes and Porchey extended this to eighteen. The course ran around the foot of Beacon Hill, starting from a little wooden clubhouse close by Winchester Lodge. Porchey was keen on the game and renowned for taking every 'advantage' he could on a course, keeping the odd spare ball in his pocket, which he would try to roll unobtrusively down his trouser leg if the original ball was in an unplayable position. He later played golf with Ian Fleming and tried the same trick, which some believe was then turned into the famous scene in which Bond villain Auric Goldfinger cheats in a similar manner. No one minded Porchey's indiscretions since he was the most tremendous fun and full of stories best kept among his golfing chums.

The weekend continued along the same lines, with tea in the Library and later a more elaborate dinner for the Saturday night. The menus followed the seasons as preferred by Lord Carnarvon, who would take a keen interest

LEFT
The Steinway piano
from 1895

RIGHT
The gramophone
in the Music Room

in what was served. Various favourites such as baked eggs, *Aloyau de boeuf rôti*, poached salmon, rhubarb fool, *filets de limande* and *profiteroles* all made regular appearances.

Saturday dinner remained a grand and beautiful spectacle, with each dish served by footmen in full livery, entering from behind the painted dining-room screen, passing round the Victorian table in a clockwise direction before departing through the Saloon door, all carefully orchestrated by Fernside.

Of all the guests, Malcolm Sargent was perhaps the most elegant; with his upright deportment and dark, slicked-back hair, he commanded attention in any drawing room. He was often pressed into playing the piano after dinner by his hostesses and was always happy to amuse the house party.

Lady Carnarvon was a talented pianist herself and Sargent persuaded her to sit down first and play the huge black Steinway, though she was soon perfectly content to relinquish her place to the maestro. Catherine put a cigarette

in her favourite holder and lit it, leaning back on the sofa to listen to the *appassionato* of the piece. Malcolm Sargent rarely gave public performances as a pianist; he was above all a conductor. As another great conductor, Sir Thomas Beecham, said of him: '... he is the greatest choirmaster we have ever produced ... he makes the buggers sing like blazes.'

Given Catherine's love of dancing, the footmen would listen carefully whilst serving dinner. Lord and Lady Carnarvon had a very good gramophone and if the word 'dancing' was spoken, it was all hands on deck. The men would roll up the carpet in the Saloon and two of the housemaids, Jessie and Betty, would stop turning down the beds and instead run to the kitchens to collect the beeswax and turpentine for Gwendolen, the second kitchen maid, who would be tasked with heating it on the huge black Croon Stirlingshire stove so it could be carefully carried upstairs and rubbed onto the oak floor of the Saloon during dinner.

The staff dining room

Gwendolen's first position at Highclere was as a scullery maid when she was sixteen years old. Her days then were spent cleaning the stone floors, preparing the ranges for cooking on in the morning and then scouring the coppers afterwards with silver sand, soft soap, and salt and lemon skins. They would then be lined up, burnished like gold, on the kitchen shelves. She had in time risen to vegetable maid and kitchen maid, by then dressed in a neat black uniform and white apron. Gwendolen still had her dreams, though, and longed to apply to become a nursery maid. Mrs Mackie, however, had other ideas, and had decided the girl was too useful to let go.

Meanwhile the cook would continue to

concentrate on the *Baba au Rhum* for the pudding upstairs. Ever a perfectionist, she had been known to chase the footmen to make them run faster along the downstairs corridors with her soufflés – determined that they should arrive in the Dining Room still properly raised and deliciously light.

It was a long walk along the corridors, pushing a laden trolley, but after the guests upstairs had finished and retired for *digestifs* in the Drawing Room or Library, the servants would all sit down to a delicious supper in their own dining room, prepared by Mrs Mackie.

The footmen occupied one side of the long oak table,

housemaids and kitchen maids the other. Fernside and Mrs Lloyd presided over mealtimes. With any luck there might be the chance of some dancing if one of the footmen was free to play the piano. Housemaids Gladys and Jessie's favourite song was the then phenomenally popular waltz composed by Julián Robledo – *Three O'Clock in the Morning*. The two housemaids would not be needed again upstairs, and Miss Smith the head housemaid would make them all hot cocoa before they wended their way up the long stone staircase behind the green baize doors to the bedrooms they shared.

As they disappeared upstairs, Stratford the night watchman would begin his rounds, with his large white dog, a Collie cross, and walking stick to lean on to save his game leg. Gladys had been downstairs late one evening near the stillroom where the jams and chutneys were made when she had seen his dog snarling at a ghost, who walked out of the kitchen towards the Gothic stairs. She refused to go there on her own after that.

Easter Sunday morning found Lord and Lady

Carnarvon and their guests making their way to Highclere Church for the service at 10.45 a.m. It was a bright April morning as the house party set off through the park. Lord Carnarvon's grandfather had commissioned Sir George Gilbert Scott, the eminent Victorian architect, to build a new

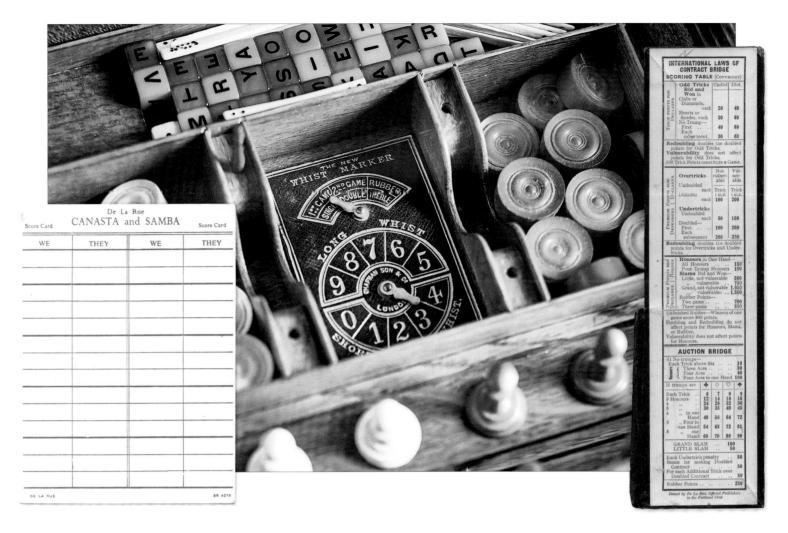

church for the family and the village. The original church had abutted the Castle and the 4th Earl had decided to move it just outside the gates so it would be nearer the rest of the parishioners.

The family filed into their pews at the front. Lord Carnarvon read the lesson from the Epistles of St John, enthusiastically and dramatically, thoroughly enjoying being centre-stage. Henry had an excellent singing voice so the Easter hymns were swelled by the clarity and fervour of his and Peter's trebles. Sir Brograve Beauchamp, by contrast, sang the hymns loudly and reassuringly out of tune, but hopefully a few seats away from Malcolm Sargent who may not have been amused.

After Easter Sunday lunch, bridge was a

mainstay of the evenings, plus other competitive games played with frequent recourse to brandy and cigars, to aid concentration. Gladys and Colin Buist, Lionel Montagu, Eve and her husband Brograve, Porchey and his old army comrade

H. C. Armstrong, who rented a house at Highclere, made up the tables.

Harry Armstrong neither drank nor smoked but was an accomplished raconteur, regaling the house party with tales of his latest adventures in Armenia and Africa, which had nearly accounted for all of his nine lives! His biography of Atatürk, *Grey Wolf – Mustafa Kemal*, was also selling quite well and he was considering his next project. His memoirs of serving in the First World War with Porchey was one possibility. An excellent if daredevil rider, he much enjoyed careering around Highclere on horseback with his old friend.

The Beauchamps left two days before the rest of the party as Brograve returned to his duties as Member of Parliament for Walthamstow East. There had been little political talk over the weekend, a relief to Brograve as the mood in Parliament was uneasy. The Stresa Front had just been signed by the British and French as part of the League of Nations, condemning German rearmament. He wondered what the next parliamentary session would bring.

For the last few years Catherine had suspected that her husband had succumbed to various temptations while in London. Porchey rather enjoyed his reputation as a man about town. He liked squiring around beautiful women, and was always the centre of attention with his story-telling skills. Aware of the rumours, Catherine did her best to ignore them but now it seemed that her husband had fallen in love again.

Fernside was most disapproving of any gossip but everyone downstairs had heard about what was going on. They knew about the phone calls and the letters ... Perhaps they knew more than Lady Carnarvon did, although she had seen her husband all too often disappear into his Study where the telephone sat on his desk.

The time came for the last of the house party to leave, the Visitors' Book was duly signed, and Malcolm and Peter kissed her goodbye, Malcolm keeping a comforting arm around her shoulders as Peter climbed back into the back of the car. Colin and Gladys set off for London. Catherine remained standing alone on the stone steps.

She knew that Porchey wanted to talk to her but there was still time for a last walk in the late afternoon. The low light cast the cedars' long shadows across the lawns whilst the dying sun was reflected weakly by the Castle windows, a few wisps of warm yellow escaping from behind the shutters and curtains. The carvings high on the Castle turrets were shadowed into oblivion by the darkening April sky. Catherine thought that, like the spring, these beautiful views were saying: 'Remember me.' Inside the Castle Mrs Lloyd was organising the housemaids to clean and close up the bedrooms. Henry would soon return to prep school, Penelope to her lessons with Doll.

Porchey turned to Catherine and begged her for a divorce.

POSTSCRIPT

The Carnarvons' marriage was finally dissolved by the courts in November 1936. A year and a half later, the decree nisi came through and immediately Porchey sailed to America to marry the woman he believed was the love of his life. She, however, changed her mind and refused him. He returned alone.

Eve and Brograve Beauchamp continued to be frequent guests at Highclere, and their daughter Patricia spent the Second World War living there with her beloved dog Tom Thumb and evacuee children.

After the court ball in 1935, the Prince of Wales did smuggle Mrs Simpson into a servant's room in Buckingham Palace to view his father the King's Jubilee procession, and Commander and Mrs Buist accompanied Edward and Mrs Simpson on holiday that summer. It was not a passing obsession for the Prince of Wales.

Malcolm Sargent celebrated his fortieth birthday on 29 April and began to pick up his career again. He agreed to a tour of Australia a year later. His dedication to music and courage during the Second World War led to a knighthood. Further honours followed both in England and abroad, including Sweden and Finland, and France where he became a chevalier of the *Légion d'honneur*. He died in 1967, the most celebrated conductor of his generation.

DIANA MOYSE

Head Housekeeper

Diana began at Highclere in 1986, helping in the plant centre run by my husband Geordie, now the 8th Earl. His grandfather lived in the Castle, which at that time was still completely private and not open to the public. Diana had never seen the house even from the outside and asked a friend who knew Robert Taylor the butler if it would be possible for her to see around it. She recalls: 'Robert was a real gentleman and one of the best-known butlers in the country.'

As she was shown each room, one shutter was opened a fraction to let in a little light before being closed again. As a result, each room remained in deep shadow so she actually saw very little. A few years later, the 7th Earl, my husband's father, was talking to her at the plant centre and asked if she would like to be a guide, as he was going to open the Castle to the public. Diana remembers clearly the grand opening of the house to visitors and talking to the press. She was stationed in the Smoking Room and it has always remained her favourite room. She is particularly fond of the clock with a 'Westminster Chime', which she believes is the only one that has always worked throughout her time at the Castle. It sits on the *pietra dura* table close to her favourite painting, a seventeenth-century still life by Jan Weenix.

In 1995 she began to help the housekeeper from time to time and since 2001 has been head housekeeper. She serves breakfast when the family is in residence and has also helped at weddings, with filming, and many other events. Her favourite season is autumn, when the shooting season brings smaller and more intimate house parties into the Castle: 'We lose boot jacks and dog bowls every year but it is part of the fun.'

Diana has an extraordinary eye for detail that would have been admired by her late-nineteenth- and early-twentieth-century predecessors. She can remember the exact position of all the furniture and photographs as in a game of Pelmanism, and an eyebrow is soon raised if the sun is catching a dusty surface or, heaven forbid, a cobweb lurks high up on the edge of a curtain!

Whenever she drives through Highclere's front gates, she feels she enters a different world. 'I just love the house: that is why I am here. The first time I saw it I fell in love with it. I am very privileged that I have met so many wonderful people and made up the rooms for some extraordinary guests.' When she met the Queen, she was told not to speak to her unless she was spoken to but forgot and just chatted away – and the Queen chatted back. 'Never in my wildest dreams did I feel I could do anything like this.'

It also has its comedic moments. She once had a phone call from the housekeeper at Highgrove, the Prince of Wales's house in Gloucestershire. It transpired that they both used the same laundry service, which had got into a muddle and sent Highgrove's laundry to Highclere. A discreet collection resolved the situation.

AFTERNOON TEA

Sandwiches

EACH RECIPE MAKES: 6 good sandwiches or 18 finger sandwiches

Everybody has their own recipes for these sandwiches but this is how we do it at Highclere.

Cucumber

One hundred years ago cucumber sandwiches were often served for tea in houses such as Highclere because this illustrated that the family had sufficient hothouses and skilled gardeners to produce the delicacy throughout the year.

INGREDIENTS

1 cucumber, peeled

White wine vinegar (optional)

Butter, for spreading

*12 slices of brown,
white or malted bread
(whatever you fancy)*

Salt

METHOD

Slice the cucumber into rounds as thinly as possible. Put the slices in a colander and sprinkle with a pinch of salt and a splash of vinegar (if you wish). Leave for about 15 minutes. The vinegar gives the cucumber a slightly stronger taste and the salt extracts the water so that the bread is less likely to become soggy.

Butter each slice of bread and lay six slices on a board. Pat the cucumber dry then divide it evenly among the slices of bread. Place the other buttered slices of bread on top. Trim off the crusts and slice each sandwich into three fingers.

Smoked Salmon

Like most good things in life, proper smoked salmon takes time to create. Old Scottish kilns take two to three days to smoke the fish over oak logs, and observe the maxim: 'A good clothes-drying day is a good fish-smoking day.' Large commercial operations, by contrast, use woodchips rather than logs and then pressurise the kilns to blast out the smoke in five hours.

Not only is smoked salmon a delicious treat, it is full of many of the natural oils we need to keep us healthy.

INGREDIENTS

350g (12oz) 'proper' smoked salmon

Black pepper

Squeeze of lemon juice

Butter, for spreading

*12 slices of brown bread
(or any bread you fancy)*

METHOD

Butter the bread and lay six slices on a board. Lay some smoked salmon on top. Grind over some black pepper and add a generous squeeze of lemon juice then place the other buttered slices of brown bread on top. Trim off the crusts and slice each sandwich into three fingers.

Egg Mayonnaise

It is often assumed that mayonnaise is a French invention. However, the Spanish claim it was created by them in the eighteenth century and was associated with the town of Mahón in Menorca. It was known as 'salsa mayonesa' before later being popularised by the French as 'mayonnaise'. Of course it is now a typically English addition to many sandwiches … and it is a staple with American salads too. President Calvin Coolidge commented that one treat he could not forgo was his Aunt Mary's homemade mayonnaise. For my part, I can never resist egg mayonnaise sandwiches.

INGREDIENTS

12 fresh eggs

Mayonnaise

Salt and pepper

12 slices of white bread

Butter, for spreading

1 large bunch of watercress

METHOD

Hard-boil the eggs in a pan of boiling water, then drain. Cool under cold running water, then peel and put them in a bowl. Mash roughly with a fork and add mayonnaise and seasoning to taste.

Butter the bread and lay six slices on a board. Spread them with the egg mayonnaise mixture, then top with watercress. Place the other buttered slices of bread on top. Trim off the crusts and slice each sandwich into three fingers.

Victoria Buns

MAKES: 6 buns

Highclere's Victorian kitchen would have been filled every day with the smell of baking as cakes, buns and breads were all made there. The great Carron ranges took a lot of fuel but were considered reliable.

A Victoria bun is a typical little cake, tall rather than wide and nicely spiced. We like to make our own candied orange peel, as its intense and superior citrus flavour makes all the difference in these buns. The leftover candied peel makes for an excellent gift, cake decoration or pudding garnish, too.

FOR THE CANDIED PEEL

1 whole orange

75g (3oz) caster sugar,
plus extra for sprinkling

75ml (2½fl oz) water

FOR THE BUNS

1 medium egg

55g (2oz) caster sugar

55g (2oz) softened unsalted butter

40g (1½oz) ground rice

40g (1½oz) currants

55g (2oz) self-raising flour

1 tbsp milk, for glazing (optional)

METHOD

Make the candied peel at least a day before you make the buns.

Cut the orange into 6 wedges. Slice off the flesh from each wedge, leaving a very thin layer of pith behind on the peel. Slice each wedge of peel into 6 long strips. To remove any bitterness, simmer the strips in a small saucepan of gently boiling water for 5 minutes. Drain and rinse, then place back in the pan with fresh water and simmer again for a further 15 minutes. Drain again and set the peel aside.

Tip the sugar into the pan with the water. Stir over a low heat to dissolve the sugar, then add the peel strips and simmer gently for about 25 minutes until the peel is soft. Leave the peel in the syrupy mixture to cool.

Preheat the oven to 110°C/230°F/Gas mark ½ and set a wire rack over a baking sheet. Lift the peel from the syrup with a slotted spoon and sit each piece on the rack. Transfer the baking sheet to the low oven for 25 minutes to dry the peel. Remove and leave to cool slightly.

Lay a sheet of baking parchment over a baking sheet and sprinkle over a thin layer of caster sugar. Toss the peel in the sugar so each piece is well coated, then spread it out in a single layer and leave for several hours, or preferably overnight, uncovered, to dry completely and become crisp.

Chop 55g (2oz) for the buns, and store the rest in an airtight container for 2–3 weeks.

The day you're making the buns, preheat the oven to 180°C/350°F/Gas mark 4 and line a baking sheet with baking parchment.

Beat the egg, sugar and butter together in a bowl with a hand-held electric whisk or in the bowl of a stand mixer for 3–5 minutes until well blended, light and creamy. It may look slightly curdled, but don't worry. Stir in the ground rice, currants and 50g (2oz) of chopped candied peel, then sift in the flour and mix until a soft mixture forms.

Spoon the dough on the baking sheet in 6 even-sized piles, spacing them well apart as the mixture will spread. Gently form them into roughly-shaped rounds, flattening only very slightly. Brush the dough with milk, if you wish. Bake in the oven for 15–18 minutes, until pale golden brown. Remove from the baking sheet and transfer to a wire rack to cool.

Crumpets

MAKES: 12 crumpets

Tea and crumpets are a quintessentially English combination. Crumpets were first made in England in Anglo-Saxon times, when Highclere was owned by the Bishops of Winchester. These were probably more like small round thin pancakes than the thick, spongy teatime treats we toast today, which are made with yeast. The holes and the thickness of today's crumpets are particularly perfect for carefully spreading with butter.

The recipe below is what Paul and his team use to make our crumpets.

INGREDIENTS

185g (6½oz) strong white flour

185g (6½oz) plain flour

16g (½ oz) fresh yeast
or a 7g sachet easy-bake yeast

15g (½oz) caster sugar

360ml (12fl oz) warm whole milk

8g (¼oz) bicarbonate of soda

8g (¼oz) salt

200ml (7fl oz) warm water

Vegetable oil, for greasing

Butter, to serve

METHOD

Mix both the flours and yeast together in a large bowl. Stir the sugar into the warm milk and pour it over the flour mix. Beat the mixture with a wooden spoon for at least 5 minutes – this helps produce the holes in the crumpets and make a thick, smooth batter.

Cover the bowl with clingfilm and leave at room temperature for about 1 hour or a bit longer, depending on the warmth of the room, until it has doubled in size.

Mix the bicarbonate of soda, salt and warm water together and beat it gradually into the batter. It should have the consistency of double cream. Cover again and leave to rest for a further 25 minutes.

Heat a griddle or a flat heavy-based frying pan over a medium heat. Lightly grease the pan and grease some metal crumpet rings (10cm/4in wide × 2cm/¾in deep).

Place as many of the rings as will sit completely flat on the hot griddle or pan and drop in your mixture (about a ladleful) to about three-quarter-fill each one. You will need to cook the crumpets in batches.

Repeat until all the mixture has been used. If you are re-using the rings, wash them well before using again.

These are best toasted and eaten warm with butter.

Scones

MAKES: about 6 scones

Originally made with unleavened oats and cooked on a griddle, scones today are generally sweetened and served with clotted cream and jam. In Devon they are spread with the cream first and then jam, and in Cornwall it is jam first and then cream – the choice is yours! The preferred pronunciation is equally contentious, as this rhyme makes plain:

'I asked the maid in dulcet tone
To order me a buttered scone;

The silly girl has been and gone
And ordered me a buttered scone.'

Lady Carnarvon's Recipe

MAKES: about 6 scones

The mixture can be made in advance and kept in a container in the fridge. The secret to good scones is that the butter and milk used are cold, the dough is handled as little as possible, and that once cooked and cooling they are wrapped in a tea towel. Dried fruit such as sultanas or cranberries can be added just before the milk.

INGREDIENTS

225g (8oz) self-raising flour,
plus extra for dusting

½ tsp salt

1 tsp baking powder

½ tsp salt

55g (2oz) chilled unsalted butter, cubed

25g (1oz) caster sugar

1 medium egg, beaten

150ml (5fl oz) chilled whole milk

METHOD

Preheat the oven
to 230°C/450°F/Gas mark 8.

Dust a baking tray with flour
and place it in the fridge.

Sift the flour, salt and baking powder into a mixing bowl.

Rub the butter into the flour and baking powder with your fingertips until the mixture resembles fine breadcrumbs, then stir in the sugar.

Add the egg to the milk and pour just enough of it into the flour mixture to form a sticky, soft dough (you may have about 3 tablespoons left). Reserve the remaining milk and egg mixture for later.

Turn the dough out onto a floured board or worktop and quickly and gently shape it into a round about 2cm (¾in) thick. Handle the dough as little as possible and cut out 6 scones cleanly with a plain 5·5cm (2¼in) floured cutter.

Place on the chilled, floured baking tray and brush each scone lightly with some of the remaining milk/egg mixture.

Bake in the oven for 9–10 minutes until golden brown and well risen.

Put a clean tea towel on a wire rack. Lift the scones off the baking tray with a palette knife, transfer to the tea towel and wrap the towel around the scones.

These scones are best eaten warm, soon after baking, and are fabulous with clotted cream, and raspberry or strawberry jam.

Tearooms Recipe

MAKES: about 25 scones

The scones that we serve in the Castle tearooms and for our formal afternoon teas are baked to a different recipe by our chef, Paul Brooke-Taylor.

INGREDIENTS

900g (2lb) plain flour

125g (4½ oz) softened unsalted butter, cubed

150g (5oz) caster sugar

55g (2oz) baking powder

1 medium egg

400ml (13fl oz) whole milk

150g (5oz) sultanas

METHOD

Preheat the oven
to 180°C/350°F/Gas mark 4.

Dust two baking trays with flour
and place in the fridge.

Make the scone mixture as left, adding the sultanas to the mix after the milk.

Cut out scones with a 6cm (2½in) cutter, place on the baking trays and bake for 17 minutes until golden brown and well risen.

Remove from the oven, place on a wire rack to cool, and enjoy with jam and clotted cream.

Victoria Sponge Cake

SERVES: 10

Apparently, as a child, Queen Victoria wasn't allowed to eat sweet things very often, but during her reign the practice of taking afternoon tea was popularised and a little sweet something to sustain the Queen and her guests in the late afternoon became *de rigueur*. Thus the Victoria sponge or Victoria sandwich cake was named and makes for a delicious addition to afternoon tea.

INGREDIENTS

4 medium eggs, at room temperature

*225g (8oz) softened unsalted butter,
plus extra for greasing*

225g (8oz) caster sugar

225g (8oz) self-raising flour

2 level tsp baking powder

1 litre (1¾ pints) double cream

About 200g (7oz) strawberry jam

Icing sugar, for dusting

METHOD

Preheat the oven
to 180°C/350°F/Gas mark 4.

Grease and line the base of
2 × 20cm (8in) sandwich tins.

Break the eggs into a large mixing bowl. Add the butter, sugar, flour and baking powder and mix everything together until well combined. (The easiest way to do this is with a hand-held electric mixer or a stand mixer, but you can use a wooden spoon.) As soon as everything is blended together, stop mixing. The batter should easily fall off a spoon.

Divide the mixture evenly between the tins and gently smooth the surface of the batter. Place the tins on the middle shelf of the oven and bake for 25 minutes.

Don't open the oven door during the cooking time or the cakes will sink. The cakes are done when they are golden-brown and coming away from the edge of the tins and a knife inserted into the middle of the cakes comes out clean.

Remove from the oven and set aside to cool in their tins for 5 minutes before turning the cakes out onto a wire rack. Remove the lining paper.

Whisk the cream in a bowl until it forms soft peaks.

When the cakes are completely cool, spread one cake with lots of thick, delicious jam, then pipe (or spread) the whipped cream over the top. Sandwich the cakes together and finish by dusting the top of the cake with a little icing sugar.

Ginger Cake

SERVES: 8–10

Despite its Asian origins, ginger has a long history in Western pharmacology and cooking. It was introduced by the Romans, who prized its medicinal properties, and was popular in Anglo-Saxon and medieval times. While ground ginger is best in baking recipes, I use grated root ginger to make teas which are warming and excellent for the digestion. On a cold wet English Sunday afternoon, perhaps after a nice long walk with the dogs, there is nothing quite like a good slab of sweet spicy ginger cake with a cup of tea.

INGREDIENTS

225g (8oz) self-raising flour

225g (8oz) demerara sugar

1 tsp ground ginger

1 tsp bicarbonate of soda

*50g (2 oz) softened unsalted butter, diced,
plus extra for greasing*

1 medium egg, beaten

*2 tbsp golden syrup (or 1 tbsp golden syrup
and 1 tbsp black treacle)*

150–175ml (5–6fl oz) hot water

METHOD

Preheat the oven
to 180°C/350°F/Gas mark 4.

Grease and line the base of a
28 × 18cm (11 × 7in) rectangular baking tin
with baking parchment.

Combine the flour, sugar, ginger and bicarbonate of soda in a bowl. Rub in the butter with your fingertips until the mixture resembles breadcrumbs. Beat the egg and syrup (or syrup and treacle) together, add them to the cake mixture, then stir in enough of the hot water to make a soft, fairly thick batter, mixing thoroughly.

Pour the cake batter into the baking tin and bake in the oven for about 30 minutes, or until golden and springy to touch. Leave to cool for a few minutes in the tin, then transfer to a wire rack and leave to cool completely.

Peel off the lining paper and cut into slices or squares to serve. The cake will keep well – getting softer and stickier – in an airtight container for up to 5 days.

The DINING ROOM

The State Dining Room is dominated by Anthony van Dyck's great equestrian portrait of Charles I on horseback accompanied by Chevalier le Sieur de St Antoine at the Gates of Paris. The other portraits in this room take their cue from this imposing painting and document the course of the English Civil War. Robert Dormer, 1st Earl of Carnarvon, is depicted as a Cavalier complete with flowing hair and flamboyant clothes. He was killed fighting for the Royalists at the First Battle of Newbury in September 1643.

Ironically his brother-in-law, whose portrait hangs on an adjacent wall, although also a Royalist, persuaded Charles I to surrender to the Scots, who in turn handed him over to the Parliamentarians in 1647 – little did either of them realise this would lead to the execution of the King two years later. Afterwards the great Van Dyck study of the royal martyr was taken down, rolled up and used to prop up a barn door until in 1660 Charles II reclaimed the throne of England for the Stuarts.

This north-facing room was originally used as a gallery in which statues were displayed until it was decided to create a Dining Room here in the 1780s. It was redecorated by my husband's mother in 1999 and nowadays rich yellow silks provide an excellent backdrop for the paintings whilst giving an impression of warmth. There is some electric heating but pashminas never went out of fashion here!

It is extraordinary as we sit beneath them now to think that these portraits must have looked down on royalty, prime ministers, Egyptologists, writers, aviators, soldiers, and travellers from far-off lands.

SWEET THINGS

Baba au Rhum

SERVES: 6

Based on a recipe by Mimi Thorisson, Médoc, France

This pudding has a long history dating back to a seventeenth-century Polish king, but became popular in French cuisine in the nineteenth century. It is traditionally a little yeast-based cake soaked in rum and filled with either custard or cream. However, today at Highclere, instead of yeast we use baking powder, which gives a more uniform result.

The addition of sultanas and a sugar syrup make this an indulgent and delicious combination.

FOR THE CAKE

50g (2oz) unsalted butter, cubed

3 tbsp milk

3 medium eggs, separated

150g (5oz) caster sugar

120g (4½oz) plain flour, sifted

2 tsp baking powder

40g (1½oz) sultanas (if using)

2–3 tbsp apricot jam or conserve, to glaze

FOR THE RUM SYRUP

150ml (5fl oz) water

150g (5oz) caster sugar

100ml (3½fl oz) dark rum

2 cinnamon sticks

2 star anise

2 small oranges, 1 thinly sliced and 1 cut into segments (removing all pith)

METHOD

Preheat the oven to 180°C/350°F/Gas mark 4.

Liberally grease a 22cm (8½in) round cake tin or *rhum baba* mould.

To make the cake, put the butter and milk in a small pan and heat for just long enough to melt the butter. Set aside to cool.

Whisk the egg yolks with the sugar in a large bowl until pale and thick, then gradually pour in the cooled milk and melted butter, whisking constantly.

Whisk the egg whites in a separate, spotlessly clean bowl until they form stiff peaks.

Fold the sifted flour, baking powder and sultanas (if using) into the egg yolk mixture using a large, metal spoon. Gently fold the whisked egg whites into the cake mixture.

Pour the cake mixture into the cake mould or tin and bake for 25 minutes, or until a skewer pushed into the middle of the *Baba* comes out clean. Remove from the oven and loosen the sides of the cake from the tin with a small palette knife, then leave on a wire rack to cool.

Transfer the cake to a serving plate with a rim (to catch the syrup later). Warm the jam slightly to make it easier to brush with and, if necessary, pass it through a sieve. Brush the cake with the apricot jam to glaze.

To make the rum syrup, warm the water and sugar in a small saucepan over a low heat until the sugar has dissolved. Increase the heat and bring to the boil. Add the rum, cinnamon sticks and star anise and simmer for 2–3 minutes. Add the sliced oranges to the syrup and cook for a further 2 minutes, then remove from the heat and set aside to cool.

To assemble the cake, remove the orange slices, cinnamon and star anise from the syrup with a slotted spoon and set aside. Gradually pour the cooled rum syrup over the cake – it should absorb all the syrup.

Decorate with the oranges slices, orange segments, star anise and cinnamon sticks (split into smaller pieces).

[**CHEF'S TIP**: To make a cream to accompany or fill your *Baba*, whisk 250ml (9fl oz) whipping cream with 1 tsp vanilla extract, gradually adding 25g (1oz) caster sugar, until it forms soft peaks. To fill, slice the cool *Baba* across the middle and spoon in the whipped cream before glazing.]

Rhubarb & Ginger Fool

SERVES: 6

Rhubarb seems to grow well for us throughout the year. The plants are prolific and can tend to take over. Occasionally this leads to interesting discussions on how best to manage it between our lovely gardener Philip, firmly rooted in the Hampshire way of doing it, and our long-time helper Genny, who equally firmly believes that Yorkshire knows best when it comes to rhubarb, or indeed most things ...

Rather than cook it in a pan (it is delicious with orange or ginger, or simply simmered with some sugar in a little water), you can roast it on a baking tray, scattered with soft brown sugar and fresh grated ginger and simply serve it with Greek yoghurt.

My mother would cook it on top of the stove in the simple way, with just sugar and water, to make a fool. When cooked, drained and cool, she would stir in whipped cream so it was all mixed together and put it in the fridge until ready to serve. Today, I often roast rhubarb in the oven and it makes a very pretty pudding if it and the cream are layered in a Martini glass rather than mixed together.

INGREDIENTS

*700g (1lb 9oz) rhubarb,
trimmed and cut into thin sticks or batons
(5–6cm/2–2½in long)*

75g (3oz) soft light brown sugar

1 tbsp peeled and grated fresh ginger

400ml (14fl oz) whipping cream

100g (3½oz) caster sugar

*40g (1½oz) crushed meringue
(shop-bought is fine)*

Fresh mint tips, to decorate

METHOD

Preheat the oven
to 150°C/300°F/Gas mark 2.

Toss the rhubarb batons in a bowl with the brown sugar and grated ginger then place on a baking tray in a single layer and roast for 20–25 minutes until soft and tender, but still holding their shape. Remove from the oven and, once cooled, set aside some of the best batons for decorating the dish at the end.

Whisk the whipping cream in a bowl until it forms soft peaks.

Spoon 2 tablespoons of the remaining rhubarb (on which you are going to put your topping), into the bottom of each of six Martini glasses.

Mix the rest of the rhubarb into the whipped cream with the sugar. Chill the glasses of rhubarb and the bowl of whipped cream until ready to serve.

Just before serving, spoon the cream and rhubarb mixture on top of the rhubarb in the glasses, decorate the top with a little crushed meringue, some mint tips and the reserved batons of rhubarb.

[**CHEF'S TIP**: Replace the whipped cream with Greek yoghurt, if you wish. Also, I love ginger and tend to cut back the sugar. Feel free to experiment and find out what is to your taste.]

Blackcurrant & *Crème de Cassis* Syllabub

SERVES: 4

Syllabub would have been eaten at Highclere during the eighteenth century. It is an English wine- and dairy-based dish that probably originates from the sixteenth century. Syllabubs were made from cream and wines and served cold.

INGREDIENTS

150g (5oz) blackcurrants, stalks removed

100g (3½oz) caster sugar

Juice and finely grated zest of 1 lemon

50ml (2fl oz) crème de cassis

50ml (2fl oz) white wine

250ml (8½fl oz) double cream

METHOD

First, chill 4 Martini glasses.

Place the blackcurrants, sugar, lemon juice and zest in a saucepan and simmer over a low heat for 5 minutes, stirring occasionally to dissolve the sugar, then remove from the heat and leave to cool.

When cool strain through a sieve into a bowl, pressing the fruit through the sieve with the back of a wooden spoon.

Alternatively, place the blackcurrant mixture in a blender and blitz until smooth. Mix in the *crème de cassis* and white wine.

Whisk the cream in a large bowl until it forms soft peaks. Reserve a little blackcurrant purée for drizzling, then gently fold the whipped cream into the remaining blackcurrant purée. Place in the chilled glasses and serve with the reserved purée spooned over the top.

Gooseberry Fool

SERVES: 8

Fools are a favourite pudding at Highclere as we can use many of the wonderful fruits that we grow here in our own gardens. They can be as fattening as you like if made with full-fat custard and whipped cream or 'slimmed' down in healthier versions with yoghurt and a splash of *crème fraiche.*

Originally a gooseberry fool would be made by mixing the sieved puréed fruit into a homemade egg custard. These days we take a shortcut and use a combination of double cream and Greek yoghurt. The results are just as delicious.

INGREDIENTS

500g (1lb 2oz) gooseberries, topped and tailed

6 tbsp caster sugar, plus extra for sprinkling

400ml (13fl oz) double cream

400g (14oz) Greek yoghurt

METHOD

Gently cook the gooseberries with the sugar in a medium saucepan for about 15 minutes until soft and pulpy, stirring occasionally. Remove from the heat and leave to cool completely.

Whisk the double cream in a bowl until it forms firm peaks then blend it with the yoghurt.

Gently fold the cold gooseberry pulp into the cream mixture, then divide between tall glasses and refrigerate for at least 2 hours. Garnish with a sprinkling of sugar just before serving.

Mango & Lime Fool

SERVES: 8

From 1795 British sailors were given rations of lime juice to prevent scurvy breaking out during long voyages. In time this gave rise to the nickname for Britons, 'limeys'.

Originally native to southern Asia, by the tenth century mangoes had been introduced to the Middle East by Persian merchants. By the eighteenth century they were grown in South America and the West Indies. However, due to the lack of refrigeration, mangoes had to be pickled before they were shipped anywhere. Pickling quickly became a popular method of shipping exotic fruit and by the early nineteenth century the word 'mango' had simply come to mean pickled fruit.

These days both limes and mangoes can be picked up in any supermarket or greengrocer. They are still one of the most delicious fruit combinations and excellent in the winter months when other, more traditional, fruits are not available except as hothouse produce.

INGREDIENTS

4 medium mangoes

550g (1lb 3½oz) Greek yoghurt

Finely grated zest and juice of 2 limes

150ml (5 fl oz) double cream

METHOD

Peel and stone the mangoes over a bowl to catch all the juice and flesh. Blend the flesh and juice in a food processor with the Greek yoghurt, lime juice and lime zest, keeping back a little lime zest to garnish.

Whisk the cream in a bowl until it forms firm peaks. Gently stir the whipped cream into the mango mixture until they are fully combined, then divide between eight bowls and garnish with the remaining zest. Refrigerate for at least 2 hours before serving.

Compôte de Poires à la Chantilly

Pear trees are trained along the walls at the back of the Monks' Garden. These produce delicious fruit much appreciated by Bella, our old Labrador, who happily potters along in search of the windfalls. Thankfully, there is usually some left for us to collect and use in this traditional recipe.

INGREDIENTS

300ml (10fl oz) water

150ml (5fl oz) ruby port

4 tbsp caster sugar

6 cloves

Pinch of ground allspice

½ lemon, for squeezing

4 ripe pears

FOR THE CHANTILLY CREAM

200ml (7fl oz) double cream

2–3 drops of vanilla extract

2–3 tbsp icing sugar, sifted, to taste

METHOD

Pour the water and port into a saucepan and add half the sugar and both spices. Add a squeeze of lemon juice. Peel and halve the pears lengthways, then use a spoon to scoop out the core from each. Add the pears to the pan, flat-side down, then place the pan over a medium heat. Cover and bring to the boil.

Reduce the heat to medium and simmer for 10–15 minutes until the pears are just tender (a skewer or knife-tip inserted into a pear should meet little resistance). Lift the pears out of the poaching liquor with a slotted spoon and put in a heatproof dish.

Return the pan to the heat, add the remaining sugar, and simmer uncovered for about 10 minutes, or until the liquid has reduced to 150–200ml (5–7fl oz). Adjust the sweetness of the syrup to your taste. Strain the syrup over the pears and allow to cool.

When ready to serve, make the Chantilly cream. Whip the cream and vanilla in a mixing bowl until it forms soft peaks, then slowly add icing sugar (to taste). Serve with the cooled pears.

[**CHEF'S TIP**: For a delicious variation for the cream, try adding grated lime zest or orange blossom water.]

Whilst studying partying and languages at university, I found poached pears an excellent dinner-party pudding and this is a modern version of the above. Smiles, my flatmate, and I would make it in advance for usually about sixteen friends as I always asked too many people. However, here is a recipe for four grown-up guests.

INGREDIENTS

4 ripe pears

1 bottle of red wine
[**CHEF'S TIP**: if you're using cheap wine, like we did, add a little cassis, or a few blueberries, which will give a deeper colour to the poaching liquor.]

230g (8oz) demerara sugar

2–3 cinnamon sticks

1 strip of lemon rind

½ tsp ground ginger

METHOD

Peel each pear and place them in a saucepan with all of the other ingredients and poach for 25 minutes over a low heat. Transfer the pears to a dish, allow to cool and cover with clingfilm.

Meanwhile, cook and reduce the wine syrup to about half its original volume. When the syrup is cool, pour it over the pears and serve with whipped cream.

Burned Strawberry & Black Pepper *Zabaglione*

SERVES: 6

Zabaglione is a classic Italian pudding made of eggs, sugar and sweet wine. The most difficult thing about including it on a menu is deciding how to pronounce the name. Make this dessert shortly before you want to serve it – the *zabaglione* doesn't keep well if made in advance.

INGREDIENTS

1kg (2lb 3oz) British strawberries, washed, hulled and halved

250g (9oz) caster sugar

8 medium egg yolks

1 vanilla pod, split lengthways and seeds removed

100ml (3½fl oz) Marsala wine

15g (½oz) fresh mint tips

Cracked black pepper

METHOD

Place the strawberries in a dry non-stick pan over a medium heat and sauté for about two minutes until they release some colour. As soon as this starts to happen, add 100g (3½oz) of the sugar.

Let the strawberries caramelise in the sugar for 2–3 minutes, then remove the pan from the heat, transfer the strawberries to a plate with a slotted spoon and leave to cool, reserving the liquid in the pan.

For the *zabaglione*, put the egg yolks, vanilla seeds and remaining sugar in a heatproof bowl. Place the bowl in a *bain-marie*, or over a pan of simmering water (making sure the bottom of the bowl does not touch the water), and cook the egg yolks slowly for 6–8 minutes, whisking continuously, until tripled in volume and light and fluffy.

Slowly pour the Marsala into the egg-yolk mixture, continuing to whisk, then remove from the heat but keep whisking the mixture until it cools slightly.

For each serving, place some of the cooled strawberries and some of their sauce in a Martini glass, add some mint tips, but hold back some of the sauce from the strawberries. Cover with the *zabaglione* and sprinkle with some cracked black pepper. Repeat for all six servings and serve immediately, while still warm.

Poudin à la Chancelière

SERVES: 6

This traditional English steamed, moulded pudding is also known as Cabinet pudding or Chancellor's pudding. While it is not often included in today's menus at Highclere, 150 years ago it would surely have amused Lady Carnarvon's Victorian guests, given the presence of the Chancellor of the Exchequer Benjamin Disraeli at the table with them.

INGREDIENTS

Butter, for greasing

100g (3½oz) Savoy cake or sponge cake, sliced, or sponge fingers

50ml (2fl oz) rum (or similar liqueur)

50g (2oz) crystallised fruits, chopped

50g (2oz) each of sultanas and currants, soaked in a little rum for 2–3 hours

300ml (10fl oz) whole milk

Nutmeg, for grating

A few strips of lemon rind

2 large eggs, beaten

1½ tbsp caster sugar

Homemade custard or single cream, to serve

METHOD

Grease the inside of a 1 litre (1¾ pint) pudding bowl or mould.

Place the cake slices or fingers in a bowl with the rum and leave to soak for 10 minutes.

Place the crystallised fruits in the bottom of the bowl or mould and fill with alternate layers of sponge fingers or cake, then sultanas and currants, until the bowl is nearly full.

Make the custard. Put the milk into a heavy-based saucepan and add a generous grating of nutmeg and the strips of lemon rind. Slowly bring to a simmer. Whisk the eggs and sugar together in a heatproof bowl. Pour the warm milk over the egg mixture, whisking as you go.

Strain the custard very slowly into the mould so that it soaks through all the layers. Place a piece of greased baking parchment over the mould, secure with butcher's string, and let it stand for 2 hours at room temperature.

Cover the top again with foil and tie with string to secure (making handles with the string to make it easier to lift the pudding out, if you like). Place an upturned small heatproof plate or saucer in the bottom of a large, deep saucepan.

Sit the pudding bowl on the plate in the pan, with water coming to just halfway up the sides of the sponge bowl. Bring to the boil, then reduce the heat and steam in the gently simmering water, with the pan covered, for about 1 hour, or until the top of the pudding feels firm and is cooked. Keep topping up the water as needed, so the pan does not boil dry.

Carefully remove the pudding from the water and remove the foil and paper top. Leave to cool for at least 20 minutes, then turn out onto a plate. Serve warm slices with some custard or single cream.

Roasted Fig Tart

SERVES: 6

Fig trees grow against the warm south-facing walls in the gardens but, because of our climate, may or may not yield fruit. One tree, however (a Brown Turkey), is trapped in a corner between two walls facing south and west and every year it fruits prolifically.

INGREDIENTS

6 perfectly ripe figs

1 × 320g (11oz) packet all-butter puff pastry (you only need half)

15g (½oz) butter, melted

3 tsp soft light brown sugar

Clear honey, to drizzle

Ice cream, to serve (optional)

METHOD

Preheat the oven to 200°C/400°F/Gas mark 6 and line a baking tray with baking parchment.

Trim the bottom of each fig so that they sit flat. This will allow the fig juices to drip into the pastry. Make 6 curved slits on each fig from just below the stem down to the base, to create wedges that will fan out slightly.

Unroll the puff pastry sheet and cut it in half widthways. (Wrap the rest in clingfilm and reserve for another time.) Cut out 6 circles of pastry using a 7·5cm (3in) plain round cutter – the circles need to be about 1cm (½in) bigger than the base of the figs.

Lay the pastry circles on the lined baking tray and brush each with melted butter, then sprinkle each circle with ½ tsp of the brown sugar. Place a fig in the middle of each pastry circle. Bake for 16–18 minutes until the pastry looks brown and crisp. Remove from the oven, and – when ready to serve – drizzle with honey.

These tarts are delicious with ice cream.

Summer Pudding

SERVES: 6

Summer pudding is a very simple pudding using old white bread and soft fruits. If you feel you are a novice at making classic English puddings, this is a good recipe to begin with. It is best made at least one day in advance and left in the fridge which gives time for all the juices to soak into the bread.

My mother often used to make this pudding in the summer and while delicious it always subsided onto the plate. Paul, our chef, often makes small individual puddings which does tend to solve this problem.

INGREDIENTS

750g (1lb 10oz) summer fruits (redcurrants, blackcurrants, white currants, raspberries and chopped strawberries), plus 150g (5oz) to decorate

2 tbsp water

150g (5oz) caster sugar, plus extra if necessary

1 stale white loaf (around 400g/14oz), cut into medium slices

Mint leaves, to garnish (optional)

Clotted cream or whipped cream, to serve (optional)

METHOD

Line a 1 litre (1¾ pint) pudding bowl with clingfilm.

Put the redcurrants, blackcurrants and white currants from the 750g (1lb 11oz) of summer fruits in a saucepan with the water. Let the fruit heat up a little before adding the raspberries and strawberries and, finally, the sugar. Cook for around 3 minutes, just to soften the fruit but not to overcook it. As the juices start to run, taste to see if it is sweet enough. Add a little more sugar if necessary, remove from the heat and allow to cool.

Cut off the crusts of the sliced bread then slice each square in half to make two rectangles. Use these to line the outside of the bowl, slightly overlapping them. Keep back a couple of slices to cover the base. Squash the bread down slightly if it looks as though it is rising up.

Spoon the cooled fruit into the bread-lined pudding bowl until it reaches the top, but reserve a cup of the juice. Cover the top of the basin with the remaining bread. Find a saucer that covers most of the top of the basin but is smaller than the lip. Place it over the top slice of bread and weigh it down with a small weight such as a jam jar.

Put the pudding in the fridge and leave at least overnight, preferably for a day or two.

When you are ready to eat it, remove the plate from the bowl and replace it with a larger plate. Turn it over so the pudding now stands on the plate and ease off the pudding basin. Remove the clingfilm, too. Have the reserved juice to hand to pour over in case any white bread is still visible. Decorate with the reserved summer fruit and mint leaves, if you wish.

Finally, serve with clotted cream or whipped cream if you like. Cream can cover up any subsidence with strategic decoration and is delicious to eat with the pudding.

Tarte Tatin

Like many good things in life, this pudding began with a mistake. Whereas in English folklore King Alfred burnt the cakes and produced something rock hard and inedible, the French, of course, burnt the apples and produced a wonderful new pudding.

Stephanie Tatin lived in the Loire Valley about 150 years ago where she ran a hotel with her sister. One day (probably exhausted) she nearly burnt the apples she was cooking in butter and sugar. To rescue them she put some pastry on top, slid the whole dish into the oven and then, when the pastry was golden-brown, she turned the dish upside down. It came out as an utterly delicious caramelised apple tart. King Alfred's cakes were presumably so blackened they were thrown away.

INGREDIENTS

4 eating apples
(we use Golden Delicious, Pink Lady or Cox's)

100g (4oz) caster sugar

50g (2oz) unsalted butter

1 x 375g (13oz) block
all-butter puff pastry

A little plain flour, for dusting

1 medium egg yolk, beaten, for brushing

Vanilla ice cream, to serve

METHOD

Preheat the oven
to 200°C/400°F/Gas mark 6.

Peel the apples, trimming a straight slice off the top and the bottom of each apple, so that when you cut it into wedges, each wedge can sit flat and upright on one of its ends. Now cut the apple into 8 perfectly uniform wedges and remove the core and seeds. Using a *parisienne* scoop will help you remove them precisely, but if you don't have one, use a small, sharp knife and cut a small 'V' shape around the core and seeds to remove them from each wedge.

Stand each wedge upright on one of its flat ends, then group and fit the wedges back together in a circle to create the apple shape. Set aside on a board and repeat with the remaining 3 apples. Don't worry if they start to turn brown.

Sit 4 non-stick deep, round individual tartlet cases (about 10cm/4in × 2·5cm/1in) on a baking sheet lined with foil (as the caramel may bubble over during baking). Be sure to use solid-based cases, not ones with loose bottoms.

Divide the sugar and butter equally between them (25g/1oz sugar and 15g/¾oz butter in each one) and melt them together by putting them in the oven for 8–10 minutes, until the edges of the mixture are just starting to be tinged brown. Remove and set aside.

While the butter and sugar are melting, dust a clean surface and the rolling pin with flour, then roll out the puff pastry to a thickness of 2–3mm and cut out 4 circles that will be big enough to cover the bottom and down the sides of the apple shape but not the top. (If you find it easier, cut the pastry block into 4 equal-sized squares, roll each one out separately, then cut out a circle in the desired size from each one.) You can use a small plate or saucer as a guide for cutting round. Depending on the depth and width of your apples, the circles will be around 17cm (6½in) in diameter.

Drape one of the pastry circles over one of the upright apple shapes, so it hangs down the sides with no excess, then gently press it against the sides of the apple wedges to make a neat round shape. Repeat with the other 3 apple shapes.

Once the butter and sugar are melted together, carefully place (as the caramel mixture is hot) the pastry-wrapped apple shapes down into each flan case, so the uncovered ends of the apple wedges sit in the bottom, tucking the pastry edges inside the case. You need the puff-pastry edges and the uncovered tops of the apple wedges to sit in the butter and sugar so that when the caramel starts to brown you get a lovely sticky edge.

Pierce a small hole to release the steam in the tops of the pastry (these will eventually become the base for each tart, once they are turned out) and brush all over with egg yolk to give you a beautiful golden-brown pastry.

Bake in the oven for 25 minutes. Once the pastry has turned golden brown check to see if the caramelisation of the sugar and butter has turned sticky and brown – if not, cook for about another 5 minutes.

Remove from the oven and, while still hot, twist each tarte tatin but leave them in the cases – this will free up the sides so when you turn them out onto the plates they won't stick to the tart case. Leave for 5 minutes then turn out and serve with ice cream.

[**CHEF'S TIP**: If you only have individual moulds with loose bottoms, line the insides completely with foil before melting the sugar and butter in them, so that the mixture can't leak out.]

Upside-down Peach Sponge
with peach purée

SERVES: 4

Upside-down puddings are reminders of childhood, and while parents struggle to persuade children to eat their vegetables, very little persuasion is needed for a peach pudding. You can swap the peach for different fruits (fresh or tinned) – pineapple works very well.

INGREDIENTS

90g (3¼oz) caster sugar

90g (3¼oz) softened unsalted butter, plus extra for greasing

1 vanilla pod, split lengthways and seeds scraped out

3 medium eggs, beaten

90g (3¼oz) self-raising flour, sifted

Pinch of salt

4 ripe peaches, halved and de-stoned

FOR THE PEACH PURÉE

1 ripe peach, halved, de-stoned and cut into 8 pieces

2 tbsp water

1 tbsp caster sugar

METHOD

Preheat the oven to 200°C/400°F/Gas mark 6.

Thoroughly grease four individual 10 × 2cm (4 × ¾in) round tins.

Place the sugar, butter and vanilla seeds in a bowl and beat together by hand, with a hand-held electric whisk, or in the bowl of a stand mixer, until pale, light and fluffy.

Gradually add the beaten eggs while still mixing, along with a tablespoon of the flour (which will prevent the mixture curdling), until you have a smooth paste.

Now fold in the remaining flour and salt, taking care not to knock out the air in the batter. Set aside at room temperature.

Cut each peach half into 6 perfect wedges and arrange them around the edges of the greased tins, each wedge slightly overlapping the next.

Spoon the batter into a piping bag fitted with a plain nozzle and pipe the mixture into the centre of each tin and over the top of the peach wedges until the dishes are full, then level out the tops to give them an even finish.

Bake in the oven for 15 minutes, or until a knife inserted into the middle of one of the sponges comes out clean.

Remove from the oven, leave to cool a little, then turn out onto a plate so the bottom becomes the top.

To make the peach purée, place the pieces of peach in a small pan with the water and sugar and cook over a medium heat for about 10 minutes, until very soft. Remove from the heat and purée in a blender.

Serve the pudding with the peach purée. It's also great with cinnamon custard or vanilla ice cream.

Boiled and Steamed Puddings

The shooting season extends from the cool clear days of early autumn through to the short dark cold days of the mid-winter pheasant shoots. Making up for the weather, puddings served then tend to become ever-more comforting and reflect one of the finest traditions of English cookery. They most definitely require a good walk before or after they are eaten. They are easy to prepare and not sensitive to overcooking or variations in the ingredients.

While I was growing up, my family had a wonderful cook called Queenie, who excelled at making puddings based on suet. These were always made after breakfast; the mixture rolled up into a log, wrapped loosely in a muslin cloth and securely tied. This was then put into a large saucepan full of hot water, which had a plate on the bottom to raise the 'log' a little, and boiled slowly until lunchtime.

Steamed suet puddings, as opposed to the boiled sort, were spooned into a pudding basin and cooked in a *bain-marie*. Paul, our Highclere chef, prefers to cook steamed sponge puddings. These are lighter than suet puddings, particularly if you cream the butter and sugar with the eggs before folding in the other ingredients.

Jam Roly-Poly

SERVES: 6–8

INGREDIENTS

225g (8oz) self-raising flour, plus extra for dusting

100g (3½oz) dried shredded suet

50g (2oz) soft dark brown sugar

Pinch of salt

150–175ml (5–6fl oz) milk or water

100g (3½oz) strawberry or raspberry jam

Custard, to serve (optional)

METHOD

Put a steamer on to heat up. If you don't have a steamer, use a large saucepan with a tight-fitting lid and sit a fully opened steamer basket on the bottom with enough water added to come just below the bottom of the basket.

Combine the flour, suet, sugar and salt in a mixing bowl. Add enough of the milk or water to turn the mixture into a dough that resembles a soft pastry. Gently shape the dough into a ball, but do not over-handle it. Roll out the dough on a lightly floured worktop into a rectangle about 18 × 24cm (7× 9½in) and spread it with jam, leaving a 2cm (¾in) gap around the edges to prevent seepage. Dampen the uncovered pastry edges with water or milk, then roll the rectangle up along one of the long sides, finishing with the join underneath.

Wrap the pudding in muslin and tie the muslin securely. Alternatively, double-wrap it in baking parchment then foil: lay a large sheet of foil on the worktop, take a slightly smaller piece of baking parchment, lightly grease it with butter and dust it with flour and lay it on the foil. Sit the roly-poly (with the join underneath) in the centre of the buttered paper. Fold the short ends of the paper and foil in to secure, then seal the top of the parcel by folding over the longer sides of the paper and foil to secure tightly, while leaving room for the pudding to expand while cooking.

Sit the parcel in the steamer or on the steamer basket. Cover the pan with a lid, bring the water to the boil, then turn down the heat so the water simmers very gently and let the pudding steam for about 1 hour, or until it feels firm on the outside. Keep checking the water level and add a little more boiling water as necessary so that the pan does not boil dry.

Remove the pudding from the water onto a rack to drain for a minute or two, then carefully unwrap, cut into slices and enjoy with custard (if you wish).

Lemon Curd Roly-Poly

Proceed as above, substituting 225g (8oz) lemon curd for the jam.

Spotted Dick

Proceed as for Jam Roly-Poly above, but incorporate some sultanas and raisins into the suet mixture, and omit the jam filling.

Steamed Plum Sponge Pudding

SERVES: 6

W.S. Gilbert, an English librettist who is best known for his partnership as 'Gilbert and Sullivan', commented that 'life's a pudding full of plums' and a plum sponge pudding is an excellent way of using a surfeit of plums.

FOR THE PLUMS

800g (1lb 12oz) Victoria plums, quartered and stones removed

60g (2oz) caster sugar

FOR THE SPONGE

200g (7oz) caster sugar

200g (7oz) softened unsalted butter, plus extra for greasing

3 medium eggs, at room temperature

200g (7oz) self-raising flour, sifted

50ml (2fl oz) grenadine liqueur

Crème Anglaise, or vanilla ice cream, to serve

FOR THE PLUM & GRENADINE SYRUP
(optional)

200g (7oz) Victoria plums, quartered and stones removed

100g (3½oz) caster sugar

200ml (7fl oz) water

50ml (2fl oz) grenadine liqueur

Juice of about ½ lemon

METHOD

Grease a 1·2 litre (2 pint) pudding bowl with butter.

Put the plums and the sugar in a large saucepan and cook over a medium heat for 3–4 minutes, until the plums have softened but still retain their shape.

Place three-quarters of the plums in a fan shape on the base of the pudding bowl, with some of the juice, then set aside to cool. You can use the remaining plum mixture in the syrup later (if using), or keep it in the fridge for another pudding.

Now make the sponge. Cream the sugar and butter in a bowl with a hand-held electric whisk until pale and fluffy.

Add the eggs one at a time, beating each egg into the mixture thoroughly before adding the next egg. Fold in the flour then the grenadine liqueur and gently mix. Spoon the sponge mix into the pudding bowl over the cooled, cooked plums.

Cover the top of the bowl with greased baking parchment, secure with string then cover the top again with foil and tie with string to secure. Place an upturned small heatproof plate or saucer in the bottom of a large, deep saucepan. Sit the pudding bowl on the plate in the pan, with water coming up to just halfway up the sides of the sponge bowl. Bring to the boil, then reduce the heat and steam in the gently simmering water, with the pan covered, for 1–2 hours. Keep topping up the water as needed, so the pan does not boil dry. To check if the sponge is cooked, pierce the centre with a skewer and if it comes out clean this is a good indicator it is ready.

While the sponge is cooking, make the plum and grenadine syrup (if you wish). Place the quartered plums, and the leftover cooked plums, in a heavy-based saucepan with the sugar, water and grenadine. Cook over a low heat for about 15 minutes, until the plums are soft (if they are not yet soft, add a touch more water and cook them for a little longer). Add lemon juice to taste. Pass it through a sieve for a finer purée, or for a fuller flavour simply blitz it with a stick blender until smooth.

To serve, loosen the edges of the pudding using a small knife and turn out onto your chosen plate. Drizzle with the plum and grenadine syrup, and accompany with *Crème Anglaise* or vanilla ice cream.

Marmalade Pudding

Marmalade pudding was much loved by my mother and would be equally popular with Paddington Bear. He might go to sleep afterwards but it would be healthier to go for a brisk walk.

The key to this recipe is the number 8, as you can see below. Using breadcrumbs helps keep the pudding moist.

INGREDIENTS

Butter, for greasing

225g (8oz) fresh white breadcrumbs

225g (8oz) dried shredded suet

225g (8oz) soft dark brown sugar

1½ tsp baking powder

225g (8oz) marmalade, preferably
old-fashioned or homemade

3 medium eggs, beaten

Custard, to serve

METHOD

Preheat the oven
to 160°C/325°F/Gas mark 3.

Put a large roasting tin, one third filled
with water, on a low shelf of the oven,
so it can heat up to make your *bain marie*.
Grease the inside of a 1·75 litre (3 pint)
pudding bowl with butter.

Put the breadcrumbs, suet, sugar and baking powder in a large mixing bowl and stir together with a wooden spoon. Heat the marmalade in a small pan, so it becomes a bit runnier. Stir the eggs into the breadcrumb mixture, then the warm marmalade. The mixture will drop softly from the spoon.

Spoon the mixture into the pudding bowl and level the surface. Cover the top of the pudding with a large piece of foil, tucking the edges under against the sides of the bowl to seal and secure, or tie with butcher's string. Place the bowl in the roasting tin and cook for about 2 hours 45 minutes, or until the top feels firm. Top the tin up with more hot water if necessary, so it doesn't boil dry.

Remove from the roasting tin, loosen the pudding from the sides of the bowl with a small palette knife and turn the pudding out onto a large serving plate. Slice, and serve with warm custard.

Orange Jelly

by **Almina, 5th Countess of Carnarvon**

Oranges originated in China at least 3,000 years ago and arrived here through trade with southern Europe in the fifteenth century. Given the British climate, they can't really be grown here so we used to enjoy the taste by using them in jellies or marmalades. Jellies were far more fashionable even fifty years ago than they are today but home-made ones are deliciously refreshing and unrecognisable from the packet varieties you can buy in supermarkets.

INGREDIENTS

550ml (19fl oz) freshly squeezed orange juice
(the juice from about 10 oranges)

Pared rind of 1 orange

Pared rind and juice of ½ lemon

550ml (19fl oz) water

85g (3oz) granulated sugar

40g (1½oz) powdered gelatine

150ml (5fl oz) double cream, to serve

METHOD

Strain the orange juice and set to one side. Put the orange and lemon rinds, lemon juice and half of the water in a pan and warm gently over a low heat. Add the sugar and stir until dissolved.

Mix the remaining water and the gelatine in a bowl and leave to soak for 5–10 minutes. Once dissolved, pour the liquid gelatine into the pan with the rinds and stir until dissolved, still over the heat. Strain to remove the rinds, take off the heat and leave to cool.

Add the strained orange juice to the jelly mixture then pour into 6 glass bowls or a 900ml (1½ pint) jelly mould. Leave in the fridge for at least 6 hours (or overnight) to set.

If you have used a jelly mould, stand it in shallow warm water very briefly to loosen the jelly before turning out onto a flat serving plate.

Serve with double cream.

Lady Carnarvon's Chocolate Pots

SERVES: 8

You can rarely go wrong with chocolate pots. Most men like them and most women cannot resist them. Dark chocolate is supposed to improve your mood, reduce cholesterol, be packed full of minerals and improve brain function. Apart from the many health benefits of chocolate-eating, it is just rather delicious.

Almina the 5th Countess's recipe includes vanilla for additional flavouring, but I prefer orange as my mother did.

This is a delicious, simple dish. It's great for a make-ahead dessert and the quantities are easily halved to serve 4.

INGREDIENTS

275g (10oz) dark chocolate,
broken into chunks
(we use 70% cocoa solids)

450ml (15fl oz) single cream

4 medium egg yolks, beaten

1 tbsp fresh orange juice
or 6 drops of vanilla essence or extract

METHOD

Place the chocolate in a heatproof bowl in a *bain marie*, or over a pan of simmering water (making sure the bottom of the bowl does not touch the water), and heat gently until melted. Remove from the heat and leave to cool slightly.

Pour the cream into a saucepan and heat until it has nearly reached boiling point. Take it off the heat before it boils and pour the melted chocolate into the pan slowly, stirring gently.

Gradually add the beaten egg yolks and either the orange juice or vanilla, depending what flavour you prefer. Combine well and pour into 8 little ramekin dishes or heatproof small cups.

When the mixture is cool, cover the dishes and put them in the fridge for at least 4 hours to set, ideally overnight (you can make them up to 3 days in advance).

[**NOTE**: Raw egg is not recommended for infants, the elderly, pregnant women or people with weakened immune systems. Be sure to use pasteurised egg yolk instead.]

Plum Cake

SERVES: 6–8

Plum cakes were often made around Harvest Festival time in the autumn. Despite the name they were full of currants or sultanas rather than fresh plums. The old Anglo-Saxon word (*plum*) meant fruit while *plúm-feþer* meant 'a rich man'. Over the ages, the cake then developed further with ever-more richness, until ultimately it became our traditional Christmas fruit cake and plum pudding.

While the recipe is termed a plum cake, the end result perhaps more closely resembles what we might think of today as a scone; however it is completely delicious, with a lovely balance of spices.

INGREDIENTS

225g (8oz) self-raising flour,
plus extra for dusting

½ tsp baking powder

Pinch of salt

½ tsp mixed spice

50g (2oz) caster sugar

50g (2oz) softened butter,
cut into small pieces

100g (3½oz) good-quality
mixed fruit and peel

1 tsp bicarbonate of soda

100ml (3½fl oz) milk

METHOD

Preheat the oven
to 220°C/425°F/Gas mark 7.

Grease or line a baking sheet.

Sift the flour into a mixing bowl with the baking powder and salt, then stir in the mixed spice and sugar. Add the butter and rub it into the flour and sugar with your fingertips until the mixture resembles fine breadcrumbs. Stir in the mixed fruit and peel.

Stir the bicarbonate of soda into the milk, then add the milk to the dough and stir just enough to combine. Gently gather the dough together, without kneading.

Dust the worktop with flour and pat the dough into a 7cm (2¾in) round shape. Place the dough on the baking sheet and, if you wish, mark it into 6–8 wedges with the blunt edge of a knife. Alternatively, leave as it is.

Bake the cake for 15–18 minutes, until slightly risen and golden, checking it frequently to make sure the top is not getting too dark (cover it loosely with a piece of foil if it is). Push a skewer into the middle of the cake, and if it comes out clean the cake is done. Remove and transfer to a wire rack to cool.

This cake is great on its own or buttered.

Lord Carnarvon's Boozy Bramble Pudding

SERVES: 10

This is one of my husband's all-time favourite puddings. You could call it a sort of flummery, recipes for which have existed for over 400 years though latterly they have been criticised for being bland and uninteresting. The bland version of the pudding is thought to be the origin of the phrase 'talking flummery', and I can remember as a child being told, when I was talking nonsense, that it was flummery. A more flattering description is that this version of the dessert is an amalgam of two classic Scottish recipes – Atholl Brose and Cranachan. Irrespective, it is an excellent combination of whisky and orange together with the more traditional oatmeal and blackberries.

INGREDIENTS

250g (9oz) medium oatmeal

750ml (1¼ pints) cold water

300ml (10fl oz) good-quality whisky

*150g (5oz) runny honey
(we use Highclere honey)*

750g (1lb 10oz) blackberries

750ml (1¼ pints) double cream

*Finely grated zest and juice
of 5 small oranges*

Mint tips, to decorate

METHOD

Put the oatmeal in a bowl, cover with the cold water and leave in the fridge for 24 hours.

Bring the whisky and half the honey to the boil in a pan. As soon as it starts to boil, add the berries. Stir gently, taking care not to damage the berries, and cook for no more than 5 minutes – just long enough for the berries to take on the flavours of the honey and whisky.

Remove from the heat, pour the berries into a cold dish and allow to cool. Once cool, drain and reserve the juice.

Strain the soaked oats and press out as much water as you can.

Place the remaining honey, cream, orange zest and juice in a pan and add the oats. Bring to the boil, stirring constantly, and cook for about 10 minutes, until the oats start to thicken and bubbles appear.

Remove from the heat and divide the mixture evenly between 10 small heatproof glasses and chill them straight away to prevent them from overcooking.

Take the oat puddings out of the fridge about 30 minutes before you want to serve them, to take the chill off them, then spoon the berries on top, garnish with a few mint tips and serve with a shot glass of leftover berry juice and whisky.

Lady Carnarvon's Preserves

Apple Mint Chutney

MAKES: 10 × 450g (1lb) jars

INGREDIENTS

*1·75kg (4lb) cooking apples,
peeled and cored*

600ml (1 pint) cider vinegar

450g (1lb) soft light brown sugar

*450g (1lb) ripe tomatoes,
skinned and chopped*

*150g (5oz) crystallised ginger,
chopped*

½ tsp mixed spice

Good pinch of cayenne pepper

½ tsp salt

400g (14oz) seedless raisins

*50g (2oz) bunch of mint,
leaves removed and finely chopped*

METHOD

Cut the apples into small chunks and put them in a preserving pan or large heavy-based pan with the vinegar. Bring to a boil, then turn down the heat to medium and simmer, stirring occasionally, for about 8 minutes, until the apples are mushy.

Add the sugar and simmer over a low heat until it has dissolved, then add all the remaining ingredients (except the mint) and simmer uncovered for 50–55 minutes, stirring occasionally, until the mixture has reduced and thickened to a jam-like consistency. Remove from the heat.

Finally, stir in the mint. Pour the chutney into sterilised jars [**SEE** right], then seal and label. Store for a week or so before using, to allow the flavours to develop.

Unopened, the chutney will keep for about 10 months. Once open, keep in the fridge and use within 1 week. Particularly good with roast lamb.

Crab Apple Jelly

MAKES: 10 × 450g (1lb) jars

INGREDIENTS

1·75kg (4lb) crab apples, washed

1·75 litres (3 pints) water

Granulated sugar

Juice of 1 lemon (optional)

*A jelly bag and stand
(or an upturned stool with muslin tied to the legs)*

METHOD

Roughly chop the crab apples and put them in a preserving pan or very large saucepan. Pour the water into the pan and bring to the boil, then turn down to a simmer and cook the fruit for about 2 hours, until it is very soft and pulpy.

Set up the stand and position the jelly bag into the top of it. Put a large empty bowl underneath it to catch the juice. Now, carefully spoon the crab apple pulp into the muslin and leave it to strain somewhere cool overnight.

The next morning, measure how much clear liquid you have and allow about 450g (1lb) of sugar to every 600ml (1 pint) of liquid.

Return the liquid to the large pan, add the measured quantity of sugar and heat gently until the sugar dissolves, stirring every now and then. Add lemon juice to taste. Boil for 30–45 minutes, or until it reaches setting point (104°C/220°F on a sugar thermometer).

If you don't have a sugar thermometer, use the plate test. Place a side plate or saucer in the freezer while you're cooking the jelly. Boil for 12 minutes, then test to see if it will set. Drop a teaspoon of jelly onto the cooled plate and put back in the freezer for a minute. If the cooled jelly forms a skin and wrinkles when you push it with your finger, it has reached setting point. If it's not ready, continue to simmer (putting the plate back in the freezer) and check at 5-minute intervals.

When your jelly reaches setting point, remove the pan from the heat and pour the jelly into sterilised jars [**SEE** right], then seal and label. Store, unopened, in a cool, dark place for up to 3 weeks.

Blackberry Jam

MAKES: 10 × 450g (1lb) jars

INGREDIENTS

2·7kg (6lb) blackberries, rinsed

Finely grated zest and juice of 2 lemons

150ml (5fl oz) water

2·7kg (6lb) jam sugar

Knob of butter

METHOD

Put the blackberries, lemon juice and water in a preserving pan or large heavy-based pan and bring to the boil. Once boiling, turn down the heat and leave to simmer for 15 minutes. With the heat low, add the sugar and lemon zest and stir at a simmer until the sugar has completely dissolved. Turn up the heat and bring the jam to a rolling boil for about 10 minutes until it reaches setting point (104°C/220°F on a sugar thermometer).

If you don't have a sugar thermometer, use the plate test (as for Crab Apple Jelly, left).

Once ready, remove the pan from the heat, and skim off any scum. Stir in the butter to dissolve any remaining scum and ladle the jam into warm sterilised jars [**SEE** below] then cover with a waxed paper disc and seal with a sterilised lid. Label and date the jars. The jam will keep well, unopened, in a cool, dark place for up to 2 months.

TO STERILISE JARS

Wash them and their lids thoroughly in warm soapy water and rinse clean. Place directly on an oven shelf, making sure they are not touching each other (do not place washed rubber stoppers/seals in the oven). Heat the oven to 140°C/280°F/Gas mark 1½ and let the bottles or jars dry out for 15–20 minutes.

MIKE WITHERS

Bee Keeper

When Mike Withers married Pat in 1973 he asked Lord Carnarvon's agent if they could move into the cottage next-door to Pat's mother. They have now lived there for so long that it is no longer simply number three Highclere Street, but has been renamed The Withies.

Like his wife, Mike worked as an apprentice painter decorator but came to work at Highclere in 1981 when Albert Saxton the clerk of works suggested that he team up with his wife. Soon afterwards a young neighbour, Richard, asked Mike for some work experience. He has stayed on working with Pat and Mike for thirty years and together the three of them are still painting the Castle.

Mike has kept bees for over sixty years, having learned about them whilst at school. He has his own hives but is also in charge of the Highclere hives. In 2015 calamity struck and three hives were stolen. Lady Carnarvon promptly suggested moving them into the park for safety. The bees now all live together in the old kitchen garden where they keep the hens company.

As a result of these twin jobs, Mike's van can be full not just of paints but also bees –

given away by the steady buzzing emanating from it at certain times. This happens when he is transporting a queen bee with her assistants in an introduction cage (a small plastic box) prior to putting them into a hive. A run-of-the-mill queen costs about £30 but Mike has some extra good ones for £35 whilst really special ones can cost up to £70. The honey is sold in the Highclere gift shop and to staff.

Like Pat, Mike has now worked for three successive Earls: 'The 6th a real character, the 7th a bit stricter and the 8th (current) Earl a lovely man but maybe originally a bit shy. He shouldn't be and the current Lady Carnarvon has brought him out of his shell. I like this one very much and Lady Carnarvon is making the estate better.

'It is a very happy environment. I have worked and lived with Pat for over forty years and she definitely wears the trousers!'

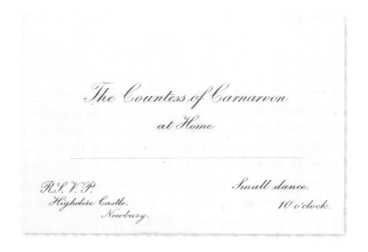

The Countess of Carnarvon
at Home

R.S.V.P.
Highclere Castle,
Newbury.

Small dance,
10 o'clock.

AT HOME

A Weekend at Highclere Today

At Highclere we are, more often than not, up and running, open to visitors, tours, weddings, and a wide range of events that require us to work at weekends throughout the year. My privilege and joyful reward is that I can reclaim some weekends for myself, filling the house with friends and family, new acquaintances, and old, enjoying the gardens, various activities and animals with sociable amusements that liven the Castle with laughter and conversation.

Weekends are planned around various events: a concert; cricket; a church fête; a Harvest Festival church service; traditional shooting; a Burns Night celebration or a ride and picnic lunch. Like my predecessors, I write letters and send 'At Home' invitations. Today, however, I can also telephone, text and email (although there remains something special about a card or letter in the post). Rather than a Groom of the Bedchamber and a secretary to help me with my administration as with previous countesses, I co-opt some of the office team to help with the logistics for the weekend.

Champagne Cocktail

A cocktail associated with the glamour of movie stars and glitzy parties, the combination of very cold Champagne, brandy and Angostura bitters is the essence of a delicious beginning to any weekend dinner party. We use our own Champagne here at the Castle, but whichever brand you prefer, I would advise sipping this cocktail slowly, and carefully counting how many you have. On the other hand, perhaps at the end of a particularly stressful week, just enjoy ...

INGREDIENTS PER PERSON

2 dashes of Angostura bitters

1 white sugar cube

10ml (½fl oz) brandy

90ml (3fl oz) chilled Highclere Champagne

Slice of orange, to garnish

1 maraschino cherry, to garnish

METHOD

Drip the Angostura bitters onto the sugar cube and place in a Champagne flute.

Add the brandy followed by the chilled Champagne, taking care to pour the Champagne slowly as it tends to bubble up.

Garnish with the orange and cherry, then serve.

Multiple demands on my time and multiple means of communication can lead to some confusion. We have several electronic diaries at the Castle. Amongst them is a general one we all use and one only my husband uses. He religiously enters who he has asked in his diary which I often forget to look at and, of course, he would never look at what I have entered, even if I remembered to enter it. In order to not confuse my husband, however, I proceed on a need-to-know basis, a marital strategy universally tried and tested.

As with every other hostess, I try to plan ahead and many weekends are marked in the Highclere diary a year in advance, especially if people are flying in from abroad. I carefully plan the mix of old and new friends, to which are added spur-of-the-moment bright ideas, whether some of our more eccentric friends or extra entertainment.

Ahead of the weekend, Paul, our head chef, is asked to set out the menus for the weekends. I declare I am happy with anything and then inevitably change my mind and his menus, when I review them. I look for a balance of meat and fish, the best of seasonal vegetables and prefer to enjoy potatoes and rice at lunchtime rather than in the evening. It is then the turn of our head butler, Luis, to confer with my husband to suggest the wines. Cocktails fall into my choice as they signal the time of day when I can do nothing more. How can you improve on a Champagne Cocktail? As a contrast, however, Luis will create a novel 'Luis Special' cocktail, full of colour.

LUIS SPECIALS

Lord Carnarvon very much enjoys a small glass of whisky before supper. He always says it is very good for him – purely medicinal. During Prohibition in the USA (1920–33) all alcohol sales were banned, of course, but the federal government made an exemption for whisky if it was prescribed by a doctor and sold through licensed pharmacies. Unsurprisingly, pharmacy chains grew tremendously in number and doctors found themselves more than usually popular.

Manhattan

MAKES: 1

50ml (2 fl oz) Scotch whisky

*20ml (¾ fl oz)
red sweet vermouth*

1 dash of Angostura bitters

Ice cubes

*Cocktail (maraschino) cherry,
to garnish*

Pour all the ingredients into a mixing glass or cocktail shaker with ice cubes and stir.

Strain into a chilled cocktail glass and garnish it with a cocktail cherry.

[Originally made with rye whiskey but at Highclere we tend to use Scotch whisky.]

Mint Julep

MAKES: 1

1 tsp powdered sugar

2 tsp water

4 fresh mint sprigs

Crushed ice

*60ml (2¼ fl oz)
Scotch whisky*

Place the sugar and water in a highball glass with 3 sprigs of the mint and gently muddle.

Fill the glass with crushed ice, add the whisky and stir well until the glass is frosted. Garnish with the remaining sprig of mint.

[You can make it with bourbon but, again, we tend to use Scotch.]

Preparation of the bedrooms for the house party begins a week in advance with Diana, our head housekeeper, and her assistant Genevieve. All the beds are made up with sheets and blankets, feather eiderdowns and throws. Many of the beds sit on old frames, with original head and footboards and horsehair bases whilst Mercia bedroom has an eighteenth-century four-poster bed. Naturally, conventional mattresses rarely fit so, more often than not, bedding is bespoke.

Many of the bedrooms around the first floor have now been redecorated, inspired by a painting found in the room, or an embroidered Chinese bed-canopy, or just the strength and simplicity of the architecture and style of the Castle. Furnishings and rugs provide modern comforts to the bedrooms which are not centrally heated. Therefore, ahead of a house-party weekend in the winter, we will turn up the central-heating boiler downstairs a few days in advance to increase the heat around the passage walls.

Bedrooms are stocked with water, towels, and other home comforts, with books and magazines refreshed and dressing gowns left ready. Radios and lightbulbs are checked and the house opens its arms again to a weekend party, as of old. Incidentally, dressing gowns are of particular importance to those guests who stay in the central rooms on each side of the house. The en-suite bathrooms are located in the four corner turrets of the Castle and are, therefore, for the corner bedrooms. There are further bathrooms along the north and south corridors, but for those wishing to retain a degree of decency in heading to a morning or evening bath, a dressing gown can be useful. However, with family in situ, there have been mad dashes of barely clad bodies running along corridors to a bathroom – the only inconvenient oversight might be to find the bathroom occupied, requiring a return dash to the bedroom to wait out one's turn.

With friends or family often bringing children or babies to stay at Christmas time, for example, the corner bedrooms

LEFT
Canning bedroom

RIGHT
Stanhope dressing room

and their adjoining dressing rooms are a modern and useful way to accommodate them. Children invariably get excited by the interconnecting doors and, rather in the vein of an *Alice in Wonderland* adventure or a C.S. Lewis wardrobe discovery, find that the door from their bedroom leads on directly to a second door, barely a foot apart, and lo and behold there's another bedroom the other side of that! With family staying, children can travel from bedroom to bedroom through door to door until they might alight on an inconveniently locked door that halts proceedings. Diana and Genevieve are careful to lock the relevant un-related guests' doors, for those who may not wish to host children of all sizes charging through their bedrooms with shrieks and giggles.

The bedrooms all have name boards above

them, which is very practical. The names often give clues to their original occupants or reference. East Anglia, Mercia, Wessex and Northumberland are named after the most prominent Anglo-Saxon kingdoms that came into being in England after Roman rule ended in the fifth century.

Queen Caroline's bedroom is so called in honour of her stay at Highclere Place House (the name of the earlier house on this site) sometime around 1730. Mary Herbert, the wife of an earlier Carnarvon ancestor, spent time at court as did her husband. In fact Mary's father was the last Speaker of the House of Commons of England following the Act of Union in 1707 and thus the first Speaker of the new House of Commons of Great Britain.

Arundel bedroom references the 4th Earl's mother who was Henrietta Howard – her family lived at Arundel Castle. Stanhope bedroom, on the other hand, bears reference to Lady Evelyn Stanhope, daughter of the Earl of Chesterfield. She married the 4th Earl of Carnarvon and helped her husband complete the interiors. This particular bedroom today remains decorated in rather fraying but beautiful red silks which date from the Prince of Wales's visit in 1895. The red damask curtains frame the wonderful views across the east lawns to the white-pillared folly, Jackdaw's Castle.

Amazingly, our restoration has already reached to the second floor. Rooms which looked rather unprepossessing, with peeling walls, broken cornicing, and without electricity or water, have been brought to life and now serve as further bedrooms for the Castle. These rooms do, however, require quite a number of extra stairs to be climbed, from the Red Hall and up the Red Staircase. Examples of the names above these small newly wallpapered bedrooms' doors are Crotchet, Quaver and Minim.

One of the larger south-facing rooms on this floor is called Canning after the Conservative Prime Minister George Canning. A passionate and great orator, he fought and lost a duel with the then Foreign Secretary Lord Castlereagh, plunging the Conservative Party into rifts until his early death in office in 1827. Renowned for his wit, it is relevant in my thoughts today – 'Here's to the pilot that weathered the storm': nothing is ever quite plain sailing and Highclere is full of surprises.

Gathering flowers in the Secret Garden to be arranged in the Flower Room [ABOVE RIGHT] which lies next to the woodshed at the back of the Castle

Fridays are always remarkably busy days in the Castle irrespective of my friends arriving. 'Friday' can signify either the end of the week or the start of the weekend depending on whom you ask. I often feel equally muddled but, with the office staff looking forward to their own weekends, make a note always to ask for help early on in the day and not at the end when everyone is trying to dash for home.

Early in the morning, I walk around the Castle with Paul, the head gardener. We will have already planned the display of plants in the State Rooms and along the corridors and galleries. In the case of Highclere, size matters. Either we need five or more plants in one bowl or large orchids, pelargoniums, hydrangeas, hyacinths, narcissi or jasmines, depending on the time of year. An early survey means we have several hours to meet any challenges.

The next task and joy is to walk down to the gardens, trug in hand, accompanied by a gaggle of dogs, to pick flowers for the bedrooms and tables. I find and collect the shapes and colours of wild flowers as well as flowers from the herbaceous borders, foliage and coloured stems from shrubs or small trees. Midwinter, however, defeats me and florists prove the more practical option.

An hour later, I am installed in the Flower Room with a cappuccino and a selection of vases. This is a well-lit tiled room tucked behind the log store and what is now the Egyptian exhibition. Making up the bedroom vases always seems to take a little longer than I have anticipated and, feeling panicked, I too often radio the office asking for help to deliver the flowers to the bedrooms. The Flower Room is near the bottom of the stone servants' stairs so, for speed, I remove my shoes and run barefoot around the Gallery, two vases at a time so I do not spill. By this time others are helping and it becomes more of a game, with one of us drawing the short straw of doing the second-floor bedrooms.

Theoretically I find flower arranging very absorbing and my husband really likes the fact I am using the seasonal foliage and flowers from our garden. Thus the next stage is to finish the flowers for the dining tables in the Music Room and Dining Room. I hope to have some spare which I leave in buckets of water to top up the arrangements as needed over the weekend.

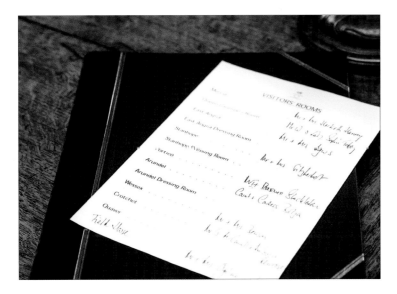

Just as in previous generations, I leave

a Room List on a table in the Saloon. As guests arrive and room allocations are identified, Luis leads the team to help carry luggage and assorted bags upstairs to the relevant bedrooms, again with amused grins to those who get the job of heaving bags up the extra stairs to the second floor.

House-party guests arrive at tea time and quickly relax with a welcoming cup of tea or, if preferred, a stiff drink and fall into absorbing conversations, puzzles, newspaper and book reading. As P. G. Wodehouse once said, 'The cup of tea on arrival at a country house is a thing which, as a rule, I particularly enjoy. I like the crackling logs, the shaded lights, the scent of buttered toast, the general atmosphere of leisured cosiness.'

I am waiting in the Saloon ready to guide guests to their rooms and make sure they know where their bathroom is and how it works. The plumbing and enormous baths owe much to Almina, the 5th Countess, who installed what was, in its time, state-of-the-art fixtures and fittings. Today, with guests in all four corners of the Castle enjoying enormous, piping-hot baths simultaneously, the plumbing and water supplies are still remarkably plentiful. There are however no showers and instead, if needed, plastic jugs in each bathroom to help rinse your hair.

Weekend itineraries are left in each bedroom, which include all the guests' names as reminders, given many of us are attaining the ages between fifty and dead, so memory

---

The Perfect Hostess

Elizabeth Paget's words about the 'perfect hostess' are amusing and worth bearing in mind:

She makes you feel when you arrive
How good it is to be alive.
She promptly orders fresh-made tea
However late the hour may be.

She leads you to a comfy room
With fire ablaze — and flowers abloom.
She shows you cupboards large and wide,
No hats or frocks of hers inside!

A writing-table meets your eye,
The newest novels on it lie.
The bed is just a nest of down,
Her maid puts out your dinner-gown.

The water's hot from morn till night,
Her dinners fill you with delight.
She never makes you stand for hours
Admiring children, dogs or flowers!

What better way to please her guest?
The Perfect Hostess lets you rest.

There are of course certain perfect guests, about whom Rose Henniker-Heaton wrote in 1931. This poem always makes me chuckle and I am sure strikes a chord with all hostesses:

She answered by return of post
The invitation of her host.
She caught the train she said she would,
And changed at junctions as she should.
She brought a light and smallish box
And keys belonging to the locks.
Food, strange and rare, she did not beg,
But ate the homely scrambled egg.
When offered lukewarm tea she drank it.
She did not crave an extra blanket,
Nor extra pillows for her head:
She seemed to like the spare-room bed.
She never came downstairs till ten.
She brought her own self-filling pen,
Nor once by look or word of blame
Exposed her host to open shame.
She left no little things behind,
Excepting ... loving thoughts and kind.

Bellini

White peaches grow against the walls of the peach house and are eagerly awaited each August. As well as being enjoyable just as they are, they are completely delicious if peeled, chopped and puréed, and combined with prosecco to make a Bellini. Apparently the drink is so named for the pink tones of paint used by the fifteenth-century Venetian painter Giovanni Bellini. However, it was created by Giuseppe Cipriani, who owned Harry's Bar in Venice in the 1930s.

INGREDIENTS TO SERVE TWO

2 large, ripe white peaches,
peeled, halved, stones removed and flesh diced

Cold Italian prosecco

METHOD

Blitz the peach flesh in a blender until smooth, then pass it through a sieve.

Fill one third of two Champagne flutes with peach purée, then top up with cold prosecco.

can be an issue. Dinner guests arrive for the evening, and all return downstairs refreshed and changed, to gather for drinks in the Drawing Room or Saloon. Always a fan of Winston Churchill's wit, I quite agree that 'I could not live without Champagne. In victory I deserve it. In defeat I need it.' By this stage, everyone has gathered and I need it.

Dressing for dinner, although no longer quite

as formal as in the Victorian or Edwardian periods, is still something of a tradition here. Earlier Earls of Carnarvon look down on proceedings: the flamboyance of the neck ties and high-pointed collars of the Regency dandies; the more sombre sartorial style of the Victorian 4th Earl, understated, but immaculately tailored with dress coats *de rigeur*.

Today smoking jackets are often the flavour of the evening, a style originally promoted by the 24-year-old Prince of Wales, Queen Victoria's eldest son, who commissioned his Savile Row tailors, Henry Poole and Co., to make a blue silk smoking jacket with trousers in a fabric to match. Matching trousers have fallen out of fashion but my husband favours a smoking jacket and velvet slippers for Castle dinners.

For ladies, the choice is cocktail dress on Friday evening and long on Saturday evening. Occasionally we revert to white tie, which looks incredibly smart but can cause *cris de coeur*s as dress studs, ties and starched collars go missing.

Remembering to advise guests of dress code is something I have very occasionally forgotten, but as Noël Coward noted on entering a white-tie-and-tail party in an ordinary (if dapper) suit, 'Please, I don't want anyone to apologise for over-dressing.'

With Champagne glass in hand, the hubbub of

a good party gathers pace in the timeless grandeur of the Saloon. A nod from Luis to indicate Chef is ready and I lead the way through to the beautiful intimacy of the Music Room, with its baroque painted ceiling, Italian-embroidery wall panels and atmospheric eighteenth-century French light sconces. The early Victorian table, gleaming in the candlelight, sits in the centre of the golden room, laid with white linen and silver to seat twelve of us for supper.

Almost inevitably the first course is a soup, a great preference of my husband, Geordie. Thereafter the main course and pudding are planned to balance the other choices throughout the weekend. If we retire to the Library, it is not for long, as an early night beckons before the amusements of the following days.

The housekeeping team close the shutters and curtains early to stop valuable heat escaping. The bedroom panel radiators, a recent acquisition, although far from attractive or traditional, are a practical solution to cold autumn and winter nights. Cosily tucked up in layers of bedding, guests will I hope report the best nights' sleep.

Breakfast is surely the most important meal of the day. Highclere certainly pays tribute to that sentiment. Scrambled eggs (with a little cream), tomatoes, mushrooms, bacon and sausages, porridge and fruit line the table near the servery. Everyone sits where they choose although some of the men determinedly hold up newspapers, whilst I am often grouped at one end of the table with girlfriends, happily chatting. One Belgian girlfriend of mine aims to descend for lunchtime rather than breakfast, whilst some Italians sit with only a little strong coffee contemplating the agenda for the day.

The agenda depends on the time of year. In January we celebrate a cold wintry month with a Burns Night Party. In March we might ride, walk and picnic in the park which, given the weather, is quite a British activity. May heralds the annual music concert in the Saloon whilst June marks the time for the village fête, horse-racing and a cricket match. Autumn returns to shooting parties and a Harvest Festival church service on the Sunday.

Marking the cycle of the year with friends is no different to my predecessors and the ritual creates a sense of place and peace. Whatever the time of year, walks in the gardens and the park give all friends immense pleasure and always, for me, recall the lines by the French philosopher, Albert Camus:

> Don't walk in front of me, I may not follow.
> Don't walk behind me, I may not lead.
> Just walk beside me and be my friend.

BURNS NIGHT

R obbie Burns is a celebrated Scottish poet who was born on 25th January 1759. Every other year I choose the nearest weekend to invite friends to celebrate the bard's birthday. Not all my guests realise, when they accept the invitation, that they are going to have to join in Scottish reeling. As they walk through the double glass doors into the Saloon there is sometimes a panicked glance but no obvious exit route open to them. Luis leaps forward with a tray of cocktails as instant fortification. We have a practice walk-through of a reel, the music begins and everyone is soon swept up into a Dashing White Sergeant. This is followed by an Eightsome or the Reel of the 51st. Worried looks are replaced by a sense of delighted achievement.

We pause in between each dance to gather the numbers and partners for the new formations and to admire the various interpretations of the dress code (black tie, long for the ladies or a tartan theme). One girlfriend, who was utterly new to the spectacle, interpreted the dress code as a tartan

mini skirt whilst another girlfriend wore a long skirt with tartan hot pants. Amidst much hilarity, they proved rather popular dance partners. If we are short of numbers with one of the reels, I persuade Luis or any of his team to join in, leaping around enthusiastically before suddenly disappearing at the end of a dance, to return a few moments later with stately demeanour and another tray of drinks.

After an hour's reeling of favourite dances, the entire party of friends processes into the Dining Room to find their places at four large round tables. We then all stand as the haggis is ceremonially 'piped' in. The procession is led by the bagpiper, followed by a friend, Charlie, bearing a sword to cut the haggis and the chef, Paul, bearing the haggis aloft. Following grace, Charlie addresses the haggis at length in true Gaelic style with a broad Scots accent, which few can follow, and the evening begins. Thereafter we follow a programme of speeches and toasts aided by Scotch whisky and delicious food.

MUSIC IN MAY

Every May, a music festival takes place in the churches and houses around Highclere and the local town of Newbury. Foremost orchestras and soloists travel from all corners of the globe to give concerts, workshops and recitals: the Royal Philharmonic Orchestra, the Moscow State Symphony Orchestra, the Berlin Philharmonic, the Hallé, Tenebrae, the Soweto Gospel Choir and outstanding soloists have all taken part over the years.

My mother-in-law, Jeanie Carnarvon, started the festival some forty years ago and it has gone from strength to strength. It is also a perfect excuse to host a weekend house party based around the concert that takes place in the Saloon in the Castle.

Music has been part of Highclere's life for generations. Disraeli, who stayed in the Castle, 150 years ago, wrote: 'The happiness of man is not merely material. Were it not for music, we might in these days say, the Beautiful is dead.'

The distinguished roll call of musical names who have

visited Highclere can be traced through the Visitors' Book. Oscar Beringer, an accomplished pianist who performed in both Germany and England, stayed in 1883, leaving a musical memento on his departure.

Jacques Blumenthal and his wife stayed at the Castle in 1886. Blumenthal had settled in London in 1848 and became pianist to Queen Victoria, and consequently a highly sought-after teacher to London society.

Almina, the 5th Countess, was given the wonderful Steinway grand piano, which today stands in the Drawing Room, by her father Alfred de Rothschild. Rothschild was himself a tremendous patron of the opera, and had his own orchestra that became famous not merely for its performances but for the musicians' immaculate dress and matching trimmed moustaches.

One spring, Dame Kiri Te Kanawa arrived to perform a cameo role as Dame Nellie Melba for *Downton Abbey*. As she warmed up and rehearsed in the Saloon, we were treated to an informal recital of various well-known arias which left a spell over the cast, crew and Castle staff who were enthralled and enchanted. I always have music on in the background when I write but just sitting, listening to it alone, lets my mind wander and relax.

During the afternoon of the concert in the Castle, the musicians arrive to practise and the staff from the office lean over the Gallery while those in the kitchens hover behind the green baize door enjoying the impromptu music and songs. Meanwhile the Saloon is cleared of the armchairs and furniture, and semicircles of gilt-backed chairs are set up around the room. At 7 p.m. up to eighty guests begin to arrive and find their seats; the voices and music soar around the galleries, and it is perhaps most mesmerising as the light through the vaulted lead glass high above the room becomes hazy and dim as the evening progresses.

Towards the end of the programme the musicians rely on small light sconces over their music stands to read their scores, but the atmosphere in the Saloon becomes timeless as the audience end the evening absorbed and lost in the sublime music.

As the Castle concert-goers slowly disperse, those staying for dinner gather and move towards the Dining Room. Behind the scenes, there may be rather more rapid movement, as our chef Paul and butler Luis invariably anticipate the need for extra guests invited to dine: a happy, yet potentially stressful consequence of finding friends amongst the audience. However, both Paul and Luis are kind enough to discreetly over-cater and stand by with extra place settings to accommodate the impromptu guests.

Late in the evening dinner guests depart often sheltering under umbrellas as they hurry into cars. May can be a very rainy month. Those friends staying wind their way upstairs through the Saloon which has been miraculously cleared and transformed during dinner by Luis and his team. As if by magic armchairs, tables, lights and plants have all been returned to their usual place.

SUMMERTIME

Our bedroom in the Castle faces east. Waking up in the summer, the early light falls towards us across the lawns and the folly, Jackdaw's Castle. Padding downstairs, the dogs are always pleased with an early-morning walk. A low-lying mist can sit across the wild-flower meadow and friends whose rooms face south have the most extraordinary views through the mist to the wooded slopes of Siddown Hill surmounted by another folly, Heaven's Gate.

Summer agendas to consider, depending on the exact weekend, can involve walking or driving to the church fête, a demon game of croquet or watching my husband's cricket team hopefully win on Highclere's own cricket pitch. The latter can cause some stress for non-English friends – what, after all, do you wear to watch cricket, a game deeply incomprehensible?

Cricket has been played at Highclere since 1840 although interest has waxed and waned depending on the proclivities of each successive Earl. There have been some recent prestigious matches such as when HRH the Duke of Edinburgh's cricket team played at Highclere against a team assembled by the current Earl's father.

Today we play about twelve matches a year, always on Sundays, and scattered through the summer months.

Souvenirs of a royal cricketing visit to Highclere by HRH The Duke of Edinburgh in 1956

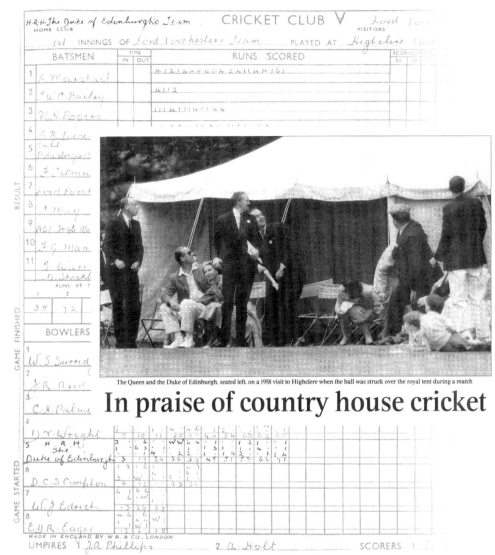

The Queen and the Duke of Edinburgh, seated left, on a 1958 visit to Highclere when the ball was struck over the royal tent during a match

In praise of country house cricket

The first challenge is to gather twenty-two men together at 11 a.m. on a Sunday along with the relevant scorers and umpires. One team of eleven men bat. The batsmen go in in pairs and try not to be out, but can be bowled out alone. The other team field and some of them bowl. Each bowler has six balls, as long as they are not no-balls, and then the bowler and end is changed. The fielding positions have names such as silly mid–off, leg gully or cow corner. Most of the positions are named roughly according to a system of polar coordinates – one word (leg, cover, mid-wicket) specifies the angle from the batsman, and it may be preceded by an adjective describing the distance from the batsman (silly, short, deep or long). Words such as 'backward', 'forward', or 'square' can further indicate the angle. Every so often, one team declares and at other times the weather will intervene to create a draw.

Even if you do not understand cricket, Highclere's pitch makes a wonderful backdrop for a lazy summer afternoon, with the soothing and familiar clop of willow against leather.

With time called for lunch, players seek out

refreshment from the burdened trestle tables in the pavilion. With an array of salads, cold meats and poached salmon, lunch is as much a social occasion as refuelling for the remaining hours of play. Summer puddings, cheese and coffee might lead some to seek the shade for a quiet snooze, particularly if Pimm's has been imbibed!

Pimm's

MAKES: 1 litre (1¾ pints) to serve 4

The recipe for Pimm's is a closely guarded secret. It was created by James Pimm during the reign of George IV, to accompany the oysters Pimm sold in his restaurants. The base is often gin, which is flavoured with various herbs, spices, fruits and botanicals. The result is a dark brown 'summer cup' that is very refreshing to drink while playing – or observing – croquet, cricket or golf. Unfortunately, given that it tastes delicious and has lots of fruit in it, the alcoholic content of a glass of Pimm's is occasionally forgotten!

Maggie, who looks after the horses at Highclere, likes to swap the lemonade for Champagne.

INGREDIENTS

1 apple, cored and chopped

½ small cucumber, finely sliced

6 large strawberries, hulled and chopped

1 orange, thinly sliced

Ice cubes

250ml (8½fl oz) Pimm's

750ml (1¼ pints) lemonade

Handful of mint leaves

METHOD

Put the chopped apple, cucumber, strawberries and most of the orange slices (reserve 4–5 slices for garnish) into a large jug with some ice. Pour in the Pimm's then the lemonade, and stir gently. Garnish with mint leaves and the reserved orange slices.

[**CHEF'S TIP**: For an alternative to lemonade, try the same proportions with ginger ale.]

Elderflower Cordial

MAKES: approx. 2 litres (3½ pints)

You'll need a ladder, a trug, some scissors and a good dry morning (so that the flowers are dry). It is also said that it must be cloudy at the moment you pick the flowers. This is probably an old wives' tale, as the elder has long associations with folklore: it offers protection against evil spirits.

Elder still grows near the remains of the old church beside the Castle and I still collect it every May.

INGREDIENTS

About 30 elderflower heads (be sure to pick white flowers, any that are yellowing or brown will need to be discarded)

2kg (4lb 9oz) caster or granulated sugar

1·5 litres (2½ pints) water

2 lemons, pared then cut into rounds

75g (2½oz) citric acid
(sold in chemists)

METHOD

Shake the elderflower heads over the sink to remove any insects, then put on one side.

Heat the sugar and water in a large pan over a low heat to dissolve the sugar, stirring every now and then. Briefly bring to the boil, then remove the pan from the heat. Add the lemon rind, lemon rounds and citric acid to the syrup, then gently put the elderflower heads into the syrup, cover the pan with a cloth and leave to infuse at room temperature for 24 hours.

Line a colander with a clean muslin cloth (or a clean fine cotton tea towel) and place the colander over a bowl. Slowly pour the syrup with flower heads into the colander and leave it to drip into the bowl below (you'll probably need to do this in batches).

When there is no liquid left in the colander, use a clean funnel and ladle to transfer the syrup in the bowl into sterilised bottles [**SEE** page 255]. Seal tightly and label.

The cordial will keep for 4–6 weeks in the fridge. Alternatively, pour some of the mixture into ice-cube trays, or plastic containers, to freeze.

To serve, pour about 2 tablespoons of cordial into a glass, add a couple of ice cubes and top up with still or sparkling water.

Bloody Mary

There is much argument about who invented this particular cocktail. Harry's New York Bar competes for the accolade with the Hemingway Bar in the Ritz Hotel in Paris. The name, however, is indubitably English, associated as it is with the Catholic Queen Mary I.

It tastes very good without any alcohol (my preference), and is then called either a Virgin Mary or a Bloody Shame. However you have it, it is the perfect cocktail for a Sunday morning and particularly restorative if the previous evening was a bit too festive.

The question of how much Tabasco or Worcestershire sauce should be included is entirely mood-dependent. Sometimes our butler Luis decides to really give it some bite and does not always remember to warn me ...

INGREDIENTS FOR ONE

45ml (1½fl oz) vodka

90ml (3fl oz) Clamato
(if you can't find Clamato, use tomato juice)

1 tbsp lemon juice

2 tsp red wine

2 tsp Tio Pepe sherry

Squeeze of orange juice

2–3 dashes of Tabasco sauce, to taste

2–3 dashes of Worcestershire sauce, to taste

Celery salt, to taste

Ground black pepper, to taste

Ice cubes

Celery stalk, to garnish

Slice of lemon, to garnish

METHOD

Mix all the ingredients together in a glass or jug and pour into a tall glass on the rocks. Stir and garnish with the celery stalk and slice of lemon.

AUTUMN WEEKENDS

The shooting season at Highclere begins with partridges in September and progresses to include pheasants when they come into season in October. It is a renowned shoot, and in October our friends are asked to a shooting weekend, arriving on a Friday, shooting on Saturday and then we walk, ride or drive to church for the Sunday Harvest Festival service.

On the Saturday morning, fortified by a Highclere breakfast, the guns are gathered outside the Castle. Instead of the ponies and carriages of previous generations, the men, loaders and pickers-up set off for the shoot drives in rather-too-clean 4×4 cars. I prefer not to rush and instead ensure lunch is well organised.

The morning is broken by a pause for soup and sausage rolls around 11 a.m. after which I will join the guns standing behind with the dogs to pick up. Given the amount of opportunities throughout the day to enjoy some delicious food, I will sometimes use the waiting time at a drive for some open-air yoga, which apparently unintentionally puts off nearby guns.

My husband occasionally stands behind a gun which may also slightly put them off form. Unlike his grandfather, however, he does not talk disparagingly about the accuracy of his guests. The 6th Earl was renowned for saying: 'I did not ask you here to look at the birds, I asked you here to shoot them.' To further alarm the guests he would see a pheasant rise in the air and shout 'prepare to shoot' followed by 'shoot!' when his utterly unnerved visitors did not even have the gun to their shoulder. The 6th Earl had a strange habit of retiring early to his bath after lunch and later saying goodbye to his guests in a state of undress after they returned from the afternoon drives for tea.

By contrast, we all still tend to go out after lunch hoping for a good walk before returning to tea in the Castle. After which, the rooms suddenly empty and everyone has taken papers and cups of tea upstairs to rest and change.

The Saturday evening celebrates the success of the shoot and, as usual, is the centre point of our weekends. The dining-room table is a Victorian feat of engineering and beauty. It can seat up to thirty people and all the leaves are kept numbered and stored in a cupboard at the back of the Dining Room. Luis, assistant butler Jorge and our banqueting team set the table in the afternoon to ensure nothing is overlooked. Always left unclothed, the rich wood gleams in the muted light. Working with white-gloved hands to keep the silver clean and fingerprints off glasses, Luis and Jorge plan the settings.

The beauty of the table is the result of detail and eye. With knives, forks and spoons carefully placed and ordered according to the number of courses, a single pat of butter, impressed with intertwined C's with the coronet, will be left in a cold pantry until it is time to put it in front of each guest's place. Wine glasses and water tumblers are arranged to the top right of each plate – a useful mnemonic to remember the order is white on the right or, as Luis likes to tell his team, like a Mickey Mouse head, with the two smaller glasses as ears. The pudding wine glass sits logically at the back, as this is the last glass a guest will drink from. Georgian silver candlesticks and mats for the flower arrangements are carefully positioned down the centre of the table, and silver salt, pepper, sauce boats and salvers are retrieved from the safe in readiness. Finally the chairs are placed at each setting.

'*Placement*' means exactly what it says – the place where you sit, although the word is French, so pronounced accordingly so staff know we are talking about the table and not an internship! The business of *placement* involves knowing your guests, and their relevant interests, and who might be interested in or share passions or pastimes with whom. My husband invariably gets involved, and declares who he would most like to sit next to, so my efforts may need to be reconsidered as a consequence. For house parties staying more than one night, the jigsaw puzzle will continue, ensuring everyone has new lunch or dinner partners, and never their own.

We have occasionally had odd numbers for lunch, and with thirteen, we will round the table up to fourteen with the place set for Teddy (a rather large soft toy). Teddy has limited conversational powers, so the setting is quite narrow to allow his neighbours to talk across him. The superstition of thirteen for dinner being unlucky perhaps originates from the Last Supper, when of course Jesus sat down with his twelve disciples, but died shortly afterwards.

When it is time to go into the Dining Room, I will ask my dinner partners to come through with me, relying on other girlfriends to follow suit. As guests filter through, our rather charmingly old-fashioned leather *placement* board is left on the sideboard for everyone to check where they are sitting. We do also leave place cards to help, although

The games table in the Library

I have occasionally written them in hieroglyphs for my own amusement and the bewilderment of guests!

We still follow the practice of turning to first one companion seated to one side for half of the dinner before switching to turn the other way and begin a conversation afresh. The key is to observe which direction my husband faces and then trying with some subtlety to ensure that everyone follows suit like a pack of dominos. The banqueting team of Luis, Jorge and Matthew move smartly round the table in a clockwise direction, beginning to the right of my husband with firstly wine and then plates of beautifully presented food to start the dinner.

At the end of the dinner, I happily suggest that

the ladies leave the room with me and we can ensconce ourselves in the Library leaving the men to their port or brandy. It is a chance to catch up with girlfriends and consider our evening amusements. I sometimes propose a general-knowledge quiz game which I referee and everyone else is divided into usually four teams. Each team has to

call itself a daft name and is squeezed into the deep red sofas from which it is impossible to make an elegant exit or grouped around armchairs strategically close to further *digestifs* and coffee.

My husband enjoys charades whilst his grandfather, as a younger man, was partial to a game of sardines, where one person hides and as the others find them they join them and hide too. Probably, a favoured game because he hoped to spend some time next to a potential new love in some dark corner and, given the size of the Castle, he might count on the fact they would not be found for quite a while by the other guests.

At the end of the evening during the time of the 6th Earl, the Castle would be plunged into darkness and the butler, Robert Taylor, would arrive with torches on a silver tray for each guest to find their way to their bedroom. The reason was never quite clear; perhaps to save on electricity or to return to the blackout practices of the war years or to hope some beautiful girl would need help to find her bedroom.

In a more mundane world today we simply continue to leave the lights on.

Continuing the traditional feel of a country house weekend, Sunday is all about the Harvest Festival church service. The church no longer structures all we do on a Sunday, yet historically, of course, weekends originated to punctuate the working week, and give employees time to practise their religions, be they on Jewish, Muslim or Christian calendars, and to have time with their families.

Most of the local village churches have a strong connective history with Carnarvon forebears. St Michael and All Angels church originally stood in the grounds, adjacent to the house since Anglo-Saxon times. It was later rebuilt by Sir Robert Sawyer from whom Lord Carnarvon is descended. Parish registers record that

> of his own liberality [he] cheerfully built a new compleat church in the parish of Highcleer, the old one being ruinous and unfitt, which was begun to be plucked down August 18th 1687, and the new church was finished so as we assembled in it on August 18th 1689.

Two hundred years later, this church was, in its turn, taken down and rebuilt two miles from the Castle in Highclere village. It remains a focal point of stillness and calm, providing the parish residents and visitors with a sanctuary from the vicissitudes and stresses of modern day life.

Autumn is the time to focus on collecting and storing foods, fruits and vegetables whilst the Harvest Festival service is all about those who 'have', helping those who 'have not', traditionally with excess goods that they have produced themselves. The estate, of course, has infinite options ranging from the sheep that graze the land to the preserves and chutneys culled from the Castle gardens.

The Castle stands on the site of the original palace and seat of the Bishops of Winchester and was occupied by monks. Today's Monks' Garden, situated to the side of the Castle, has its roots both literally and historically in this period. Sixty-one pear and apple trees are listed as thriving within the walls in 1260. The church relinquished its hold on the estate when it was sequestered by Edward VI in 1551, for it to be subsequently bought by my husband's direct ancestor, Sir Robert Sawyer, in 1679.

Crab apple trees still grow along the west-facing wall whilst a solitary quince tree grows in the lawn just near to them. Crab apples make a delicious jelly – not something you can readily buy from shops. Jellies are a lost art, but much used and enjoyed at Highclere. Quinces are large hard yellow fruits, only edible when cooked, whereupon they become utterly delicious and fragrant and a great accompaniment to game or cheese courses.

Fig trees also grow in corners of the Monks' Garden. The south-facing walls give them protection, and warmth. The first fruits are eaten freshly picked from the tree, or included in baskets of fruit at the table. Later in the season we bake or grill them – deliciously soft, wrapped in Parma ham with Stilton pushed into the tops and warmed through in the oven.

Behind the fig trees are pear trees espaliered against the walls and Bella our matriarch Labrador is often to be found nosing through the fallen fruit as she is rather partial to pears. The various apple trees are laden with fruit – a fraction of the harvest is consumed immediately, but the majority stored, wrapped, or cooked and frozen for later in the year. In fact,

there is such an abundance of produce that it becomes a full-time job to harvest, cook and bottle this profusion into jams, jellies, pickles and chutneys. I usually find that I am the lead 'Stillroom Maid', and definitely a part-time one, so not nearly as proficient as many of my predecessors who would shudder at some of my shortcuts.

As a tribute to the history of the Castle and the monks' knowledge and use of herbs, in 2014 we planted a Healing Herb Garden near the Castle. Approximately thirty different species of herbs are planted within box beds. Lavender, for example, can aid sleep, whilst its oil is an excellent antiseptic; sweet woodruff can be used to scent linen and ward off moths; lovage aids digestion whilst infusions of it help urinary problems; rosemary is uplifting and sage helps fever and apparently snake bites ... We use the mint and other herbs today as tisanes after dinners and lunches.

After Sunday lunch and an afternoon walk, a final cup of tea prepares our guests for their departure. The Visitors' Book is laid out for signing. Luis and Jorge help carry any last luggage downstairs. The cars slowly wend their way down the drive, passing the huge cedar trees that dominate the park, over the bridge before leaving Highclere's world behind.

The house seems oddly quiet and I potter around clearing up, going for a last evening walk before returning for a TV supper with my husband. 'Friendship,' said A. A. Milne's Christopher Robin, 'is a very comforting thing to have.'

In days following thank-you letters arrive, a wonderful reminder of a brief time amidst the working week. I put them in drawers of desks and rummaging through my disorganisation later I always have marvellous discoveries.

The sense of responsibility and trust that comes with running and maintaining a house such as Highclere can at times feel a little overwhelming. With loyal and long-standing staff who have continued to steer our collective ship forward, weathering fair weather and storms, Highclere has been undergoing a steady and beautiful transformation both inside and out.

ACKNOWLEDGEMENTS

I am, as ever, tremendously grateful to my husband Geordie for his support. Hannah Windmill and David Rymill are brilliant research assistants, whilst Hannah, in particular, doggedly kept me to agendas. Sally Popplewell has turned to her editing skills to help me especially when I had little time and lots to do. My sisters support me as always and Lucy in particular has contributed her calm help. I am very grateful.

Paul Brooke-Taylor, our head chef, produced outstanding dishes to both eat and photograph, as well as working through the recipes in great detail with me. We were ably helped by our assistant chef, Robert Avery. They were endlessly patient, occasionally revealing interesting language and always determined to do their best.

It was a great pleasure working with David Griffen who photographed the food as well as some interiors and detail. Adam Hillier and Elizabeth Vickers have also taken some beautiful photographs reflecting the seasons as well as the interiors over the past years. Some of my husband's excellent photographs have been included and one of mine which was clearly lucky rather than planned.

John Gundill, our Castle general manager, has never failed not to interrupt me but his stories and wit are light relief and unique. Luis Coelho and Jorge have leapt around offering enthusiastic support. Alexander Terry has opened Champagne late in the evening and worked with me through very late hours (thank you), while Louise Speers and Alex Popplewell aided the list-making, recipe photography and food testing.

I am very grateful to the Library and Archives Canada as well as the Henry James Center Creighton University, Omaha. Thank you all very much.

It has been delightful to work with Trevor Dolby, Lizzy Gaisford at Penguin Random House and Tim Barnes, book designer. I thank them for their support and unceasing work to produce a beautiful book. And I would not have met a great team without Ed Victor – thank you.

It is a team effort but above all I am lucky to live in an extraordinary home. My husband, Geordie, and my son, Edward, have always encouraged my efforts to write about it.

BIBLIOGRAPHY

Those readers interested in food could consult two famous books: the first by Mrs Beeton and the second by the great French chef, Auguste Escoffier.

Diaries and letters of the 4th Earl of Carnarvon are both at Highclere and in the British Library, which also holds the diaries of Malcolm Sargent. Elsie Carnarvon's diaries are in the Somerset Record Office and I am lucky her writing is so clear. Diaries and letters from Disraeli, to Henry James, John A. Macdonald, to Stanley Baldwin reflect the times and voices and can be found in bookshops or on the internet.

Andrew Roberts has written a masterful biography of Lord Cranborne – *Salisbury: Victorian Titan* – and Robert Blake's biography of Disraeli is invaluable. *The Life of Benjamin Disraeli* by G. E. Buckle is older but interesting. *Mr and Mrs Disraeli, A Strange Romance* by Daisy Hay explores their life whilst A. N. Wilson's three books *Victoria, The Victorians* and *After the Victorians*, explore the period in detail. *The Age of Reform* by Sir L. Woodward is a standard text followed by *England 1870–1914* by R. C. K. Ensor.

If you enjoy houses, try *The Victorian House* by Judith Flanders whilst *The Life and Letters of Lady Dorothy Nevill* is a window into life and society in the nineteenth century.

Leon Edel's *Henry James: A Life* must be the first biography for admirers of the author, but you could try *A Private Life of Henry James* by Lyndall Gordon. I enjoyed *The Correspondence between Henry James and the House of Macmillan*. It gives every struggling author hope. If you wish to read Henry James, *Portrait of a Lady* and *Daisy Miller* are good first choices.

There are many books to choose from about Edward VII, from *The Heir Apparent: A Life of Edward VII, The Playboy Prince* by Jane Ridley, to *The King in Love* by Theo Aronson, *Edward VII* by Anthony Allfrey, *Edward the Caresser* by Stanley Weintraub, whilst *The Big Shots* by J. R. Ruffer, which gives the flavour of the sporting weekend, is to be found in many shooting country houses. *The Edwardians* by Vita Sackville-West, again, gives the flavour of the time.

A number of books are relevant to the stories in the 1930s, such as *George and Marina* by Christopher Warwick, *Malcolm Sargent* by Charles Reid, *Tunes of Glory* by Richard Aldous, whilst *Edward VIII* by Philip Ziegler and *That Woman: The Life of Wallis Simpson, Duchess of Windsor* by Anne Sebba give insights into the challenges faced by the abdication. The pens of Nancy Mitford and Evelyn Waugh through letters and novels give the tone to country-house life between the wars. They are more than worth reading.

INDEX

Page references in *italics* indicate photographs and illustrations; recipes and ingredients are listed in **bold**

1 3 5 7 9 10 8 6 4 2

Preface Publishing
20 Vauxhall Bridge Road
London SW1V 2SA

Preface Publishing is part of the Penguin Random House group of companies
whose addresses can be found at global.penguinrandomhouse.com.

Penguin
Random House
UK

All images © Highclere Enterprises LLP
except © Mary Evans Picture Library pp.11, 19; © RIBA Collections pp.12-3, 14;
© iStock, p.52;© The Mullan Collection/Mary Evans p.79 right;
© Sasha/Stringer/Getty p.191

All images by David Griffen
except Highclere Castle archives pp. 15, 18, 19, 20, 23, 26, 27, 30, 31, 79 left,
80, 81, 82, 85, 89, 91, 130, 131, 135, 136, 141, 142, 143, 145, 146, 147, 189, 190,
192, 193, 194, 195, 197 bottom, 202, 203; Adam Hillier pp.2, 4-5, 128,
134, 204, 211, 265, 269, 270, 271, 272, 273, 282; Michael Wiseman p.8;
Mary Evans Picture Library pp.11, 19; iStock, p.52; RIBA Collections pp.12-13,
14; © The Mullan Collection/Mary Evans p.79 right; Elizabeth Vickers pp.102,
283; Kenneth Gillham p.129; 8th Earl of Carnarvon pp.132, 231, 236, 277, 278,
281; Sasha/Stringer/Getty p.191; 8th Countess of Carnarvon p.275

Image on endpapers © RIBA Collections

First published by Preface Publishing in 2017

www.penguin.co.uk

A CIP catalogue record for this book is available from the British Library.

ISBN 978 1 8480 9498 7

Designed by Tim Barnes, herechickychicky.com

Set in Hoefler & Co.'s Surveyor, derived from early nineteenth-century
map engraving.

Copyedited by Laura Nickoll

Recipe testing by Emma Marsden and Angela Nilsen

Printed and bound in Italy by Graphicom Srl

Penguin Random House is committed to a sustainable future for our
business, our readers and our planet.

This book is made from Forest Stewardship Council® certified paper.